s. f. pfister

Droplets
the soul's journey home

ICENI
BOOKS
Tucson, Arizona

To my wonderful wife, Nora, and to the love we share. To my sons, Jason, Mikel, and David, who have honored me with the joys and pains of fatherhood and who humble me daily as I witness the glorious potential of human life and behold "what God is doing now." To my dear friend Jill, whose pain was the impetus for this book and whose good spirit was part of the inspiration. And to all who seek their fulfillment in love, to all who suffer in ignorance of their eternal nature, and to all who desire a deeper understanding of their lives and whose hearts have remained open to the wondrous joy of Being.

TABLE OF CONTENTS

INTRODUCTION

God asks no man whether he will accept life. That is not the choice. You must take it. The only choice is how.

—*Henry Ward Beecher*

Enlightenment with the promise of eternal happiness in an all-knowing blissful state of consciousness is a goal very few of us have set for ourselves in this lifetime. Consciously reuniting with our Lord in this Moment, in a loving reunion that would reveal to us our Lord as ourselves and free us of the illusions of past and future, mine and yours, good and evil and the suffering that is inherent in those illusions, is either perceived as too lofty a goal or the pursuit would seem to demand the sacrifice of a life we have grown all too accustomed and are unwilling or perhaps unable to give up. Perhaps the whole notion is a bit too "unreal" and so it seems that under "normal" circumstances we have little interest in a personal quest for truth and for a deeper understanding of the human experience. Of course, there are those who have no interest in the possibility of a higher state of consciousness or in the world of Spirit, and seriously doubt that God exists at all. Many more are not aware that such a state of consciousness is possible or that there is a choice available. Their view of life is one of struggle, competition, and "survival of the fittest" in a world that they can see, hear, and feel. It is, on the face of it and as it is perceived through the five senses, a direct and honest approach to the challenges of life but one that will inevitably leaves those who have adopted it empty and dissatisfied in a conscious or unconscious state of anxiety and persistent need.

1

Our various religions have attempted to bring to us an understanding of some of the teachings of those who had broken the bonds of our illusions and have experienced this ultimate state of consciousness—one that had brought their awareness to a direct and immediate experience of the omnipresence of our Lord as the source of Life and the eternal essence of this Moment. Religion has created structured belief systems from the teachings of these exalted individuals and has satisfied, in those faithful, the need for assurance in an unsure world with the promise of salvation in a conceptualized spiritual utopia perceived as the domain of a loving God in an altogether different kind of reality that lies beyond this existence.But for most, the quest for happiness is seen fulfilled in the relative world of career, profit, and acquisition, and in the prospects of loving relationships, marriage, and family backed up with a social life, television, hobbies, sports, vacations, food, alcohol, recreational drugs, sex, sexual fantasies, and, of course, orgasm. That quest for "enlightenment" and a direct experience into the true nature of our lives would seem impractical and the time needed in its pursuit impossible to find in this hectic and demanding world. The concept seems just too abstract to be taken seriously and tends to fall into an existential limbo that is difficult to navigate and certainly difficult to incorporate into our "normal" lives as perceived through the five senses. And so it is left to our priests, ministers, rabbis, and holy men to explore in some "other-worldly realm" that we are not meant to know, at least while we are alive, and is frequently associated with weird cults and counter-culture groups whose bizarre activities too often end in tragedy.

For the most part, religion has left us one step removed from the process of self-discovery. Our energies are misdirected into the practice of ritual and the dogma of beliefs that rarely provide methodologies that would allow for a direct and immediate experience of our Lord, in this Moment, as this Moment, and the fulfillment of the glorious potential that we have in our lives as fully aware, sentient beings. The possibility of higher states of consciousness is neither encouraged nor even acknowledged. The average human being is left powerless and insignificant in the "grand scheme of things," leaving them to focus on securing their more "down to earth" needs and relative identity. Ours is a destiny seemingly determined by an unknown yet, as we've been told, loving God who is perceived in conflict with a dark and sinister force that at times would appear to have the advantage, leaving many of us to suffer as victims of a pervasive evil. It is here that our fear of the unknown and the insecurities of our isolation and ignorance rule. It is here that our Lord is reduced to a "concept" and His immediate presence obscured in the relative, limited processes of the mind. It is here that the illusion of our lives has exiled us from the sacred grounds of Eden and to the truth of our Being. The wisdom and peace available in a direct and immediate experience of the Eternal One as the essence and source of this Moment and as the core of our existence alludes us in the "mind stuff" of relative life.

The assorted "self-help" gurus are a draw for those of us who are having their difficulties "making it" in this relative world of ego, success, and "peace of mind." Their focus on securing a relative egocentric identity brings no awareness to the illusion of our lives and to the inevitable failure of the ego/mind to fulfill our deepest desire for love and our innate longing for spiritual fulfillment. There is little awareness that the "material world," as perceived through the five senses, and any prospect of success and happiness taken from it, will inevitably leave us miserably short of the transcendental and glorious experience of the Eternal One as the essence of this Moment and to the radiant role our Lord has set for us in this grand and majestic play that is this Life.

There is far more to our lives than the five senses would have us believe. It is from within the limits of these five senses that ego has necessarily been formed. It is here, within this self-aware state of consciousness which would have us appear separate from our experiences and dependent on them for our security, that we have gathered a personal identity as to whom we *think* we are and what we *believe* life to be all about. This "shroud of illusion" that ego and mind have created is indeed a necessary evolutionary process, but one that ultimately will need to be lifted if we are to truly know who we are outside those limitations and the suffering inherent in them. Free of the illusion of mind and the identity we take from it, we would be opened to a direct and immediate experience of our own true essence as an expression of our Lord, the eternal Source of Life, as It manifests in this Moment, as this Moment.

This is easy enough to say, and I assure you that if we could somehow suddenly lift this "shroud of illusion" and clear all the perceptions we had gathered about ourselves and about our lives, it would, initially, leave us strangers in a very strange world. All that we knew and loved in our egocentric, mind-based identity would have been removed and our senses would be stretched to their limits attempting to understand the magnitude of this new experience. It may initially be an experience of deep loneliness, the utter despair of complete emptiness in the sorrow of losing everything we had come to love and understand. It would be the total destruction of the world we once knew and all that had once given us pleasure and joy. We would find ourselves alone in an immense and overwhelming universe that would be, at least for a time, void of definition and empty of meaning.

As difficult as it may be to appreciate, there are spiritual practices that would have the participant focus on making this extraordinarily devastating event happen by rejecting the material world and living an austere life in denial of it. It is believed that once the focus on the material world and the illusions presented in it are gone, we would be infused with knowledge of the eternal, unseen world of spirit and come to a profoundly deeper *knowing* of who we are in the peaceful silence of that unseen world, free from desire and the illusions of mind. With help from more enlightened guides, the student is prepared for this terrible destruction, which would enable them to transcend the illusion of mind and the subsequent relative understanding of life and be open to the Love and the universal deep peace of Now, our ever-present Lord and Creator.

As it was for me, there was no preparation or even a desire to lose my "relative" identity. With God's grace alone, I unwittingly became a humbled witness to the great Mystery that is this Moment. I was opened suddenly to this Moment of miracles and given the opportunity to witness this extraordinary yet initially frightening existence as I suffered the loss of a life I could never reclaim. Understandably, this would hardly seem something I had been "graced" with, as the pain and sorrow of this great loss were devastating. Yet, as I came to understand this process and as I emerged from this dark and painful experience, I did so with the realization that it is within this illusion of ego/mind and the ignorance inherent in an isolated, narcissistic egocentric identity, that we are depriving ourselves of the glorious experience that is this Creation and of the sacred role we play in its fulfillment. As my "new world" came into focus and as I went beyond the sorrow of loss, I found that within the emptiness there was a wisdom, a wisdom not of the mind and the transient egocentric identity, but rather a wisdom that emanated from the innate eternal Spirit of Life—the wisdom of the Soul.

It is here within this immense silence and deep sense of peace that true self-knowledge can be gathered as we step away from the illusion of our egocentric lives. We would find that it was within the illusion of the isolated ego that we had filled our hearts with fear and our minds with the definitions that had severely limited who we are and obscured our Lord's presence as the Source and essence of Life as It manifests as this eternal, ineffable Moment of miracles.

As we transcend mind and become a pure and present witness to this glorious Spirit of Life that is indeed the essence and Source of this sacred Moment—that is our Lord and Creator—we would, in our becoming aware, have fulfilled our destiny by truly knowing who we are as an expression of this ever-present Spirit. In our complete presence, we would open ourselves to the divine and glorious mystery that is the nature of this magnificent Creation, fulfilling It in our joyful role as witness. We would, in turn, have made our Lord joyful in the ecstasy that is this knowing as we come to the realization and experience that we and our Lord are One.

This book is intended to open you to the marvelous possibilities of your everyday Life as it explores the human experience. It will hopefully plant within you the seed of "higher knowledge"—knowledge of the Soul—as you continue on your quest for self-realization and fulfillment. It is a quest we all are on, a journey we all must take. Some know of it and are consciously searching, others do not. Like it or not, it is our destiny to discover who we are in this

Moment beyond the illusion of ego, the confines of beliefs and the limits of the five senses, into that sacred field of "Beingness" that surrounds and permeates every aspect of our lives. This is the dawning of a new age of consciousness and the seeds of this new awareness are beginning to sprout all over this planet. As this "seed" of awareness grows within you, you will come to know that our Lord is both here and now, in all you perceive, as that perception, waiting to join with you in a union of complete Love and total, divine Peace.

I am not a guru. I have not traveled to the Himalayas in search of the meaning of life, nor have I spent years at the feet of enlightened masters in a quest for truth. I have no degrees or titles that would give me any right to speak to you about your life. In fact, there is not much, at first glance, that anyone would find extraordinary about me.

I was born in New York City in the summer of 1944 and raised on the north shore of Long Island. My mother's faith was Roman Catholic, and it was in that faith that we worshipped; I even served as an alter boy for a time at our neighborhood church. My love for Jesus and my faith in Him were poetic; that is, until puberty set in and my confessions became far too uncomfortable as I was asked to describe those "impure thoughts" I was having. Of course, the more I tried to avoid them, the more frequently they seemed to arrive and the more dread I felt at having to confess them at my next confessional. My love for Jesus was consumed, for a time, by my guilt and the subsequent avoidance of church. I was thirteen when my family mercifully moved. As we were not a particularly religious group, the importance and influence of the Catholic church had evaporated in our new Protestant environment where God had become somewhat more forgiving and less demanding, much to my hormonal relief.

With the family move, I abandoned my black leather jacket and the rebellious "greaser" look as we had moved "up," and it seemed time to adopt a new persona. I became a jock in high school, instead, a "four-letter man," captain and quarterback of our football team. I was an above-average student but can't imagine what those days would have been like without the escape of sports. Ours was something of a dysfunctional family, although not so different from many of the families of friends I knew at the time. Troubled by the specter of alcoholism, physical and mental illness, and occasional violent episodes, love was sometimes difficult to find. My parent's unresolved problems and their inability to address them were a source of ongoing heartache. It took its toll on all of us in different ways and not too many years later my family would dissolve in an ugly and bitter divorce.

After high school I applied and was admitted to the United States Merchant Marine Academy at Kings Point. In retrospect, I have no idea what I was doing there except that it was close to home and inexpensive. With the help of my influential high school football coach, I had secured the necessary senatorial sponsorship, and off I went. It took a year before I knew with certainty that this was not the direction I wanted to go with my life and I was forced to resign. Thrown into the ugly world of unskilled labor, I struggled to find appealing work until a family member secured a New York City union carpenters position for me, and I worked two years in apprenticeship before I was drafted into the Army.

In July of 1965, I began my journey from New York to Fort Gordon, Georgia, to begin basic training. I was miserable and overwhelmed by the tearful, painful goodbye from my "dysfunctional" family. From our small-town draft board, about sixty of us were bused to the induction station on Whitehall Street in Manhattan. "Beatniks" picketed and protested outside the building, but none of us really knew why or cared. After the final physical, we were carted onto the train that would take us to Georgia. It was a sorrowful time for most, and the empty, sad faces of those around me only added to my pain. However, it wasn't long before our misery evolved into comradeship and lasting friendships developed. None of us thought seriously about the prospects of dying in Vietnam, although evidence of the possibilities was everywhere. I watched boys become men and I don't regret the service. If not for the prospect of war, I believe it can be good for some young people to take time away from home and get in touch with their own inner resources in unfamiliar environments loaded with challenges in service either to their country or to their fellow man. It develops char-

7

acter and confidence and prepares one for the world. Basic training also put me in great shape, and I was pleased to win the battalion trophy as "sharp shooter" before it was done.

After basic training I was transferred to Fort Belvoir, Virginia, to begin my "advanced training" in the Army Corp of Engineers. I spent several months there in training, and upon completion my orders were somehow mixed up and I was left stranded in Virginia. I was not disappointed, for most of those who had graduated with me had received orders that would send them to Vietnam. By then, we had lost our "gung-ho" attitude and had become more aware of the corrupt political game being played out there. Without orders, there was some confusion as to what to do with me. I could type, so I was given a clerical position on base. I made rank quickly and within a year had achieved the rank of E-5, with my own section to command. The service had turned into a nine-to-five job, and I had about seven months left before my tour of duty was up.

It was in late January of 1967 that my life would suddenly be taken from the ordinary to the extraordinary. I had taken a weekend pass and had planned to visit my sister at her home on Long Island. She was my older sister and we were close, as were my younger sister and brother. There was a lot of catching up to do, and we talked well into the early hours of the morning. Finally, exhausted, we said good night and went to bed. While I was lying in bed waiting for sleep to come, I felt a strange sensation, an unfamiliar sudden surge of energy that slowly began to move up my spine. It was completely unlike anything I had ever encountered, and as it reached the base of my skull, I experienced what I can only describe as an explosion inside my head. With this "explosion," that inner consistent sense of "I" in what was once a familiar environment had been blown away and took on mysterious cosmic proportions. I had some how been unceremoniously awakened from this dream of Life. Free now from the restraints of a limited mind and superficial egocentric identity, this mysterious and most miraculous Moment was revealed to me. Like Dorothy, I wasn't in Kansas anymore. I had abruptly been taken from a world I thought I knew and had come to a place of complete mystery and magic. My experience of life would never, nor could it ever, be the same again.

I was overwhelmed and terrified by what I was experiencing. I had become insignificant in the face of the cosmic display now before me. My ego had been shattered. I had lost all sense of who I was. Frightened and confused, I got up from bed and headed for the bathroom. As I finished splashing water on my face, hoping to somehow "snap out of it," I raised my head. The reflection I was looking at in the mirror no longer felt like me; I truly did not recognize the image I was looking at and I turned away, horrified. All illusions of who I thought I was and what I thought life was had vanished and I cannot describe the unbearable loneliness I was experiencing. Now that there was nothing familiar, I had become a witness to everything around me. I felt completely isolated and alone and could take comfort in no one or nothing.... I wandered into the kitchen. It was then that something very significant happened, as within this chaos and confusion my sister called out to me from her bedroom, "Are you all right?" From deep within me a compassionate "silent witness" who did not want to fill her with the same fear and panic I was experiencing, replied, "Yeah," and said no more. There had been something left, a witness to the destruction, a me beyond mind and beyond ego! A me that would bear this "dark night of the soul," frightened and alone. A me, I would come to find out, that is at the core of our existence and is the key to our salvation. I had come to the experience of Soul.

I went back to bed, my mind spinning and heart pounding in the anxiety and fear of this overwhelming event. Was I losing my mind? What had snapped? Would I ever be all right again? What was this that had so completely altered my life!? I eventually simply passed out, and finally got some rest. The next morning my nightmare had come true, and I found myself a stranger in a strange world. I left my sister's home early without eating breakfast and with very little interaction, as now even she had become a stranger. I drove to my parents' home about an hour away. I found myself equally disoriented and estranged from my parents. My father, concerned about my behavior, asked if I had taken any drugs. If only that had been the explanation! However, I had not, nor had I ever, and I knew he could not possibly come to terms with what I was going through. I was on my own, frightened and disoriented, an isolated witness to everything around me, including, to my great despair, myself.

In the ensuing days and weeks and in spite of the trauma of this most difficult time, I was becoming deeply and completely certain that what I was now experiencing was the true nature of Reality, that this was "*It*," and it unnerved me further to find no one else as mystified and awed by this incredible Moment. It appeared to me that everyone was either mad or in some sort of hypnotic trance of denial. Could they not sense the incredible magnitude of this Moment of miracles? Why were they not mystified and rapt in awe with all that was around us? What dream were they dreaming that kept them from this? In spite of these clear and powerful revelations, I still found myself nonetheless overwhelmed, frightened, alone, and confused in what would have otherwise been just another day.

This was the beginning of an extraordinary journey. Eventually, with help no doubt from my guardian angel and from kindred souls like Alan Watts, Gopi Krishna, and Krishna Murti, who had passed this way before me and had written their experiences down in books, I came to understand that what I had experienced that fateful night was a *spontaneous Kundalini rising*. For those who recognize the term, let me assure you that, like the word *love*, without the experience, it would be meaningless. For those who do not, have patience. I will try to clarify it later on as I take you on my journey.

This is meant to be a simple book—not to be studied but to be experienced. I have italicized certain words that, in themselves, have no real meaning but point to the "*something*," far more than they could ever convey. At times I use a line of periods to have you pause and take the time to consider what is being said. I use analogy and metaphor in an attempt to communicate concepts that have to do with ineffable experiences, and although the result doesn't perfectly represent the reality I'm striving to present, it is as close as I can get. I may seem repetitious at times. Over the eons, we have been mesmerized into thinking in a way that has kept us asleep, unconscious of our vital nature. It is a powerful illusion we suffer in and I felt it necessary to repeat and repeat again the depths of that illusion and point, as best I can, to what lies beyond. In general, I would ask you to read this book slowly and in a quiet time and place that would be conductive to introspection. It is not a book to be read for information, so you should put your attention on what you are feeling while reading and explore your emotions as you contemplate what's being said. Instead of putting all of your focus on whether you believe what you are reading or whether the arguments are intellectually sound, be open to the possibilities of a knowledge that transcends the mind. I emphasis again that words alone are inadequate here and could never convey my whole experience. As you will come to find out, that "experience" lies peacefully within you beyond the words, within the silence, waiting to fulfill you.

This book is an exploration into the human predicament. It is a book about ourselves and about the consciousness we share. It is a book that will offend many and is frankly intended to, and I make no apologies. It is a "wake-up call" to our humanity and to the peril it is in. It is though, finally and completely, a book about Love.

I am not a scholar in the classic sense, yet I do take a great deal of delight in finding how easily all of what is to follow echoes the themes and is supported by great works of literature, from the Bible to Emerson. I pray that it will inspire your inner quest, enlighten your experience of "everyday" Life, and deepen your faith in our Lord.

Chapter I
"IN THE BEGINNING..."

The Now-moment in which God made the first man and the Now-moment in which the last man will disappear, and the Now-moment in which I am speaking are all one in God, in whom there is only one Now. Look! The person who lives in the light of God is conscious neither of time passed nor of time to come but only of one eternity...

—Meister Eckhart

I am compelled to begin this book with a vision, for it would seem that without a center from which to start, without a basic understanding from which to build, we would have nothing to refer to in order to weigh information for its veracity and thus develop our own inner core of "higher knowledge," our own internal sense of truth. Within this inner core we can begin to accept or, more importantly here, reject what may be so in our lives and so begin this journey into Magic.

Now imagine, if you will, an unbounded, infinitely deep, endless ocean, an ocean so pure that it is not visible. It is absolutely still, not a ripple, lying in complete and utter silence all around you. Know that the essential qualities of this ocean are the purity of *wholeness* and the eternal perfection of *nothingness*. This is in lieu of the essential components hydrogen and oxygen that would, once combined, make up the essence of an ordinary ocean, but like hydrogen and oxygen, these essential qualities of *wholeness* and *nothingness* are found everywhere in this extraordinary ocean as this ocean. In this eternal presence, time and space do not exist because they would need something other than what is to be measured and here there is no other. *It* is in its *wholeness* complete and there are no words that can begin to describe the level of perfection and the incomprehensible creative potential that is this *Wholeness. It* is nothing less than absolute divine perfection waiting to be realized. *It* has no needs or desires. *It* is totally and eternally fulfilled in *Its* silence and through *Its* expression. Be clear, though, for as an integral and mysterious aspect of this "ocean's" complete perfection, *It* must also be absolutely *Nothing,* the great abyss that makes this unbounded, timeless wholeness possible or *It* simply could never be. *It* is and must be everything and nothing at once for *It* to be whole, for *It* to be Holy. It is a vast eternal duality that is the *One.*

It is all that there is and in *It* all that could ever be. There is nothing more nor could there be any more. *Its* essence is total completeness, everything and nothing with an unlimited potential for creative expression. *It* is absolute, omnipotent, omnipresent, and ineffable. *It* is the Eternal, ever-present timeless spirit that is this Life. *It* is the creative *Source* of all that is or could ever be; "the Power, the Kingdom and the Glory." ...... *It* is all we believe to be Heaven. ...... *It* is the perfect Love we seek, fulfilled. ...... *It* is what we have come to know as "consciousness," the mysterious essence of life at its core. *It* is the cause and substance of this eternal, ever-present, ever-becoming, mysterious *Moment.* ...... *It* is the *Ineffable,* the *unspeakable One.* ...... *It* is the *Spirit of our Lord and Creator!*

Take some time and do your best to perhaps intuit such a presence, right here and right now. The pure eternal light of consciousness that is this "ocean," that is the miracle of "self-consciousness," and the source of all that is, the essence of your being, is here and is now in all you see and hear and think you know—an incredibly vast *Wholeness* wherein all of our needs and desires would be fulfilled in Its presence. Within Its hold we would find total bliss and complete contentment, nothing left undone, ... perfect eternal peace, ...

the pure creative intelligence of endless possibilities, ... absolute, incomprehensible beauty and perfection, ... unconditional, faultless Love. If you can begin to feel such a state of being, if you can begin to sense such a presence, if you can begin to imagine yourself a part of *It*, then you may have just begun to imagine ...... "*That*"!

Now imagine further, for suddenly from deep within the perfect stillness and silence of this eternal *Spirit*, out of *Its* perfection, as a part of *Its* perfection and as a creative expression of *Its* wholeness, the *Ineffable One* "speaks." And with this voice there came a mysterious and powerful vibration, a tumultuous sound, and that sound was the word of *God* and was with *God*. This colossal event comes as a spontaneous and creative act of the *Eternal One*, as it is from "*That*" where all things must come or could have come. And as the word of our Lord resonated, as our Lord sang the song of Creation through the stillness of this formless, endless "ocean," Droplets of "water" began to take shape and come into being seemingly independent of their *Source*. As they vibrated and began to separate from the whole and take form in *Its* eternal presence, a fragile membrane formed around each Droplet, creating the illusion of separate entities in an infinite and dazzling display of different shapes, sizes, and potential. And yet these Droplets remain a part of the ocean, a part of "*That*," with, as their essence, all the essential qualities of wholeness and the eternal that are "*That*," just now seemingly separate from the whole.

It was then that something even more miraculous, something even more mysterious, would come into being as some of these Droplets, "vibrating" as it were, in this state of separation yet still holding all the essential qualities of "*That*" as their essence, became independently *self-aware*. As those qualities of the Eternal Spirit manifested in these Droplets, it became possible for the Droplets themselves to become *aware* in the consciousness at their core. And for the first time, in the light of this consciousness that is the *Source* of life and the essence of our Lord, our Lord would become ignorant of Himself as these Droplets formed. In that seemingly independent state of self-awareness, these Droplets were caught in the uniqueness of their form—in their individual "vibration"—that had been created by the appearance of a membrane formed in this evolutionary process of "becoming," one which would temporarily isolate them from the whole.

It was from within this conscious state of fragmentation that it had become possible for these Droplets to, for the first time, become forgetful of their *Source* and ignorant of their essential nature as within this "membrane" the qualities of self-awareness and the desire to know had been born. These then were the mysterious gifts of life bestowed upon these Droplets by the Creator as a part of the perfect plan that would be in fulfillment of the Creator.

This potential and desire to know must necessarily begin in ignorance, and yet in their ignorance and in spite of their ignorance, these Droplets could not have nor would have come into being without "*That*" as their *Source* and so are totally dependent on *It* for their existence and are instinctively drawn to "*That*" for their fulfillment. It was not until the isolation and subsequent suffering inherent in that state of "self-awareness" that these Droplets could possess the potential of realizing "*That*" as their *Source*—as their essence—as they were perfectly and unconsciously a part of and in union with "*That*" until then. And joyfully, it was not until this Creation that this great *Spirit of Life* could come to know *Its* own splendor, which can now be realized through the growth of awareness, the acquisition of knowledge, and through the glorious witnessing that is the miracle of "self-awareness" and the most precious gift that these isolated Droplets now hold.

So it was that you and I and all of our kind, the family of man, was created, as was this most splendid universe for us to play in. We had been created, as the scriptures tell us, in "God's image," giving each and every one of us the potential of knowing God through knowing ourselves as we, like the Droplets of our imaginary ocean, contain within us the same essence of Wholeness and the Eternal that is this Holy Spirit—that is "*That.*" This incredible gift that is our lives has at its core the spirit of our Lord we call Soul. It is pure consciousness, the essence of our Lord, shrouded in a veil of ignorance and the illusion created by the "membrane" in the appearance of separateness. Beneath appearance and the ignorance inherent in self-awareness, we are all a perfect expression of the Spirit of God as Consciousness in search of Himself. I use here and will continue to use throughout the remainder of this book the masculine to refer to what has no gender, no form or substance, that which cannot be known, defined, or conceived of through the intellect, yet is the glorious *Source* of all that is.

If we are to truly know our Lord, it would be only through a direct and immediate experience of the "essence" of the Droplet we have come to know as Soul. Through it, we would come to realize all the majesty and splendor that is our *Source*, the essence that is ourselves and all that exists. Through a deeper knowing of ourselves, we would come to know God in all His splendor. Within the silence of this Moment, we would know Him as this Moment, as ourselves. And so it is the mystical revelation of those who have come to know and experience the unity of Life at *Its* core, "I am *That*, you are *That*, all of this is *That*."

Cast from the "Garden of Eden" that is this "ocean," having been blessed with the "fruit of knowledge" and so becoming self-aware, we all began this glorious journey of self-discovery on the road—albeit a rocky road—called Life. A road that is guiding us all towards the experience of ecstasy that is in the glorious and conscious reunion with our *Source* and Creator. And like the cycles of the natural world, we are born and die only to be reborn again as within each life cycle we gain knowledge and insight into our true nature, likening each life to a golden thread of a majestic tapestry being woven to completeness, ... to wholeness, ... to Holiness.

Although we Droplets appear separate, we are bound together not only by our essential nature and our common *Source* but also by an intricate energetic web that binds us to each other, to nature, and to God. In that connection, no act we do is done in isolation. Everything we do has an effect, and in this universe there is, as Droplet deepak chopra calls it, a "perfect accounting system" that lets no deed or action go unanswered. Whatever we do in this world will be returned to us whether in this life or in some life yet to be lived.

This concept of past lives, reincarnation, and the long-term effects of our actions has been provocatively revealed to us by Droplet brian weiss through his direct and immediate encounter with those whose past lives were disclosed to him. He has an extraordinary story to tell. As a therapist, he found hypnosis useful in his work and one day accidentally regressed a troubled patient into a past life during one of their sessions. This was the beginning of a long and insightful journey for Droplet brian weiss, a journey that would completely change the course of his life and one which he has documented in captivating books and through his lecture series. He has come to know with certainty that the Soul is immortal and that we have all died and returned to this life many, many times. The "past-life regressions" of numerous Droplets reveals a pattern of life and death that will inspire and free you from fear. The implications of the effects of our actions, as what has come to be known as "karma," are fascinating. The enormous importance of how we deal in our interpersonal relationships in this lifetime is immeasurable. Our spiritual understanding of this Life and our place in it rises and falls on the understanding of these relationships. I would strongly encourage you to take a closer look into the mystery of reincarnation and the long-term effects of our actions by reading Dr. Weiss's book *Many Lives Many Masters*.

Be warned, though, for as high as this knowledge is and as fascinating some of the accounts of past life involvement may be, it is only a small part of the story, a story we must learn to forget. To know with intellectual certainty that the Soul is immortal is nonetheless a knowledge taken from the processes of mind and will serve little more than egocentric needs if not taken to direct experience. Our immortality is an aspect of the God Head within us. That eternal essence transcends time and space and cannot be experienced through mind. All relative knowledge of this Divinity must be let go of if we are to allow God and Soul to reunite and truly come to know who we are. The Eternal cannot be known through concept;

it must be experienced in a knowing that transcends mind. You are not your mind or any concept taken from it. You are the Eternal.

There is a destiny that makes us brothers;
 None goes his way alone;
All that we send into the lives of others
Comes back into our own.

—*Droplet edmin markham*

The law of "karma"—that is, whatever you put out into the world will be returned to you—is perfect, as is all of Life. I say that having had the direct experience that what we have here is absolute perfection. There is not a grain of sand out of place, nor a single moment of your life to regret. As difficult as that may be to believe at times, the experience of the perfection of life at its core is total and undeniable. There is simply nothing wrong here; our Lord is perfection and all that is must be. The karmic consequences that have brought you to this moment are more than debts to be paid; they are also the vehicles to your understanding. There are no mistakes, only different ways for you to learn. Yours is not to reject or have remorse over any part of your life but to go deeply and consciously into each experience and become aware, to accept and embrace completely the experience of this Moment, to learn to forgive and to love in that experience with the knowledge and faith that it could be no other way and that God has given this to you as a means for your return to Him. However painful or however joyful your experience of *Life* may be, know that it is a gift for your awakening and should be accepted and explored consciously with an open, receptive, and grateful heart.

You must come to know that your pain and your fear are a measure of your distance from that Spirit of Life that abides within you, as your essence and as your *Source*. All that has come to you has come as an act of compassion, no matter how horrific it may appear. It is a debt that needs to be paid, an understanding that wants to happen so an opening can occur that would bring you and, as a result, all of this humanity closer to our Lord.

There is a tendency for the shallow mind to take this knowledge of the workings of karma and excuse itself of compassion. Statements like "I wonder what he did to deserve such misery?" creates an attitude that is demeaning and judgmental and will only serve to burden those who carry it with the same karmic misfortune, and isolate them further in the illusion of mind. Your brethren feel what you feel and suffer as you suffer. They are the Divine in turmoil and pain. Your open and compassionate heart is the path to your freedom and to the Divine. It will serve to heal your wounds and the wounds of humanity. What you do for one, you do for all. As you relieve the suffering of others, you are bringing an awareness of our Lord and His love for us into this Moment through your actions. It is an open, compassionate, and loving heart with which you must live your life, with no other reason than the promotion of love. In a total acceptance of this Moment, you will become an instrument of that Love, free from the bondage and needs of an isolated ego, free from the ignorance and limitations of mind.

Avoid the negative gossiping you might do about others. What the "other" provokes in you should be acknowledged and explored, especially when that other lowers your vibrational frequency and puts you in an egocentric state of superiority and/or threatens your egoist sense of self, which can lead to an unfortunate variety of destructive, unproductive actions. Look inside and try to find the source of these negative emotions and expose them with your awareness. In recognition, they will be transmuted into the higher frequencies of the Divine within you. Of course, there are people in this world that are best avoided and for good reasons that need to be understood. But the petty, day-to-day caviling that only promotes your own egocentric identity and hides the reality that we are all the Divine in search of Itself, should be avoided. Relieve yourself of this negativity that would limit your identity and promote a competition for Life. Through this witnessing and the application of "higher knowledge," your love and compassion will grow and they will enrich you and the lives around you in ways you can barely imagine.

You will come to know that this Moment is perfect, that there is not a grain of sand out of place nor a single moment of your life to regret and that you have become a witness to Life perfectly revealing Itself. You will come to realize that this experience of Life is all the magnificent, sacred, and divine "energy" of Love revealing Itself to you as you, and will manifest to you in many different ways but is all and forever "*That.*" It simply and completely could be no other way.

Droplet william blake, in this profound and penetrating poem, has expressed his transcendental experience of the unity of life and the enormous potential available to all who would open to this Moment in full awareness:

To know the universe in a grain of sand
And Heaven in a Wild Flower
Hold infinity in the palm of your hand
And Eternity in an hour

We have imagined together a somewhat simplified yet perhaps not so far off vision of Creation. "New physics" posits a more scientific but not a very different theory of creation in books like *The Dancing Wu Li Masters* by Droplet gary zukav, wherein the physical world seems to vibrate into form out of a most subtle field of existence that can only be described as "nothing." In our vision, as our Lord "sang" this glorious Song of Life and produced the unique notes that would vibrate in *Source* and give rise to the trees, the ocean, the stars, the planets, all the wonders and potential of this magical universe, *It* did so with all the Love and Joy that is *Its* eternal nature. From within this ecstasy, Droplets were formed that would mirror our Lord in their creative potential and capacity for love and compassion. These Droplets, created by the "Song of Life," seem for now apart from the whole by virtue of the illusion of the membrane formed and the gift of mind and self-awareness inherent in that membrane. They suffer in isolation and ignorance of their *Source* but have been given, by their very presence, the incredible opportunity to experience the rapture of knowing and reuniting with their Creator in this wonderfully mysterious and miraculous play that we call Life. In this vision, *you* are the Droplet, *you* hold the secret, *you* have the answer and yet the *you* that is the illusion of *you* as presented in an unconscious, separate entity, must be set aside for this glorious reunion to happen and for your perfection to be realized.

This is a journey of learning to Love and of learning to let go. Through the complete and unconditional Love of this Moment and in that conscious, joyful surrender to what is, we will come to unite with all we have been blessed with by our Lord as we continue on this magical journey. It is through our loving and in our total, unconditional acceptance of this Moment, which would give rise to our complete presence, that we lose the isolated identity formed in ego and mind and open ourselves to our full potential, to this Moment of miracles and to this Eternal Loving Presence. The Eternal that is within us will join with the Eternal that is this Moment in a divine expression of Love and union. And so it was that Droplet feodor dostoyevsky proclaimed:

> Love all God's creation, the whole and every grain of sand in it. Love every leaf, every ray of God's light. Love the animals, love the plants, love everything. If you love everything, you will perceive the Divine mystery in things. Once you perceive it, you will begin to comprehend it better every day. And you will come at last to love the whole world with an all-embracing love.

Chapter II
THE MEMBRANE

There is an endless world, O my Brother! and there is the Nameless Being, of whom nought can be said. Only he knows it who has reached that region: it is other than all that is heard and said. No form, no body, no length, no breadth is seen there: how can I tell you that which it is?
—*Kabir*, Tagore, 76

Droplets! It's a fun word, and I like thinking of us all as Droplets—each with their own unique sense of individuality so defined by the "membrane." For a Droplet of water to be formed, a membrane must first be formed, although it is truly an illusion to think of it as something other than water or, as in this case, something other than "*That.*" This "membrane" gives us the appearance of being separate, isolated and alone in our relative state of self-awareness in contrast with this ever-present, eternal Now, the infinite Nothingness that is our essential yet unrealized nature and the essence and *Source* of all that is. How, you may ask, does everything come from nothing? I am happy to announce that there are no words that can begin to fathom the nature of this great Mystery. Yet so it is. For from the purity and stillness of Nothing, which we have come to call Consciousness—that is this "ocean"—comes all that is in that which appears as something to our senses. But the word "Consciousness" cannot begin to define or have us understand what it is referring to and you, most likely, may not feel comfortable with this notion of "Nothing" as the core and the essence of your existence. You are accustomed to the form and concept delivered to you through your mind and your senses. Yet it is the mind and your senses that too have been given life and have come into being out of this "Nothingness," the eternal, ineffable spirit of our Lord and Creator, the alpha, the omega, the all that is or could be. It is from within the identity taken in the mind and the senses that the illusion of your isolation has been formed and is what is causing the suffering inherent in ignorance of our *Source*—the unspeakable mystery of Life at Its core and the essence of your being.

Your fulfillment, then, is assured in a conscious return to *Source*, free of the illusions of mind and the limited identity taken in it, as you reunite with the spirit of our Lord and Creator as yourself. Here the love that is our Lord would fill this eternal Nothingness as you realize Its source as yourself. The concept of God being separate from His creation would dissolve in His presence. As you come to this Moment completely present and dissolve in His embrace, you would realize you are *That*; and all that is, is *That*. And so it is that we can come to a *realization* of this most profound and extraordinary Mystery through the dynamic state known as "no mind." This coveted state of " no mind" would allow for a direct and immediate experience of "*That*," in the eternal silence of the Now moment. In that experience, free from mind and egocentric desire, we would find the joy and peace in the eternal presence of "*That*"—the love, beauty, mystery, and unity of Life at Its core. Until then, we would seem to exist as a separate isolated entity that is formed in the creation of this *membrane* and the appearance of mind. It is from within this mindful, self-aware state of isolation that "ego" has been born, by which I mean the illusion of a self identity that would appear independent from "*That*." ...... Herein enter the intellect and the madness of civilization.

Our ego/mind, which would seem to define us as something other than "*That*" in a never-ending banter of words, memories, concepts and desires, is truly an illusion because there simply *is* nothing other than "*That*." This "membrane" is truly nothing more than a *tension* between "*That*" and not *knowing* "*That*." But not knowing must necessarily come from something that is capable of knowing, and so we have the ingenious machinations of mind and the ability and desire to "find out" incorporated into this phenomenon of egocentric identity as we took of, or perhaps as we were blessed with, this "fruit of knowledge" as conscious beings. This gift of awareness, which is truly an expression of our *Source* and which is now incorporated into the membrane, brings with it intelligence, and is the light which illuminates our new-found state of self-awareness. It is also the how and why we began this journey of self discovery—the how and why we would become fully conscious.

It is within this state of "tension" that exists between the world that is *real*—the world of unity—and the world of illusion created by the isolated experience which we now know as *mind*, that "knowing" begins to happen. And so, having the appearance and experience of being a part from *"That"* —on our own, so to speak— in this awesome and mysterious universe, there has been, in the initial stages of the evolution of man, a natural insecurity, a fearfulness inherent in our newly formed "self-aware" state of ignorance. In that state of ignorance, one in which we are still most assuredly engrossed, we don't know who we are, why we are or for that matter why there is anything. We appear on the scene afraid and alone and necessarily begin to gather an identity in that experience of isolation and in those relative "things" around us. These experiences are incorporated into the "membrane" which, in a way, crystallizes this fragile illusion of ourselves and creates an identity as to whom we *think* we are. We take our identity in the relative thoughts produced in mind with little attention as to how it is we can think or from where these thoughts arise.

This fragile, wonderfully unique *relative* identity called ego or "lower self" will be with us all the days of our lives until we come to know and experience our *Source* and the unity of life at its core. Ego, by its very nature, cannot have that experience of unity. Its existence relies on the illusion of its isolation. In a complete awareness and understanding of the Now Moment, the isolated ego simply does not exist. The illusion it has of itself can only exist in its experience of being separate and apart from life, unconscious of the unity inherent in Life as perceived from the "higher-self" experience. It has taken its identity from the experience of mind, one that can never be in this Moment, but rather one identified in past experience and what it *believes* itself to be as it constantly references what *was* for identity. You could not be reading these words and have them make any sense if this aspect of mind were not in place. Each word is recognized and their meaning *remembered* in the reference library of mind that is not and cannot be present as it chatters on. Ego is hopeful and dependent on its fulfillment in the mind's illusion of a conceptualized future, an imaginary promise, that has no reality outside of mind but one potentially powerful enough to blind you to this Moment and keep your focus in the mind as it strives for your fulfillment in the illusion of tomorrow. And so, our egocentric identity is oblivious to Now, the only true reality that is or could ever be. Nothing has ever happened nor could it ever happen outside the Now, the glorious and mysterious presence that is this Moment.

Mind is unable to fathom the mystery that is this Moment because of its transient nature. It is simply a tool to be used and enjoyed when needed. Like a hammer, it can be useful, even essential for building a home, but it is not capable nor would its nature ever allow it to become that home. And so, in ignorance of our true nature, the mind simply does its job as best it can. Mercifully, we are becoming aware, however painfully, of its limitations and the hold it has had on our eternal spirit, a hold that has kept us imprisoned in the constant chatter and endless banter of mind as it "hammers" away at life in the illusions of past and future, which it has had to create as it names, calculates, and tries to define this world and ease the tension of our ignorance. Mind cannot *know* the Eternal; it is merely an expression of the Eternal. That Eternal aspect of ourselves is an *experience* that lies outside the constant activity of mind in the peaceful silence of our own Being, and yet, as you will come to know, is the reason and source of that activity, indeed for all that Is.

In a state of stillness wherein the "tension" is completely eased, that is, in a state of "no mind" in which there is a pure and complete awareness of Now, we would lose our transient relative identity and the illusion of separateness that is inherent in egocentric consciousness. The light of love and the peace of unity, which is the true essence of this eternal Moment and is at the core of our existence, would radiate from our Being which is now realized in the Now as

Source. As we lose the illusion of separateness that the ego/mind has created through this process of silent discovery and so become *conscious* and *aware* enough to *let go* of it—that is ease and release the *tension* that isolates us in the illusion of mind—we would come to *realize* who we truly are through this exploration and subsequent illumination of our inner essence. This inner essence is truly our divine nature, our "higher self." It is essentially our *Source* manifested as us in search of itself. ...... It is this *Soul* of ours that can, through an enlightened incarnation, realize Itself as God through, ironically, these vehicles of body and mind once they are understood as tools/gifts and as expressions in form of the Holy Spirit within us and not the "who" we are. Total identification with the body, mind, and emotions would be, in a way, like believing you are the car you are driving. It may be a powerful vehicle that can take you to many interesting places and open you to extraordinary experiences, but without you, what would it matter!?

As we become aware of the silent, eternal presence of Being and of the illusion the mind/membrane has created, and come to witness this state of *tension* in which we exist, we can begin to let go of that illusion of separateness and start to experience the unity, magic, and joy of this eternal Loving presence. If that Love and knowledge of the spiritual significance of our lives had been an important part of our initial experience of life in a loving and supportive family, then we would be well on our way to that deeper understanding. And yet, the influence of suffering that is inherent in ego identity can be a powerful catalyst for transcendence and the reason Jesus saw those who suffer truly blessed, for more than one have come to our Lord through pain and the desire to be free from it.

Developing a deep faith in our Lord and His wisdom, having realized how we have been so graced with this glorious gift of life and with a clear vision of the limitations of mind, the innate wisdom and impetus for letting go of our shallow, egocentric pursuits would be revealed. With a loving and compassionate heart that would ensue, we could begin to dissolve the membrane in a conscious, loving, and joyful surrender into *"That,"* as we come to know It as our essence. In the ecstasy of this eternal presence, free from the tension of ego and with a silent mind, we would consciously reunite with our *Source* and *Creator* and so fulfill our destiny. We will come to know the joy of eternal Peace that had been obscured by the illusion of separateness and the constant chatter of mind, and experience the ecstasy of *His* eternal Love, the Love that has always been ours, the Love that we seek, the Love that we are!

⁂

Well now, that may all sound easy enough; however, there is a bit more to it than that. For as we continue to evolve out of our state of ignorance and detachment towards that potential state of awareness that will awaken us to our true nature, there is much to overcome, much to learn, and far more to *unlearn*. With each birth, we are born again into ignorance and taken from the profoundly deep yet temporary security of the womb, finding ourselves incredibly vulnerable. If we were karmically fortunate enough to have been born into an environment of love and support, the membrane does not "thicken" quickly. In other words, feeling secure, the ego structure need not develop rapidly—we are not so tense—and we can remain in the Light of Love, ... innocent and happy, a most auspicious beginning! This, of course, would seem the ideal. We, of course, do not live in an ideal world—relatively speaking. Our experience of separation leaves us ignorant not only of our *Source* but also out of touch to the energetic *way* of Life. The limited ability of our five senses to go to the "unseen" eternal world of spirit imprisons us in the transient, relative, and superficial world of ego where suffering is born. For within that world of ego all things must necessarily pass. Our desire for fulfillment and our need for identity have been sought-after in the many "things" of the transient world of form and illusion. We will necessarily suffer the loss of this superficial, false identity and the inevitable failure of fulfillment in the world of form.

Within this limited perception of Life, the birthing process is too often viewed as a dis-ease that requires a cure and not the natural "flow" of Life's energy. The intervention of technology, the fear and ignorance that surround the birthing process, and the good intentions of those involved have made for many a horror story. But it certainly doesn't end there. Abusive or inattentive parents, the influences of a disturbed society, any early childhood trauma, or the karma of past lives can and do create the need for protection. The membrane/ego "crystallizes" and the inherent, although for the most part unrealized, connection to our *Source* is clouded and darkened further. We quickly enter the world of mind and remembering—a most powerful illusion—and lose touch with this Moment and deepen our disconnection from *"That"* ...... from *God*, the eternal essence of our lives. It disturbed Christ when He pleaded to "Let the little children come to me, and do not hinder them, for the kingdom of heaven belongs to such as these" (Matthew 19:14). The innocent, the pure, the trusting; there is nothing in their way, and it is a time that should be honored and protected. It is also an incredible opportunity for us, as parents, to experience and to practice unconditional perfect Love and to be truly in touch with our divine essential nature.

Childhood is and should be a magical time filled with the love and security that only a parent can give to a child. It is a time that this "unseen" world of Spirit plays an important role in the development of our children's ability to love as they venture into the relative world of form. But the ignorant, distorted, and fearful egocentric influences of aggressive, impatient, critical, demanding, abusive, neurotic, inattentive, absent, or intolerant parents can do great harm by further "insecuring" this Moment and creating more fear, tension, and the need to protect. These energetic "blocks" of fear, anxiety, and insecurity that crystallize into the membrane become obstacles to the flow of the Life energy that we are all "vibrating" in. These blocks can turn into the ego structures of neurosis and psychosis that can become more intense as the Life energy tries to move through them—as we "grow." Many on the spiritual path have come to experience this phenomenon of holding on to an identity which is locked into the mind's pain and suffering and intensified by the powerful negative energy associated with it. They have learned the importance of spending time with and coming to understand the nature of these blocked energies so the process of dissolving and/or transmuting them can begin. Many who are far from the path have become hopelessly lost in a painful identity that is difficult to let go of and suffer, as a result, from the fear, anger, and frustration of their isolation, opening themselves to the addictions of escape and a life of perversion.

The importance of not creating these negative influences through the practice of unconditional love and total acceptance during those initial seven or eight years of childhood is the sacred role of parenthood, and whose importance cannot be overstated. Indeed, we will all need to drop the ego structure and return to this Moment like children if we are to know the Kingdom of God. Having and knowing this aspect of unconditional love as a part of our initial experience of Life can make this journey so much easier, our experience of Life so much richer and our contact with the Divine so much nearer.

Naturally, the membrane will "thicken" anyway. Birth, with all the trauma of separation, the difficulties of passing from one world to the next and the needs and sensitivities of this new body all begin the process. Still, under normal circumstances, at birth the membrane is very transparent, so we are very close to our *Source*, and it is difficult to see ourselves apart from our experience. Ego hasn't formed, so there isn't much to remember, and we are very much a part of and in the *Moment* although not terribly conscious of *"It"* yet. As time passes and as we learn who we are in relation to the other "Droplets" around us, we identify ourselves as a separate "I." Our membrane thickens and crystallizes into the relative identity being formed, a natural and indeed necessary growth process if we are to survive relative egocentric life, as we begin the process of undoing our karmic debt and coming to full awareness.

Adolescence, with the onset of puberty, hormones, boy/girl-friends, the future, competition, "drugs, sex, and rock and roll," and everything else that makes the teenage years both wonderful and miserable for us all only adds to the clouding and thickening of the membrane. The mind/ego are very much in control now. We are going out into the world of our parents armed, or should I say *armored*, with our and others' sense of who we are and how important or unimportant we see ourselves. We are imprisoned in mind, in the illusion of past and the definitions we have formed in identifying ourselves, and become slaves to the illusion of a future we perceive will one day fulfill us or cause us to suffer in the anxiety of uncertainty. We have intensified our disconnection from this Moment in the illusions of mind and the process of securing the illusion of ego.

To not have a deep spiritual connection to Life at this time can be a recipe for disaster. If we as parents and teachers have not passed on this "higher knowledge" which would open our children to the unseen world of spirit and the unlimited potential of present-Moment awareness that can lead them out of the illusion of mind and into the unity, power, and Love of the Now Moment, then we have left our children to wither on the vine of the material world. They are detached from *Source* and deprived of the nutritional "soul food" of higher knowledge.

Education that does not provide a clear sense of the majesty and mystery of Life, with emphasis on the importance of our inner journey back to *Source*, and without reverence and gratitude toward our Creator, is of little use as a tool for personal growth and may create a dangerous barrier of deception. The exploration, naming, and manipulation of the relative world of form can be a fascinating, unending, and very demanding activity. But it will produce only shallow achievements if derived merely from the illusion of mind and ego as it will do little more than support the illusion of the mind and ego. Without an appreciation for the unseen world of spirit and for the moral and ethical values inherent in the higher knowledge of Soul, with Its immediate connection to our Lord, we have abandoned our children to this relative world of illusion, its inherent ignorance, unholy needs, wanton greed, and the fearful influences of the "politically correct." Look around! They are bombarded constantly by a world lost and corrupted by the illusion of separateness and tempted by the paraphernalia of escape that arises from the pain of that isolation through drugs, alcohol, and a distorted, hedonistic view of our purpose here. Even the most mundane references to our Lord have been removed from our schools, leaving the unseen world of the Spirit without credibility. They will gain no direct insight from the perverse view of the world peddled by an unconscious, exploitative media that profits from the *sins* inherent in this detachment through the glorification of violence, sexual deviancy, and callous, unconscious egos. These are the ear marks, as history has shown, of a culture in deep spiritual crises. Truly, the illusion of ego is in control here with all the chaos, tension, isolation, and madness that is the ego as it attempts to find identity and security in a world *it* has "made up." It has become consumed by the "story" it would have of itself, blinded to the reality of Life and to the glorious joy of Being. It is a joy that is eternally waiting to be realized, in this very Moment, once we have freed our Soul from the illusion of ego and time.

Whether as an adolescent or as we develop into adulthood, we find the built-in mechanisms of psychosis and neurosis that can develop as we try but too often fail to find a secure ego identity in the limited "relative" world of illusion and the five senses. We merely exist in this "mass-consciousness" state of isolation, which is not easily reflective of our individual divinity, and which clouds and obscures the spiritual heritage that would lead us to a realization of the unity of Life. In this delusion of mind, these mental dis-eases manifest as a result of an increase in the *tension* that is inherent in our ignorance and isolation. An awareness that is limited to a disturbed, isolated ego with limited deranged information will get hopelessly lost in the darkness of isolation if a connection to *Source* cannot be made. Mental illness manifests from the inability to form an identity in this relative world of illusion because of some great trauma, fear, and/or isolation that may have been experienced and then became crystallized into an identity early in one's life. Or, as Droplet brian weiss has revealed, these difficulties could be the possible effects of past-life traumas.

The attempt to fit one who is lost and confused into a narcissistic world lost in its own illusion of itself is hardly "mental health." The blind cannot lead the blind! Surely, our love and compassion with the application and understanding of this "higher knowledge" should be applied here, not the random use of powerful, mind-altering drugs or techniques used to "shock" away destructive tendencies. Droplet r. d. laing may have been the first to recognize the failure of psychiatry and the difficulty of defining "sanity" in this world of illusion. Although his controversial views and his own troubled life came and went quickly in the public eye, his work remains a starting point for many who would like to add love, compassion and a strong spiritual perspective to their therapy. That clearly defined line between science and religion, the physical and the mystical had been mercifully blurred by Laing. His work may have been the beginnings of the humane treatment and spiritual understanding of the lives of the deeply disturbed.

The pervasive use of behavior-altering drugs in our children is nothing short of criminal and a sinful disservice to Life and Its processes. It is horrifying to note that suicide is the number one killer of our teenage sons and daughters. Our shallow, materialistic approach to the problems of this life and the simplistic approach of removing the symptoms of the dis-ease that arise from a life lived in ignorance of our Lord are no doubt creating more disturbance in our mass psyche. Any attempt at understanding this life without a clear recognition of its spiritual significance is at best incomplete, and at worst a lie and a perpetuation of the illusion that isolates our soul and intensifies our suffering. We are all the Divine in search of Itself. Those who dedicate their lives to ending the suffering of mankind must come first to that understanding and "higher knowledge," adding to their work the love and compassion taken from the perspective of Soul. Too many well-meaning Droplets have brought the pain of their own traumas to their work, giving them little more to offer those in need than their compassion and their empathy. Not that compassion and empathy aren't necessary; it's just that it isn't nearly enough to take those in need out of suffering. To become a true healer of mankind, the healer must come to first "heal thyself." Only then can the peace and love of His eternal presence, now radiating from the healer, be brought to this Moment and guide those who are lost and in need of His love home again.

Jesus' first law and most urgent and passionate plea was to "simplify," and to not let the accumulation of possessions and the incessant need for more "things" outside ourselves cloud the membrane with an identity in those "things" which keep us from Him. This law, more than any other, we have ignored and abused and this has caused untold suffering. Clouding the membrane early on in the frantic need to secure the isolated ego's identity, sometimes in "things," will only make this journey that much more difficult. There is good advice in measuring someone not by what they have but by what they can do without. It is in simplicity that we will come to know who we are in this Moment, in and through the "eyes of God," whose essence lies at our core, free of the trappings of relative life and the illusory, narcissistic identity through which the mind/ego has you mesmerized.

The "energies" of this relative world can be overwhelming and complicated as well as fun and magical. The key here is to simplify and to know with *conviction* that this life we are living is a spiritual journey; "*It*" could be nothing less or nothing more. It is a journey of self-discovery and insight into the mysterious nature of our Lives and the glory of God's creation. We are here to free our souls from the prison of egocentric life and open ourselves to the divine Love that we were meant to be, that we truly are. We cannot allow the superficial trappings of this relative world to overwhelm or identify us. We must not get lost in the false, transient identity of the ego and its limited awareness, which would keep us unaware and out of touch with Now. We must be sure to avoid the addictions of this life that would limit our identity to their power over us. Our purpose here is far greater, much deeper, and infinitely more fulfilling.

In this world we'll come into contact with many other membranes. Some Droplets will be a lot like us, and we'll call them "friends" and explore together. Others will be light, yielding, and disarming, offering no threat, and easy to go deeply with, even to love. There are those we will marry and so, given the time, gain the powerful opportunity to grow in awareness together, as ego and its limitations are revealed in the relationship. Others will be frightened, lost and in great need, and will suffer terribly in their isolation. Some will become dark and unyielding, narcissistic and well armored, deeply insecure and difficult to reach. (This type often finds "accomplices" in their perversion. The Droplet hitler was this type, and managed to coerce many others as insecure as himself with the promise of a "savior".) There are those poor souls who have not been able to integrate a relative ego identity or a more significant spiritual awareness into their experience, so they suffer from the absence of both in a world of delusion.

The inherent dictate of the mind to "find out" has spawned the "intellectual," those of us whose life energy has been directed primarily to the head and who may have closed their hearts to the ravages of Love. With an ego that is filled with the fear and insecurity all of us have inherited, their view of the purpose of Life is often a superficial, impulsive one of conquest and gain, rather than one of exploration and insight into the mysterious nature of this existence. Their ego/mind creates and can manipulate this relative world of illusion very well and *must* remain in control of it for security. Many have rejected religion as "opium for the masses" (actually, as you will see, not a bad analogy), and in so doing have "thrown the baby out with the bath water" by creating and living an extremely insecure and shallow life surrounded only by what they know and what they can control and/or manipulate. Their experience leaves little or no room for anything that is spiritual, the "unseen" or the "Mystery" that is the essence of this Creation and which lies in the silence of this Moment that mind deplores. The brighter they are, the easier it is for them to manipulate the illusion that comes with this isolated experience of Life, and the more successful they may be on this level of ego; however, it will be more difficult for them to leave the illusion behind and to uncover a deeper, richer meaning and purpose for their lives. How they suffer and/or shut down when "Life" inevitably comes along and upsets their plans. Taken too far, these Droplets tend to detach themselves from their bodies and/or their hearts, leaving them empty and dissatisfied with, at times, a "know-it-all" attitude as protection. In failure, they may adopt a "victim" status and reject an "unfair" life that has "no God." Their judgment and rejection of others is a way of securing a false sense of superiority in the illusion of the isolated ego; yet in reality, they are closing off all portals to the mystery of Life and to their role in "*It*" (although every role, as you will come to see, has divine purpose).

Knowledge derived from intellectual pursuits is essential for surviving and exploring the relative world, but can present a formidable hurdle for gaining *direct* experience into the truly miraculous and mysterious nature of Life. For this, the mind must be taken to its limit and then surrendered. It must be understood that the mind is an instrument for our use and must not become something that enslaves us. The world of mind, ideas, beliefs, and exploration can and will lead us to something more than we are and is the vehicle, the *gift*, we Droplets will use on this journey of self-discovery. How else could you be reading this? Education and the exploration of life is of the utmost importance; however, it's not about boosting and securing the ego's need for identity with degrees, titles, and status, but rather humbling and awing the ego with an understanding of this miraculous experience that is Life through the gaining of "higher knowledge" and heightened awareness, and, out of that, to the experience of *Wonder!*

> To me, every hour of the day and night is an unspeakable perfect miracle.
>
> —*Droplet walt whitman*

There is, finally, no intellectual *knowing* of "*That.*" It is an *experience* that transcends the intellect into an altogether different realm of knowledge and way of knowing. Truly, not even the simplest of one-celled creatures can be understood intellectually; they can only be given a name and/or manipulated. The final mystery that is theirs and our own existence remains a marvel, a miracle and truly a testament to the creative wonder of our Lord.

Jesus warned the intellectual with the words, "I will destroy the wisdom of the wise; the intelligence of the intelligent I will frustrate" (1 Corinthians 1:19). His is an experience of unity in a direct communion with *Source*. His soul and our Lord are as One. In that awareness, He would frustrate the intellect in its attempt to know the unknowable or define the unspeakable. He would confuse and humble the relative mind that isolates and keeps us from that *awareness* of unity, and open us to His vision of this ineffable *Moment* and to the glorious Mystery that is the essence of our Lives. "*That*" is beyond the intellect.

The mind/intellect is indeed a manifestation of consciousness; from where else could it have come? Yet it is a very small aspect of whom we truly are an expression and certainly not a true representation of our full potential as long as we find our identity in it. It is beyond the mind and the limitations of thought that essentially binds us to a "relative" identity and to the mental "story" of our lives, into the transcendental spaciousness of Being that lies at the core of our existence where our unlimited potential in *Source* can be realized and true self-knowledge gained.

It is our mind that sets us apart from the natural world and allows for our search for meaning, our sense of wonder, our creative expression, and our extraordinarily diverse individuality. These, then, are the marvels of our lives! However, undisciplined, as a tool for the ego, the mind can destroy any connection we have with Life, with God, and ultimately with ourselves. We Droplets have *believed*, among other things, that we were of a superior race, a superior religion, and/or a superior political persuasion. Secure in those *beliefs* and limited by that *knowledge*, we have committed and continue to commit the genocide that is the hallmark of our race, a tragic and terrible reminder of our dark side—that is, a membrane darkened and thickened by the process of securing the isolated ego—which can and has created identities that are capable of almost any act, no matter how horrific, in order to strengthen and preserve the illusion of itself.

The mind—the intellect—cannot complete this journey for us, but without it we could never begin. This desire to know what is unknown is the driving force of Life in search of Itself. Take caution as to what you fill your head with each day. Don't allow yourself to escape into the banter of an unconscious media and to be exploited by or find your identity in programming that glorifies violence, promiscuity, and the ignorance and destructive qualities of narcissism. We are not here to be entertained from morning till night by the mindless forces of culture as the patterns seem to suggest. Nor are we here to be defined by religion, politics or anything else that would have us stagnate in egocentricity. Break the patterns that would define who you are and so limit your experience of what Life is—what God is. Seek your own truth in a direct experience of "*That*"! Come to this Moment and to the Silence of Being; there is much for you here. Find and wonder at the miracle that is your Life in this Moment, then explore and celebrate the glorious role you play in it. Ask yourself often "Who am I? ...... Why am I? ...... Why is anything?" for these are powerful questions when asked passionately and explored sincerely in the power of this Moment.

Listen to Droplet albert einstein, who took the mind to its limit and found that

> the most beautiful thing we can experience is the mysterious. It is the source of all true art and all science. He to whom this emotion is a stranger, who can no longer pause to wonder and stand rapt in awe, is as good as dead: his eyes are closed.

How we all come to these varying degrees of detachment and dependency depends a great deal on our karmic "load," the degree of insecurity in which we went out into the world and the identities we were drawn to in our search for security. Religion, career, politics, money, and power come quickly to mind with nationalism or racism not far behind. How we look, what we drive, how much money we have, what we *believe* or where we are on the social ladder of success, w*hatever* can give us a place to belong and feel secure is all lore for the ego. Most, if not all, of the relative life man has created reflects and feeds off of this deep need and insecurity that is fostered by the appearance of our isolation.

Whether we pump ourselves up as being of a superior race or a Yankee fan, it is, ironically, that need to belong to something more than we are that is the impetus which will eventually lead us back to our divine heritage, provided we can acknowledge and identify that *need*. Through introspection and focus, we can learn to acknowledge and experience the insecurity that all of us detached Droplets share. Once acknowledged, it can become the impetus and the means for our return to our *Source* and Savior. When it is not acknowledged, it is our own self-imposed hell of fear and superficial pursuits in the endless, narcissistic isolation of the ego and our futile and too often destructive attempts at securing it.

I have come to experience that there exists in the realm of knowledge a "higher knowledge." This "higher knowledge" is obtained not from books, although it can certainly be reflected in books and is a measure of the author's clarity. It does not come from theory or opinion but rather is acquired from within this mystical experience that transcends relative life and is universal and undeniable to all who have come to it. It is from within this experience of the infinite, in the eternal silence of this Moment, that this mystical "higher knowledge" is transmuted. This knowledge has an energy in it that compels those who hear it and are ready to hear it to need to know more. It is a knowledge that instinctively eases the underlying tension of our isolation. It rises from a source deep within our being and infuses the intellect by its presence with a genuine sense of truth and hope beyond the lie of ego. This infinite *Source* of all we know and experience is obscured by the relative, false ego identity that is lost in the mind's illusion of time and space, and whose wisdom is unobtainable through the five senses. It is in the transcendental experience of pure consciousness, the Spirit of our Lord—which has given rise to form and life to the senses—that this "higher knowledge" is transmuted.

It is from within this field of "pure consciousness" that all true knowledge is taken, for It *is* where all that can be known arises. It is from within this field of pure consciousness that all knowing happens, for It *is* where knowing has come. It is from within this field of pure consciousness that we will truly come to know who we are, for It *is* who we are.

Ego arose out of the illusory experience of self as a separate entity and the initial fear inherent in ignorance as a means of dealing with this mysterious world of the unknown. The ego, in an awareness of itself, one which isolates us from this unified field of consciousness, simply ignores Now and is kept occupied while it finds its identity in the illusion of past and future, and in the manipulation of the more familiar, relative world of form and the limited experience of life through the five senses. We live in the illusion of being apart from all we are a witness to, and although we can at times intuit and begin to sense this aspect of the eternal, it is avoided and feared as something other than what we perceive ourselves to be. In truth, the ego would like nothing more than eternal life as it has been endowed with the desire and the quest for life eternal; however, it is within the experience of the Eternal that the illusion of the ego is revealed and its demise ironically assured. The Eternal is, nonetheless, our inner essence, the core of our existence, and it is within the experience of this silent, perfect stillness, in the state of "no mind" that you will find your fulfillment in a peaceful, joyful reunion with our Lord as who you are.

Droplet eli jaxon-bear is an accomplished spiritual master who has brought "*Nothing*" to his practice as a therapist. He has come to *know* the source of our fear and has allowed himself to fall deeply into it, and then through it, and has come to that place of complete and total peace. He has brought the love, compassion, and "higher knowledge" of this unified field of "Beingness" into his practice, and has been a guide for many who seek, who suffer, and who are lost. Coming to "Nothing" has enriched his understanding of the source of our suffering and has brought him deep insight into the nature of ego through the use of, among other things, the "enneagram."

For those of you who have never heard of the "enneagram," I'll define it simply as an ancient Sufi concept that describes nine basic personality types that each of us, to one degree or another, fit into. Three have emphasis on our identity in the physical body, three in the emotional body, and three in the intellectual body. The enneagram has us look at our ego structures so we can free ourselves from those stereotypical identities, so described, through a recognition of the "lower self"—the ego—and its limitations. In so doing, it allows us to open to our "higher self" through a "witnessing" of the lower self. In other words, we free ourselves from the illusion of the "membrane" and the personal identity in which it has become crystallized.

As an example, let's say you are a Number Three in the enneagram teachings. In that illusion, your security and sense of self is taken from a strong desire to have your "self-image" in the relative world be recognized, praised, and acknowledged by those around you, especially those who have achieved a level of success you admire. You may put great effort into the acquisition of titles and degrees and post them in prominent places. You may strive to be a part of the elite society of your community and volunteer your services to worthy causes, not so much for the cause but rather for the philanthropic status it may bring to you. You may be drawn to politics for the status it holds or theatre for the acceptance and praise. You may be very demanding in your work and of those who work for you. Anything less than perfection is seen as failure and as a direct affront to your status and identity. It is a world of deep insecurity with a constant need for recognition and accomplishment. There are, of course, highlights of achievement and the recognition that keeps you in the mode; however, the underlying insecurity is never satisfied and the anxiety and tension never eased. Those who live it may always be "on," fun and interesting to be with; however, they may suffer terribly in their quiet moments and are uncomfortable alone. If you were a Number Three and could begin to recognize the "box" in which you are imprisoned, opening the lid to the possibilities outside your self-imposed prison would bring with it a richer understanding of who you are. It would be marked at first with an undoing of your relative identity. That may be painful and difficult to let go of. However, once accomplished and once your identity has moved from the transient to the eternal, you will begin to experience a genuine sense of joy and peace in your life, and perhaps live your life fully for the first time.

Droplet eli jaxon-bear's work with the enneagram is masterful. Look to his website at *www.leela.org* and embrace the effects of this "higher knowledge" as it manifests through him and his work. The enneagram is a fascinating look at ourselves and a good start at recognizing and exploring our situation, and it will open you to the unlimited possibilities of your life.

Droplet gangaji's understanding and spiritual awareness are in no way shadowed by her husband Eli. She is a dynamic spiritual teacher who has come to *Source* and is a clear expression of the wisdom of the Soul. You are also invited to her website at *http://gangaji.com* for an inspiring look into the world of Spirit. Now listen to her as she speaks of the eternal.

There is a great secret that beings throughout time have announced, the secret of an extraordinary treasure, the treasure of the nectar of life. It is nectar of pure beingness, recognizing itself as consciousness and overflowing in the love of recognition.

If you imagine yourself to be located in a body, then you will move that body from place to place, searching for this treasure of nectar. But, if you will stop all searching right now and tell yourself the truth, you will know what is known in the core of your bones. You will know what these great beings knew and attempted to describe. You will know it with no image of it, no concept of it, and no thought of it. You will know it as that which has eternally been here. And you will know it as yourself.

⚜

My soul is a candle that burns away the veil;
only the glorious duties of light I now have.

—Droplet st. john of the cross

The membrane, then, is that "veil of illusion" that shrouds our perception and creates a barrier between whom we "believe" we are and of whom we truly are an expression. However thickened that membrane becomes—that is, however strong the relative ego identity is—it is proportional to our suffering and insecurity, and vice versa. And so we have the endless cycle of births and deaths and the accumulation of karmic debt that continues to perpetuate our isolation and our suffering until the membrane is dissolved, the debt repaid, and that veil of illusion is burned away.

As we become aware of the eternal nature of the soul and allow Its presence to color our relative life, and as we continue to acquire this "higher knowledge" of the soul, we can naturally dissolve the membrane in an easing and a letting go of that false ego identity that is clouding our perception of Life. As we become totally present in the Now, we will easily flow into a conscious and loving reunion with our *Source*—with *"That"* which is our essence—allowing us to realize we are and have always been *One* with our Lord and this Creation. In that awareness we lose the fear, insecurity, and suffering of the isolated egocentric identity, and inherit all the Love and acceptance, all the joy and security, all the wisdom, compassion, and

41

creativity that is in the ecstasy and grace of a loving reunion with our *Lord.*

Filled with Brahman are the things we see,
Filled with Brahman are the things we see not,
From out of Brahman floweth all that is:
From Brahman all—yet he is still the same.
OM ... *Peace—peace—peace.*

—*The Upanishads*

Chapter III
CITY LIFE

People who have not been in Narnia sometimes think that a thing cannot be good and terrible at the same time.

—Droplet c.s.lewis

Cities hold a particularly strong draw for the ego. They are the materialization of all aspects of the human mind/ego. Everything can be found there and the ego can swim in the security and the ecstasy of its own creations without the distractions of nature or reminders of the "Mysteries" of Life. It is an extremely mental/ material environment. Living in *apart*ments, Droplets can go on infinitely satisfying urges and never need to know or question their source. Life goals can be established and sought-after, supported by an arena created just to that end. An incredible amount of energy is spent that does little more than comfort and attempt to secure the isolated narcissistic ego identity in its illusion of separateness and in its need to have and be more. The illusion that is our lives and the ignorance inherent in it is reinforced each year as ego celebrates New Years Eve, a commemoration of our detachment from the Moment in the nostalgic glorification of the past and with a hope for happiness in a future that can never come. It is a celebration that seems to unconsciously emphasize our need to find happiness beyond the restrictions of mind by temporarily intoxicating it into oblivion.

Remember Narcissus who, having seen his reflection in the water and having fallen in love with it was then compelled to live his life at the water's edge, mesmerized and in love with his own

43

image. It would be here at the water's edge that Narcissus would waste away and die in the pursuit of a love that could never be. We too may be slowly "dying," lost in the ego's illusion of itself reflected in the illusory world of "mind stuff." We are oblivious to the potential of our own destruction as we do all we can to secure the image we would have of ourselves in the pursuit of a love that too can never be.

I lived in New York City for many years and enjoyed much of it, especially the other Droplets. I love the city in the fall, the holidays, the pubs, the restaurants, the museums, the theatre, the innate creative spirit of man. There is much to feel good about. I also learned about the many "boxes" we put ourselves in both mentally and physically—boxes that would define and identify who we are and limit us to the illusion of the mind in the endless pursuit of securing the ego. It was, in fact, *Mysteries Outside the Box* that I had envisioned for the title of this book those many years ago. There is always something to do, something to create, something to consume, somewhere to go. We are never in the moment, and we are oblivious to our own destruction, living in the reference library of mind that is in a constant repetition of the past in the hope of success and fulfillment in the future. Even those whose vision of life and of themselves has become deeply distorted through trauma and/or perversion can find like-minded Droplets with similar deviant life styles in which to get lost. There is, everywhere, much for any ego to identify and secure itself in, many mental "boxes" that would limit our awareness. The mind is in a constant state of "chatter," always "on," always doing. Within this endless mental activity, there can also be much to escape from, should things go wrong, or we wake up to the emptiness of our lives consumed by superficial egocentric pursuits, giving drugs and alcohol fertile ground to plant their addictions of escape.

I have often pitied professionals like Droplet mickey mantle whose strong ego identity was formed during his extraordinary career in baseball (one in which I took unending delight) but left him empty and vulnerable to the addictions of escape in the *Moment* of his retirement years. "No one can serve two masters" (Matthew 6:24), and the building of the ego in the illusion of relative life is in direct opposition to the building of a spiritual life in His eternal presence. That doesn't mean one does nothing or denies the uniqueness of one's character and the gifts we have been blessed with. A world with only monks in it would be rather boring, I think, and not reflective of our Lord's creative spirit. What it does mean is that we must come to recognize the *gifts* given to each of us that have made us uniquely ourselves, and express them in this world with the full knowledge and acknowledgement that "there but for the grace of God go I," and leave the isolated and unnatural "look at me, I'm so great" egocentric view of who we are behind. Humility is the key word here. Not the humility of low self-esteem but rather the humility and grace that is in an *awareness* of how we've all been so blessed!

> *Life in the world and life in the spirit are not incompatible. Work, or action, is not contrary to knowledge of God, but indeed, if performed without attachment, is a means to it. On the other hand, renunciation is renunciation of the ego, of self-ishness—not of life. The end, both of work and of renunciation, is to know the Self within and Brahman without, and to realize their identity. The Self is Brahman and Brahman is all.*
>
> *—The Upanishads*

"Success," whether sought-after or accomplished, can be an awful trap to escape from, leaving many "has beens" in the public eye, with no identity in the Moment that can give them comfort, subjecting their vulnerability to the addictions of escape or locked into a mind/ego addicted to dwelling in the glories of the past. For those who have "made it," they often become consumed with the fear of losing "it," or for those who have not yet made "it," consumed with the desire to have "it" and in that quest and to ease that fear, the unbridled insecure ego will demand a very high price: ...... your soul!

The conquest of the illusion of Life and the comfort and strength of the spiritual life that would accompany it would make even the most spectacular career or fortune pale in comparison. Becoming aware of our Lord's almighty presence in your every experience is to gain a vision of the world that is unshaken by events, free from suffering, and filled with a divine peace. Listen to the words of Christ and come to truly know, for "What good will it be for a man if he gains the whole world, yet forfeits his soul?" (Matthew 16:26). And by "soul" He is pointing to the "higher self," the spiritual connection to our Lord, the eternal spirit of Life that is our essence and our heritage. To lose that connection in the pursuit of money, fame, power, and the trappings of the material world is a corruption of our essential nature by the ego in the endless pursuit of its identity and security. We would suffer the loss of the true meaning of our lives and the peaceful inner essence that is the Soul.

We did initially come together in cities to comfort, share, and protect. They were the centers for art and learning, a place to socialize and explore our human predicament. Unfortunately, it seems that much of "art" has gone from a genuine search for meaning and a glorification of God's work to, for the most part, a repulsive, self-indulgent "ego trip" and learning a way to produce ourselves for the consumer marketplace.

With the mind/ego in control, "nature" becomes a concept. The opposite sex, the nearest thing to a *natural* phenomenon to be found in the city, is merchandized and obsessed over. The insidious influence of cell phones, CD players, the banter and divisiveness of talk radio and newspapers, only add to and strengthen the illusion and power of the mind/ego, leaving us further isolated and detached from this Moment and our essential nature. These same egocentric influences are systemic throughout the human experience. As such, the "burbs" don't offer much of an alternative, for here nature is pruned, clipped, and generally put up with. Everything is given a name, a place, and an owner, and the *Mystery* is pasteurized with plenty of shopping.

I have no doubt, and it is my experience, that in this all too familiar state of consciousness we have unconsciously been "possessed" by mind. It is forever "on" in a constant repetition of past experience that would have us become identified with the relative knowledge gained from those experiences. In that "reference library" of mind, we live our lives from a purely "relative" perspective that has programmed and imprisoned our essential yet unrealized nature into a false identity supported by man-made environments that flaunt and encourage the ego in its quest for security and identity. Tell me, can you shut mind off at will? Can you become free of it on demand? Have you become a slave to the ceaseless machinations of mind? Would you know who you are outside the familiar chatter of mind? As you ask yourself these questions, you may begin to sense an opening happening. As we begin to recognize and transcend mind, there is a presence, a spaciousness, an ineffable feeling of being more than we are that rises as we begin to sense the silent emptiness of pure consciousness. It may be a little frightening at first; however, herein lays the key to your freedom. For as you begin to perceive the Mystery of your life in *"That,"* the all and the nothing, your inner identity is taken from the transient to the eternal, and true liberation becomes possible. Do not resist the mystery of this presence; rather, open to it and surrender.

When the Mystery is not alive, and when your identity is stuck in egocentricity, boredom and complacency take its place and the need for more becomes the dictate of the mind. We are meant and are driven to be more, and ego knows this energy. Herein lies the very tricky and difficult dilemma of the human experience. For being unconscious and out of touch with the miracle that is our lives, we put ourselves in the mental "boxes" that initially give us the needed identity ego seeks; yet, by its very nature, limits and falsely defines who we are. In the illusion our spirit continues to cry out for freedom. Unrealized as our need to transcend mind and as a drive of the ego, this desire for freedom can take us even further from ourselves in the pursuit of some concept or belief outside ourselves we feel may satisfy our innate longing for freedom. We can get even further lost in the muck of the material world and the illusion of mind/ego in its futile attempt to escape the confines of conformity in unending "alternative" pursuits as it ironically and hopelessly uses itself to escape itself in a never-ending cycle of illusion. We can become hopelessly lost and/or completely crystallized in yet another transient, shallow "mind-based" identity by continuing to look outside ourselves for fulfillment.

Here then is the "higher knowledge," which can identify this energy that demands that you become more than you are. It is the God Head within you that longs for and cries out to you for your heightened awareness so that you can come to the glorious realization that *you* and *It* are as one. Understood as *"That,"* it can lead you to who you are, for it is within you that this immense silence of Being awaits and true freedom can be found. Your life can finally be truly lived in a joyful fulfillment that is forever new in miracle and can never know boredom. As you still your mind in the light of this higher knowledge and release yourself from the need for egocentric identity and come to the quietude of your inner essence, you will come to know God as yourself.

I have walked with people whose eyes are full of light but who see nothing in sea or sky, nothing in city streets, nothing in books. It were far better to sail forever in the night of blindness with sense, and feeling, and mind, than to be content with the mere act of seeing. The only lightless dark is the night of darkness in ignorance and insensibility.

—Droplet helen keller

The mania to "produce" our children by teaching them so much so soon is robbing them of their childhood and the development of their basic instincts and intuition. These are the non-intellectual, the "right brain" functions that are essential for creating a whole human being and are unimportant to the ego, which is based and survives in the intellectual "left brain" functions. Our children most of all need our love and attention. Through it they can feel secure and loved in this Moment, as a part of this Moment, and as part of God's creation. The city can only offer what man's ego has created in order to secure itself in the illusion of separation, and it is mired in the insecurity, fear, and isolation that are the ego. The obsession to secure the future is an "unacceptance" of this Moment and who we are in It, and it is filled with the fear only an isolated ego knows, locked away from and in contempt of the silent miracle that is Now.

I feel great compassion for the children who are born and raised in cities, so detached from their essential nature and so quickly burdened with the egocentric illusions of life. The ease and flow of nature, the infinite and the "Mystery" replaced with the intensity and shallowness of mind stuff. Children subjected to the shallow importance and manic competition over the "right school," the "right grades," and the "right career" are being denied their ability to "be here now," and this is a denial and a rejection of who they are in the Now. What you are in this Moment *is* what you are; it is all there is and all you will ever be, and it must be accepted and explored *Now* in this *Moment!* The wisdom and innate intelligence of an open and loving heart, regardless of age, can only be experienced in this Moment, and are the keys to true self-knowledge. It transcends and leaves the shallowness of the intellect far behind, yet will eventually fulfill the intellect as it finds and expresses the wisdom of the soul and reveals the impulse behind knowing ourselves, indeed behind knowing.

All of life has purpose, and even the incredibly diverse and at times perverse, confused, addicted, and shallow identities that can come from a lifestyle limited to egocentric pursuits can serve as a reminder of how desperate we are for fulfillment and the necessity of *Being* with nature and in finding our identity in and as a part of the natural world, outside the city and not limited to the transient ego identity, the "mind stuff" that will surely suffer in its isolation and wither away.

> *A happy life is not built up of tours abroad and pleasant holidays, but of little clumps of violets noticed by the roadside, hidden away almost so that only those can see them who have God's peace and love in their hearts; in one long continuous chain of little joys, little whispers from the spiritual world, and little gleams of sunshine on our daily work.*
>
> —Droplet edwin markham

In many respects, the cities are now being replaced by the computer. We have created yet another "box" in which we can find all of the ego-satisfying facts and fantasies without leaving the house! Combined with television, we can live most of our lives in a box within a box, rarely having to experience Life directly. Either or both of these "boxes" can be powerful addictions for the detached soul imprisoned in mind, as they offer a safe place to hide and be entertained. Although I do love my computer with all the Droplet connections and the fabulous wealth of information available, there is room for concern. It can be one of the many things that have us, instead of us having them, by directing too much energy to the head. I am reminded of the film *The Matrix*, wherein the illusion of life is so expertly created by machines that humans are no longer aware of reality and had become unconscious "produce" for the machines. In a similar way, the ego can and has created environments wherein *we*—that is the essence or soul of our being—becomes "produce" for its survival. As Mr. Spock would have said, "Fascinating."

Many years ago the book *Four Arguments for the Elimination of Television*, by Droplet jerry mander came to me. This is an extraordinarily insightful work, written by a man who worked many years in the television industry. It is a book that everyone should read, and certainly anyone who has children must read. The powerful illusion that this medium creates and the negative effect it can have on our children by taking them away from the flow of Life and putting them in front of nothing more than a box of flickering lights that promotes questionable values and ethics should concern us all. If you have any doubts as to addictive quality of this medium, shut it off for a week. This medium has replaced much of the everyday family interactions that are essential to our children's growth and to the building of character. It is a barrier to our creative impulse and creates a powerful disassociation between who we are and this Moment. It does, however, make the ego happy, as it has been created by the ego to satisfy, pacify, entertain, educate, and keep the illusions of the ego strong. But don't panic! I would not want to see this medium abandoned completely, as it can have, in the hands of those responsible, enormous value and purpose. It can also offer an insightful look into the workings and madness of egocentric pursuits once they are understood. Everything in moderation can be applied here, as we must come to accept, explore, and understand *everything* that has been set before us; but do take caution not to subject your children to the "garbage" that the ignorant, narcissistic ego can produce in its exploitation and abuse of Life.

Clearly, the cities have been created for and by the ego to give it entertainment, identity, security, and purpose, and I suppose that in that security lays the hope for the soul. But like *The Matrix*, we are living in an illusion created by a lesser force that lives off of our life energies. The desire to "become" someone better, richer, or more famous is the innate desire of the Soul to return to our *Source* and Creator, but it remains the barrier to that quest if only the ego is served. For now, there is little more to do here than accept the wisdom and order of God's plan and find our place in it. I do, however, foresee a more enlightened time when cities would be more integrated with and supportive of the natural environment and not such arrogant, isolated ego statements—and our identity not so dependent on egocentric structures but more open to, in tune with, and with a reverence for this miracle of Life and the natural world.

We have within us the God-given spirit and ability to create incredible beauty, perform great acts of love, and achieve deep wisdom. We can and should express ourselves in many ways to communicate where we are and where we are going. City life, television, the ego, and the separation and insecurity that are self-awareness are where we are right now in that process of becoming. Let it be and let your first step have you become a witness to the process so you can learn from it and not become another exploited victim of it.

I have a ball court next to my workshop, and every spring a particular weed manages to push nearly three inches of black top out of its way in order to sprout and grow. The "Life force" in that little weed to become what it was meant to become is incredibly strong. Do you think that desire to become is anything less in us Droplets?! ...... Love will find a way, in or out of the cities, with or without television and computers. Watch and see!

To believe this terrible machine world is really from God, in God, and unto God, and through it and in spite of its blind fatality all works for good—that is faith in long trousers.
—Droplet george terrell

All that is happening is happening for you! You are what you are seeking, free of mind, free from fear, free of the endless egocentric pursuits that call to you outside yourself for fulfillment. And so you ask, "What is life without goals, without striving for more, without hope for the future, without mind?!" And I would answer that your life is complete as it is, in a freedom from mind that has no need of future, no need for power and security, no need for anything more. Here and Now is your fulfillment in a loving, joyful experience of our Lord as yourself. Fear not, for you will not turn into a zombie with a frozen smile on your face, unable to think as many have interpreted this state of "no mind." Rather, you will join with this eternal Moment as the dynamic, ever-present, loving and creative spirit of Life that you truly are in the Now, joyful and grateful.

Chapter IV
EVIL

Of the good in you I can speak, but not of the evil.
For what is evil but good tortured by its own
hunger and thirst?

—from The Prophet *by Droplet kahlil gibran*

As stated, this membrane of ours can be thickened and clouded by almost *any* concept so long as it remains on a mental or intellectual level in the unending process of securing the fragile ego. As an example, no group of Droplets I've encountered are more self-indulgent, self-righteous, narcissistic, and more difficult to go deeply with than the "religious" ones (alcoholics being perhaps the exception). As the mind structures and crystallizes the membrane with concepts and ideas that would, in that mental activity, secure the ego's identity, we grow further and further from our immediate *Source* and more towards a superficial transient identity, albeit unique and mesmerizing. Given the powerful concepts of God, the specter of His fearsome antagonist Satan (evil), and "righteous" living as security, these religious zealots' identities are formed from the concepts and dogma of their beliefs and the world becomes a "them/us" situation that can, and has—like many other "beliefs," justified the atrocities man commits against man, against nature, and against God. They may judge the rest of the world that does not conform to their beliefs as "evil" and in so doing, limit God only to what *they* can understand. In their ignorance, they are creating an even greater barrier to our Lord with those limited "beliefs."

You must and will come to know that *All* of this *Moment* is the Holy Spirit expressing Itself as this Moment and can be found *only* in this Moment, *Now*. The Kingdom of Heaven is indeed at hand *in this Moment*. ...... It *all* happens here! Silence your mind and raise your awareness to an understanding of *"That"* in this *Moment*, and you will come to know. As the ego becomes saturated with this "higher knowledge," it becomes its servant, and life is naturally lived more from the heart. Knowing happens from a place deep within, at the level of soul and not limited by the experience of ego. The source of "evil" is a membrane clouded by narcissistic delusions and/or beliefs that leaves one out of touch with this living and ever-present Holy Spirit. In the darkness of their own perversion and deeply in the illusion of their separate identity, this "evil" can at times be given far more power than it deserves, when many others, lost in the same fear and isolation that is the ego, "convert" to believing the same thing, often with an empty emphasis on achievement in the world of form as a substitute for true self-knowledge.

Truly here is where the failure of the mind and its inability to finally fulfill us is so blatant. Clearly, concept has replaced experience and the glorious prospects of this Moment are lost to the mind/ego and its need for identity. Our Lord's presence as the Source of this Moment and as the core of our existence has been obscured in "beliefs" and the limited machinations of mind—beliefs that may have pointed us in the right direction but hold us back from a direct exploration of our lives and the great mystery it holds, for fear of losing the comforting "knowledge" taken from these various beliefs. This "knowledge" gained from these beliefs has foolishly attempted to define that which cannot be known through the intellect. Without the security of beliefs, though, we fear falling back into the eternal black hole of ignorance as we approach this ineffable Source of our existence, the great abyss, the "Nothingness" that defies explanation. Locked safely into the prison of mind and the concepts that falsely define who we are, we find a temporary yet necessary, given the anxiety of our ignorance, false understanding of ourselves, one that would ironically keep us from realizing, through direct experience, the who we truly are, as an expression of our Lord in this, the only reality that is, the all and the nothing, ... the

Now Moment. "Knowledge" that cannot or does not take us beyond the dense fear of ego into the glorious flow of life, continues to cloud the "membrane" in the structure of "knowing" that can, if not taken far enough, limit our immediate experience of this, the Now Moment. If there is something to be considered as "evil," this then would be it, and anything else that would keep us from a direct experience of our Lord as the essence and Source of this Moment, should also be considered "evil." Now we can begin to gather why Droplet carl jung so poignantly declared that "religion is a defense against religious experience." Strong religious conviction can ironically keep us from our Creator for fear of losing those mental concepts we would have of ourselves and our Creator. In what must necessarily come in a direct experience of the ineffable Spirit within, free from mind, we would open ourselves to our Eternal essence. This direct and immediate experience of our inner Source and Lord, would overwhelm and make insignificant any mental concept we would have of ourselves or of Life.

Evil, like darkness, is, in and of itself, non-existent and is given identity only in the mire of ignorance where there is no light. The darkness of fear and ignorance are evil's fertile garden, but they can be easily dissolved with the light of "higher knowledge," the divinity of awareness from that level of Soul, and a heart that is filled with Love—the product of a life lived with an intuitive eye towards the unseen world of Spirit, an ear to the eternal silence of Being and with a trust in and love for our Lord and *all* He has created ......
NOW.

Let's consider the myth that is the story of the Droplet lucifer. In it one of God's most trusted angels who, having gotten lost in the illusion of self in a knowledge that was ignorant of the true nature of Life, *thought* himself to be better than God. He somehow crossed the line that put him in union with our Lord and became a separate entity with free will and great power (hmmm, sound familiar?). His *knowledge* became limited to his own self-interest, and his actions took him further from his *Source* and *Creator*. Actually, if Lucifer did exist, we would owe him a great debt, as it was his sacrifice and his subsequent banishment from Heaven—this metaphorical "ocean"—that created the dynamics of separation, perversion, suffering, longing, and finally the glory of reunion with our Lord. This "reunion" cannot be overglorified as it encompasses the whole of creation and is an ecstasy beyond imagining. It is the complete fulfillment of our lives in the realization that we are *That*, and in *That* we would radiate the eternal Love and peace of our Lord as ourselves. As *That* becomes aware of *That*, there is an overwhelming ecstasy in the jubilance and joy of recognition.

It is in the suffering inherent in separation that the impetus for our return to our Lord is found. Lucifer, or more accurately the dynamics of separation, was brought into being at the dawn of creation, and he was given his name out of the anxiety and in the ignorance that came with our becoming "self-aware." We simply had to find someone or something to blame for our suffering and for the pain of our ignorance.

Truly, we can continue to suffer in ignorance of our *Source*, and in the illusion of separation blame Lucifer for our pain, or we can choose the process of reunion with "*That*" which is our Lord and ourselves, through the dynamics of heightened inner awareness, the acquisition of "higher knowledge" and in becoming completely present, free from the illusion of mind. It is within those dynamics that we will be rewarded with the Love and compassion that is in the presence of the Almighty as the *Source* and essence of this Moment.

Perhaps it could be said that anything that would keep us from that experience should be considered "evil." An undisciplined ego and a mind lost in the illusion of itself would keep us from true self-knowledge and is a powerful destructive force that could easily be construed as evil. Ironically, the self-proclaimed religious leaders of our time who have mastered the "Scriptures" and who have come to judge the world from that perspective have perpetuated an "evil" far more divisive than if Satan himself were at work. They have obscured our Lord's holy and immediate presence in the muddle of mind, in ignorance of and detachment from a glorious state of consciousness that is in the silent presence of Now, free from Scripture yet rich in the "higher knowledge" of our Lord.

In the creative process, there must necessarily be something destroyed. As the flower blossoms, the bud is no more. However, to identify only with the destruction of the bud and blame "evil" as the cause is severely limiting the whole picture and perpetuating the illusion that there is something more than God going on here. "Evil"—the destructive energy that appears in opposition with the creative force of Life—does have its place in the overall play of creation, and may even be experienced as a "dark, ungodly force," but there is more going on here than our intellects can possibly come to understand, at least at this juncture. Hatred, murder, rape, war, greed, and all the other negative, destructive qualities we humans possess are the product of our ignorance, our narcissism, and the perversion of an isolated insecure ego. What else could it produce?! Thank God for conscience and the compassionate influence of Soul, or we never would have made it this far.

An identity that has become dense through the crystallization process and has become identified and obsessed only with the illusion of ego can become an "evil" in its "unholy" needs and the desire for self-gratification. It can be a powerful force whose experience can be a terrible drain on the unsuspecting. This "heavy" solidified ego identity can be taken even into death, and the "negative" energy of those lost souls' transitory identity may be experienced as an "evil" dark force. These souls may have to live through many lifetimes of suffering in their own self-imposed version of "hell" before the karmic debt they have created is satisfied and they become aware and humbled by their own divinity.

I have seen the effects of this "evil," and I have witnessed the powerful destructive force it can manifest. I know how it can draw many who are lost and unaware into the dark side of life. I have been sickened and deeply saddened by the sight of a young pregnant mother staggering through city streets, drug addicted and defiled. My blood ran cold as I listened to the confessions of callous, heartless murderers. I know of the countless millions who have lost their lives to the horrors of war. I have known young men forever traumatized by the brutality of war and have lost loved ones to the addictions of drugs, alcohol, and obsessive use of tobacco. I have watched natural beauty polluted and destroyed by greed and corruption. I know the brutality of the mob, the cruelty of the disturbed and wounded soul, and the terrible pain that evil can inflict on the innocent. Yet I fear no evil, for I have come to know our Lord and trust in His Love. There is a higher order and purpose to life that no "evil" could ever disturb. What appears as evil may at times shroud this vision of hope, but it can never be more than just a passing aspect of this great Mystery of life in search of itself.

Too often we are seduced by this "evil," and in our desire to end it we feed this negative energy and create a greater evil as it manifests in war and the violence of hatred and revenge. Evil cannot remove evil; only our Love can remove evil, for it is our Love that is reflective of our Lord and His eternal presence. When we are faced with evil we are faced with souls who are lost and who suffer. Their greed, their lust, and their ignorance must be brought to an end, but not at the cost of our souls. We must be resolved to bring Love back into the Moment, and through our actions that Love will be revealed.

If we are suffering in this experience of Life, it is because we are ignorant of the will of our Lord and detached from a true awareness as to the glorious nature of this *Moment* and our role in it. The greater the suffering, the further away we are from an understanding of who we are. The degree of suffering becomes a measure of our own ignorance. We are blinded by this veil of illusion and live in the darkness of our ignorance. No words can take us to that exalted experience of Grace that would end our suffering, although some can inspire and give direction. It will come in a *realization, a direct experience* of who we are in this Moment, free from the limitations of mind and ego. It will come from a spiritual life lived in faith and dedicated to a clearing of the membrane that would bring our awareness to the only reality there is …… this eternal Moment. In a conscious surrender of the ego and in a state of "no mind" we will come to a direct and immediate connection with *"That."* In that wholeness, in that emptiness, true knowledge of what we have been blessed with will be taken. In that awareness there is no evil, there are no mistakes; there is only God's will, God's work, and God's Love of which we are all most assuredly an expression. Until that understanding is achieved, faith is our only recourse.

Faith is a big word here and suggests more than passive submission to circumstances. We must make every effort to understand and include ourselves in this process of becoming, and make every effort to do what is right and honorable in the face of adversity, as well as avoid the addictions of "evil" with a trust in the processes of Life. Within each of us lies the Love and Compassion that is our Lord, and it is our destiny to bring it to bear on those who are lost and in need of this love. We must use the gifts of free will and the process of discovery to come to an understanding of our lives beyond the superficiality of ego, and avoid the temptations and addictions that would lure the insecure ego and imprison our Soul. When we come to love and have faith in and for this process of becoming, it will open our hearts to the needs of others and prepare us for His presence as we become the fulfillment of this Moment.

> *It is not an unworthy thing to wish to count for something and to do great work in the world; but we shall count in the final audit not by the measure of our capacity, our business, our energy, but by the tenacity and vitality of faith and our love.*
>
> *—Droplet richard roberts*

SIN

Let's consider the dilemma of the Droplet julian of norwich:

After this I saw God in a Point, that is to say, in mine understanding, by which sight I saw that He was in all things. I beheld and considered, seeing and knowing in sight, and with a soft dread, and thought: What is sin?

Sin, to answer Julian, is the *perfect* expression of being out of touch with *"That."* In that isolation, we have found our identity in the transient nature of mind and body and in that identity we are susceptible to pain and injury, and to our ability to inflict pain and injury. And yet in truth, we have never been born nor will we ever die. We are that ever-present eternal spirit in search of Itself, veiled in the illusion of ego and the temporary identity of mind and body. All that is, all that was, and all that will be finds its source in *"That,"* and in *"That"* all things are perfect. Our Lord's plan could have it no other way. Come consciously to *"That"* as *"That"* through these *gifts* of mind and body, and you will be free from the stigma of sin and the limited identity of mind and body.

If you have lost your way, your suffering will be your guide back to Him. While lost, you may have "sinned"—a relative term at best—or witnessed the sins of others, so ask: against whom or what and/or why? Then go deeply into the experience and to the motives and find your way back. You will find that you can only "sin" against yourself in the darkness of your ignorance and that you can only defile what has been defiled in you. Only ego is capable of sin and only ego can identify it. A heart that is filled with love and a mind that has faith in this process of becoming cannot sin or be sinned against.

The ego, the "lower self," has within it the God-given desire to become more, to have more, and to be fulfilled. However, as long as only the lower self is served, you will be chasing horizons forever in an endless pursuit of limited pleasure and transient desire, never knowing why and never being truly fulfilled. From that egocentric perspective, evil can appear a vibrant force that lures and temps unsuspecting souls into its hold. Within the limitations of the body and mind there would truly seem to be a "dark side" to life that can be heartless in its cravings for power, control, and pleasure. It is however, your "higher self" that has the answer to your quest for happiness, and your suffering will be the wake-up call.

Revere your life and treasure the incredible gifts of life that are yours to enjoy, but turn your longings from the constant needs of an insecure ego and come to acknowledge the potential for your fulfill-ment in the eternal unseen world of spirit and in the power of Love. Know that every being has equality in God's eyes and that there is no "sin" that will not be forgiven by the power of this Love. By your complete presence, you will be embraced and the "sins" committed in the darkness of ignorance will fade away in the power of Love's pure Light.

Forgive yourself and those who may have "trespassed against you." We are all on this glorious journey of self-discovery. Do not be led into egocentric temptations, but be delivered from "evil" through the higher knowledge of who we are meant to be. Every moment *is* perfect; there is not a grain of sand out of place nor is there a single moment to regret. Know this and there is no sin, know this and there is no evil, know this and there is no "kingdom of darkness" bent on our destruction, know this and there is only ...... *"That"—the Kingdom, the Power, and the Glory!*

DEATH

The darkness and mystery of death can, at times, appear as an evil force that is working against our desires. The loss of a loved one can be a terribly painful experience. The love and the connection that was created *appear* to be lost. That physical presence of the beloved is no more, and we can no longer find our comfort and pleasure in them as we seem to have lost that place of exchange. A sincere contemplation of our own death is unimaginable and perhaps frightening outside the familiar sensations of body and mind. Even in faith and with a strong belief in heaven and an afterlife, the mind is challenged and fearful with the prospect of no body and no mind.

From the perspective of ego, the death of the body is the end, for it can only feel its existence in relative life and is ignorant and isolated from our eternal nature. Indeed, in that "relative" field of being, that is in the world of form, all things are transient and must pass. However, we have within us all a point of reference that is beyond the limits of ego and our five senses. From the perspective of Soul, we are not locked into the false transient identity of ego, limited in time and space, but rather hold an eternal, ineffable understanding of ourselves and of those we love. From that perspective we are *all* a part of and are swimming in this great sea of Love.

Everything and everyone we have ever loved and everything and everyone we will ever love has come from this eternal Spirit of Love and will return to that eternal Spirit. It simply and completely could not be any other way, for we are all a part of and an expression of this Great Spirit of Life. Truly knowing this through a direct and immediate experience of our eternal nature, the suffering of loss would be no more, for what would be lost? If we could drop the illusion of separateness, realize the connection we all share with our Lord, and come to this Moment of Love in Love, nothing could be lost and no one ever abandoned. If in life we come to realize our eternal nature, then death is a time for celebration, for although we may leave the body that once served as the vehicle for the soul for this glorious lifetime, the soul that has longed for reunion will have been freed from its limitation and find the eternal love and compassion of the Holy Spirit that has always been here for us and for those we love. In that Love then—in our return to *"That"*—what would be lost? Outside of this vision, oblivious to that Presence, there can only be the suffering of the isolated ego in the relative appearance of eternal loss. If the unseen world remains unseen and our awareness is limited to the ego and what superficially *appears* to be, then our suffering will be great.

Take the time, try and come to an understanding as to why we suffer in this illusion of isolation. Feel how we have limited our identity to the fear and ignorance of the ego without consideration for our *Source* and for the *Source* of all that we are a part of. Feel this eternal presence in all that is and know the peace of God. Do this and your relationship with the Almighty will improve immediately and your pain will surely be relieved as you realize you and all you experience could not be here without the eternal presence of our Lord as this Moment. If you are suffering the loss of a loved one, consider closely where they have gone, where they came from, what gave them life, and what has given you life. Truly, only the ego in exile can suffer here, isolated from this ocean of Love and afraid. Embrace your pain, go deeply into your suffering, and you will come to the eternal presence of the Love within you. Come to this Moment in the peace and silence of "no mind." Know His love and join with your beloved. Holding on to your pain and identifying

62

only with the limited, ignorant experience of ego will only serve to deepen your suffering and isolation with little hope of realizing the fullness of our Lord and what is actually going on here.

Dying is the unavoidable fact of Life, whose timing comes in and through the karmic consequences of our lives. It may come unexpectedly or be inexplicably cruel. In the illusion of separation and in the ignorance of the ego, it will come painfully with the sorrow of finality and the illusion of total loss. There is, of course, a place here for compassion in what Droplet kirtana sings of as the "beautiful sadness" that is inherent in the loss of form, and I do not mean to trivialize the pain of the loss of a loved one. However, as we come to the realization that we are not our bodies and that we are not our minds and we can let go of these false identities, then, in surrender and with faith, death comes as all things have come, with God's blessing and in God's grace regardless of circumstances. "Even though I walk through the valley of the shadow of death, I shall fear no evil for you are with me" (Psalm 23:4). Indeed, the Spirit of Life will be with us then as It is with us now and has always been with us. We could not, would not, exist otherwise. We are *"That!"* Knowing this, the essence of Life that gave that unique presence to our beloved can never be lost and will live forever in the eternally creative and loving presence that is this Moment of Love.

Bring your total awareness to this Moment, live it completely in joy and with Love, without pride and the illusion of ego, and then nothing can ever come as loss because you will come to know it was never *yours* to begin with. Know that in death, there is nowhere to go but to this eternal Moment of Love, and the Kingdom will be yours again. It is from *"That"* you have come, it is in *"That"* you have lived, and to *"That"* you will return, and it all and can only happen in the Now, this eternal Moment.

Understanding this deeply, bringing the experience of your eternal nature to this Moment, living a life of forgiveness in the light of the Love and Compassion that are the essence of our Lord's presence within us, can ease or even delay your death and the death of others. The limited ego has created an identity out of the many experiences of Life, and there may well be associated pain and trauma in those experiences that have caused energetic "blocks." The body experiences these blocks as dis-ease that will manifest in an assortment of illnesses if not dealt with and released. The miracle that is spiritual healing can come to us as we open to the eternal nature of our Spirit, imprisoned in ego identity, and join our Lord in this Moment of Love, forgiveness, and compassion. Dis-ease is released, body armor dropped, and health can be restored as we let go of the illusory, pain-filled egocentric identity into which we have crystallized. As we become aware of our eternal nature in the Now, we are freeing and healing body and mind from the anxiety of a false identity in ego, and realizing them as the gifts and tools of life that they are. We are free now to enjoy and use them creatively in the dance of Life!

Death, or at least the death of the body, will come to us all no matter what, but death is more than the process of our simply "passing on." It is a clarion call to the illusion of our lives and to the transient nature and the shallow identity of body, mind, and ego, whose "moment of glory" will surely and most necessarily pass. It is a reminder of the pain inherent in our exile and the desire of the Soul to have us find fulfillment in our own eternal nature, free from the restricted identity of mind and body but rather as a pure expression of this eternal Moment.

There is in death a shift in our "vibrational patterning" as we are approaching our Source, as we approach "That." If in life we have adopted the "higher knowledge" of the Soul and have come to appreciate and experience the fullness of this Moment as the only reality that is, death will be little more then a transition in perspective as we lose entirely our identity in the more dense physical body and our focus easily shifts to the experience of Soul. We naturally begin to vibrate at a higher frequency. If we have not become solidified in egocentric identity we can easily "move on" and join with angels on this higher vibrational plane. However, if our energy is heavy with egocentricity, if we have lived a life of ignorance and selfishness, if we have "sinned" against our fellow Droplets and have not been able to "let go" of the illusion of mind and the fear inherent in it, we will remain in the malaise of "low vibrational" frequencies.

In this state of consciousness, dying can be unnecessarily traumatic and painful as we are *forced* to "let go" of our superficial identity in the illusion of mind. "Moving on" would be difficult and so our return to this plane will be assured as we continue on our quest for self-realization. A return, it should be noted, that will leave you no better off than when you departed and may even carry with it the burden of a good deal of accumulated negative karmic debt.

If you knew with certainty that tomorrow you were going to die or that your beloved was going to pass on, tell me, where would your focus be, how would you live your last day? ...... Don't wait, surrender to this eternal Moment, to the Love, *now*!

Listen to Droplet kabir as he writes to us of *The Time Before Death*:

> Friend, hope for the Guest while you are alive. Jump into experience while you are alive! Think ... and think ... while you are alive. What you call "salvation" belongs to the time before death. If you don't break your ropes while you're alive, do you think ghosts will do it after? The idea that the soul will rejoin with the ecstatic just because the body is rotten—that is all fantasy. What is found NOW is found then. If you find nothing now, you will simply end up with an apartment in the City of Death....

All that you are looking for is with you Now. Come to this Moment completely present, free of the illusions of mind and ego, absorbed in His embrace, and you will come to know that every moment *is* divinely perfect, that there is neither a grain of sand out of place nor a single moment of your life to regret. This eternal Spirit has given you your life and has brought life to all you love. This eternal Spirit will bring you and all you have loved eternal, unconditional Love. Be grateful for your beloved, be grateful for the loving. Love your life, ... love your death.

The practice of meditation is a methodology which teaches us how to "let go" and be present. Its practice is essential, I believe, to becoming aware and to bringing those transcendental "unseen" qualities of the spirit into everyday life. I have practiced meditation for over thirty years and continue to enjoy the peaceful surrender into *"That"* which is the meditative experience. I will go more deeply into those experiences later on. For now, though, I would like to pass on one experience as it relates to dying.

During my more intense period of the practice of meditation, which took place during a six-month retreat in the first half of 1970, there were several instances wherein I did spontaneously leave my body. It was strangely a very comforting feeling, not one of disorientation or confusion. It came easily and quite naturally without any feeling of loss, but rather with a peaceful sense of having joined with something *more*. In that experience, outside the confines of one's body and as a witness to one's own body, there is a sense of "fluidness" and a flowing into something of great comfort.

Years earlier, I had read the *Tibetan Book of the Dead*, and although I found it interesting at the time, it didn't mean much until I read Droplet james moody's book *Life After Life*, which recounts the experiences of many who died and were "brought back." The parallels with the *Book of the Dead* were uncanny, and I knew with certainty we must indeed survive our bodies. Both books detailed the experience of dying with an initial "hovering" over one's deceased body, and then the movement through what is described as a dark tunnel. A brilliant, celestial light radiates at the end of the tunnel, and encounters with loved ones that have already passed on and/or revered spiritual guides await the departed soul there. The "crossing over" was described in both accounts in amazingly similar ways. My "out-of-body experiences" only supported the theory that we do survive our bodies and that we are more than our bodies. The fact that we do not readily have at hand the experience and memory of past lives and that *we* can somehow bear witness to the machinations of the mind would seem to suggest that *we* are not our minds as well. So then, who are we?

There is a Zen koan that says, "Show me your face before you were born." A koan is a question that has no intellectual answer and is used in the Buddhist faith as a means of leaving the mind behind and opening to the Eternal. The struggle to know what one looked like before one was conceived leads one directly into the spiritual world of the unseen, unseen yet very significant. It is here in this unseen world of spirit that we would come to realize the true nature of our being as an unbounded source of Love and creativity. Ours is a quest to know that world in this world as its *Source* and as our destiny.

To allow only egocentric pursuits to control and drive your life will leave you empty and lost in your passing on, at least initially. (We cannot be abandoned or rejected in spite of ourselves; our destiny still remains.) But a spiritual life lived in love and forgiveness with integrity and focus, one that avoided acts of violence, destruction, hate, and the relentless needs of an isolated ego, will put one more easily in touch with our *Source*—the essence of our "being-ness"—when the time has come to pass from this life. Those who have not will suffer the terrible loss of that loving connection in their vanity and egocentric pride, and bear the awesome burden to "undo" the karmic debts of their actions. Truly then, what can it serve you to have gained the whole world and to have lost yourself?

You are not your body and you are not your mind; live a life that is grateful for those *gifts* and one that takes wisdom, delight, and pleasure in them. Live your life with a daily focus on the Mystery and splendor that is the eternal *Source* of all there is as this Moment, and your passing and the passing of those whom you have loved will not bear the terrible pain of eternal loss as you come to know that God, Love, and this Moment are eternal and the very essence of who you are.

Some might feel that the "logical" conclusion to all that's been said is that there is nothing to do! If everything is perfect and under His guidance, why do anything? What you would have missed here is that you and your "free will" are also His perfect expression. Who you are, what you feel, and what you do are all a dynamic "Part of the Plan." It is true that who and what we are at this Moment are perfect; it could not be any other way in our process of becoming. There have been many perfect mistakes—"sins" if you will—and it is vital to our healing, our growth, and to our awakening to accept all that we have become. Reject nothing, remorse over nothing, but explore and understand everything that has happened in your state

of ignorance and separation. If you will go deeply enough, you will come to understand and to forgive, not only those who may have hurt you but also yourself. We are the prodigal son who has left the beloved "farm" to search out our dreams. We have suffered and sinned in our ignorance and in our exile, but we will return one day, guided by our pain, with the knowledge and faith that all we ever needed, all we ever longed for, was right in our own back yard. ......
It is time to come home.

We should celebrate and be joyful for who we are, take stands on moral and ethical issues, and rebel against injustice towards our fellow Droplets and those things that would cloud the membrane and so create "evil." Make use of the God-given creative forces within us to express our love for Life. In the words of the Droplet j. j. van der leeuw in his wonderful and highly recommended book *The Conquest of Illusion,* "Life is not a problem to be solved; it is an experience to be lived."

So live and know that you are loved, and live with the faith and courage to love. Don't allow yourself to be bogged down in stagnant psychic patterns that would define and limit you. Take yourself to your limits; go beyond your "comfort zone" in Love. Live—don't just exist; it is an essential part of the clearing of the membrane. Try new things, be free, and explore all of life! Free will is God's most mysterious gift; use it responsibly and enjoy! Just let's not take ourselves too seriously, remembering that nothing has come from *you,* so don't take the credit. What may come comes *through* us, and we should be grateful and give thanks daily for His gifts. Listen to the Droplet rabe'a basri:

> O God, if I worship You for fear of hell, burn me in hell, and if I worship You in hope of paradise, exclude me from paradise, but if I worship You for what You made me on mother earth, bestow on me the courage and will to carry it on.

...... Oh, what a precious gift this Life is! Be grateful, become aware, and open your heart to Loving!

Free will, though it makes evil possible, is also the only thing that makes possible any love of goodness or joy worth having.
—*Droplet c.s.lewis*

Remember that the membrane can be clouded with even the most righteous concepts and most pious of knowledge. Don't allow them to become the burden of the intellectual possessions that can keep you from the Kingdom as surely as those material possessions. In *The Essene Jesus—A Revelation from the Dead Sea Scrolls,* by Droplet edmond szelesky, it is written,

> Thus He speaks of the impossibility of a rich man's entering the kingdom of heaven on account of his unnecessary possessions and of the effect of these on his consciousness. Likewise, He says that the scribes and Pharisees with their burden of intellectual possessions can in no wise enter the kingdom of heaven.

Does that mean that too much learning is evil? Of course not, but it does mean that too much *knowing* and the egocentric identity that may be taken from that knowledge can block or cloud your relationship with the *Moment.* This Kingdom of God and your relationship to It is not a belief—It is the Mystery! He/It/That is all around us in this *Moment* as a living, *unknowable* presence that must be "experienced" with an open, receptive heart and not with an analytical, controlling mind. The egocentric world of beliefs, theories, ideas, and words must be taken to their limit and let go of here, and the essence of our Lord that dwells within us released from the prison of ego and mind so we are allowed to simply BE.

There is much in our state of separation that is destructive and much to avoid. We Droplets have much to learn and far more to unlearn if we are to be relieved of our exile. However, to create "evil" or "Satan" as a reason for our suffering would be akin to driving down the road blindfolded and blaming "bad luck" for the accident. There can be no scapegoats or excuses. There is only God at work here and only *we* in our ignorance can be responsible for what we create as "evil" and what we perceive as "evil." Remove the blindfold, become aware, and put a trust in the Holy Spirit that guides us. No concept of evil can survive the realization of His eternal Love. That Love is who you are, why you are and all that you are seeking.

Chapter V
MUSIC

Music doth soothe the savage beast.

The "intricate energetic web" mentioned earlier, which connects us not only to one another but also to the natural world and ultimately to God, is essentially *music*, that is, the "energetics," the sound or vibration that is this Creation, in what could poetically be called the "Song of Life." The physical world around us, including ourselves, becomes "frequencies and waves" when looked at from a purely scientific perspective, leaving nothing truly "physical" at its core, but rather, all is a great melodic oscillation, a grand cosmic symphony. In this glorious "Song of Life" we are either resonating and "in tune" and so enjoying a deep communion with this Moment or we are in "discord." That is, we, as a tonal note in this symphony of Creation, don't quite fit, don't seem to harmonize, or are "out of tune." Being out of tune for us creates *dis-ease* and can manifest in either emotional or physical distress.

Droplet john beaulieu is internationally recognized as a pioneer in the field of "music therapy" and is the founder of BioSonic Repatterning Enterprises. His work uses music—vibrations, rhythms, and tones—to allow patterns of trauma to be broken and to realign the body "energetics." This can begin to dissolve or move these energetic "blocks" and ease the unnecessary tension from the nervous system, allowing a healing to occur in an opening to the flow of this Life force energy that we are all *resonating* in. To state it more simply, we are put in harmony. A visit to his website, *www.biosonic-enterprises.com*, is certainly worthwhile.

Now don't oversimplify this and confuse what has been said. I know the attraction we have for the "maverick," the individual who has rejected conventionality and gone off on his own. Nothing is more abhorrent than the vision of humanity wherein everyone is the same. But this is not what is meant by being "put in harmony." All who have managed to put ego aside and allow the love within themselves to blossom; all who have opened their hearts and exhibited the saintly acts of a Christ; all who have willingly sacrificed their lives for a cause or a love greater then themselves; all who have displayed their creative genius and produced great works of art in a reverence for life and a glorification of the Creator, not for their own aggrandizement but rather for the common good; all these have come into "tune" and are flowing harmonically in this great, creative, loving river of Life, ... a crescendo in the symphony of Creation. A soul "out of tune" would be one limited by ego structure and locked into the malaise of a mass identity, the "mind stuff" of relative life, ... unrealized and unfulfilled.

Music therapy is an interesting and beautiful methodology for healing, and its insights can have application even in the understanding of the movement of planets and the very process of Creation itself. However, music that we simply *enjoy* can bring us into this Moment and is an experience that can be a relief from the constant chatter of the mind, allowing for a "softening" of the membrane. It gives the isolated ego—the "beast"—an opportunity to relax through the non-threatening, harmonic joining that is the experience of music. To allow music to flow through you and inspire song, dance, and the flow of emotion is fun and exciting and can bring one closer to God by simply "letting go" and being in the Moment.

I loved the "dynamic meditation" which came from Droplet bhagwan shree rajneesh's teachings and which is described in greater detail in his book *Meditation: The Art of Ecstasy.* It is a highly energetic "dance to the music" sort of thing, wherein you let go of everything, completely uninhibited, and go wherever the music takes you. It can really get your energy moving and is a wonderful release of tension and can be, in total surrender, an extraordinary cathartic experience. But then, having gone absolutely and totally free with the music for some time, the music would suddenly stop and so then would you. Being as still as you could hold yourself, you would find yourself suddenly left wide open to this Moment, alive and very aware, if only for a moment. It is a wonderful experience!

I have a pleasant pastime that, at least in my mind, allows music to become "consciousness." As I am driving or watching some activity, be it a sporting event or simply people walking through a mall, I enjoy listening to a favorite classical piece. I put the volume up high enough to block the noise of whatever the activity is around me, and then simply *be*. As I am watching and listening, the movement of people and objects around me spontaneously become an integral part of the music. The long procession of cars coming and going, the random directional signal, the passing of birds overhead, the stately presence of trees, the rhythmic cadence of pedestrians, or a leaf blown across my field of vision are all now merging with and a part of the music in perfect synchronization and harmony. What is most profound about it is that it easily becomes a thoughtless process and life around me is seemingly produced by the music for no other reason than to be a part of the music. All of the "normal" thought processes are gone as I come to the Moment in music. My own actions and reactions become a spontaneous, non-judgmental flow with the rhythmic flow of life around me. Try this yourself and be amazed how the "savage beast" can be pacified as music replaces the chatter of the mind and opens you to a perfectly harmonic sense of Now in the "consciousness of music."

There are so many artists whom I've enjoyed listening to, who have inspired, touched, and comforted me. There are many that have expressed their connection with a deeper part of themselves through their music. Of course, mine is a "baby boomer" perspective, but nonetheless, when the Droplet john denver wrote *Rhymes and Reasons* and *Sweet Surrender*, he was surely in touch. When Droplet cat stevens wrote *On the Road to Find out* and *Miles from Nowhere*, he too was in touch. When Droplet rod stewart sang *No Holding Back*, he was touching on something more than himself. What could be more profound or more heart rending than Droplet louis armstrong singing *What a Wonderful World*? How about the beatle Droplets and *Let it Be* and George's *Here Comes the Sun*, or Droplet joni mitchell's *Both Sides Now; Little Love Affairs* by Droplet nancy griffith, or Droplet jennifer warnes's first album, which I've worn out and would give anything to replace! Lose yourself in the haunting melodies of Droplet enya. How close was Droplet billy joel with *A Matter of Trust?* How much can you read into *The Question* by the Moody Blues? If you don't spring a tear while listening to *Amazing Grace,* I would have cause for concern (especially when played on bagpipes!). Does your heart swell and your spirit rise while listening to *Pachelbel?* I hope so. Don't miss the incredible beauty of Droplet kirtana and the love of her awakening. Is it Droplet mozart or bach that does it for you? I could go on and on, as there is no end to this list. Music has been the expression of our passion, love, pain, and en*joy*ment of Life ever since we Droplets could bang on rocks. Even the primitive and rhythmic beating of drums can create a magical atmosphere in which to get lost if you allow yourself to open to it and let go.

The theme of Love has been and continues to be our most popular subject expressed through music. As the children of Love who are searching for that Love, what else would it be? Take some favorite love songs and replace the beloved referenced—"darling," "baby" or even "Peggy Sue"—with "my Lord," "sweet Jesus" or "dear God" and feel what it is you really need and are searching for! Our longing for love and union with something more than we are *is* the energy that guides us back to Him. Love is our essential nature, and through the practice of love we are connecting with our higher self. The loving experience expressed through music can open the heart and be a daily reminder of our purpose here. In the immortal words of Droplet gracie slick,

> When the truth is found to be lies, and all the joy within you dies, don't you want somebody to love, don't you need somebody to love, wouldn't you love somebody to love, you better find somebody to love.

The longing of the Soul to be released from exile and be fulfilled by Love is reflected in the loneliness of ego and its desperate need and desire to be loved. Ego can only look to the "other" for its fulfillment and that quest can be manic in its pursuit, especially if the "other" has opened the heart to glory of Love and revealed the vulnerable illusion of ego. No finer expression of the compulsive and obsessive need for love and the desire of the ego to secure it can be found than in the Police's haunting song "Every Breath You Take." I loved this song the first time I heard it. It clearly reveals the insecurity of the ego and need for love we are all experiencing, and it sings the obsession that can manifest in the ego's compulsion to possess the illusive object of love. It is a beautiful, melancholy song that exposes the failure and fragility of ego ("since your gone I've been lost without a trace") and the longing of the Soul as it cries out "pleeeeaaaaasssssssee" in a desperate desire for union with the "other," a union that can sadly never happen in egocentric consciousness. Mercifully, I have never been on the receiving end of that kind of obsession; however, I have known and been possessed by that need and desire. It is, if understood, the first step towards the Divine as we lose ourselves to something more than we are. However, if this need for love is not understood as a "gateway" to the eternal as the Soul longs for reunion now manifest in egocentric desire, it can burn you at the stake in a hell of your own creation. Your possessiveness will not only destroy you but your beloved as well, as the "drama" is played out ("I'll be watching you"), and your beloved eventually becomes the cause of your suffering as you blame and accuse him or her for not fulfilling you. Let this song remind you of the desperate need we all share for Love and let it open your heart to the only place where it can be found ...... yourself. Become a present witness to the miracle of Life and your need for love ...... Become the lover, become the Love, and as you do, all of your relationships will be love relationships as the illusion of ego and the tension that had created it vanishes. The longing of the Soul is eased in the Love you were so desperately searching for ...... the love that you are.

It is not a good sign of our times, although indeed a sign of our times, to find so much music (if indeed it can be called music) expressing so many of the symptoms of souls lost in a membrane that is clouded, distorted, and detached and whose messages naturally express the hate, the violence, and the perversion inherent in runaway egos. Impressionable, disillusioned, and detached young people who have witnessed the pain and hypocrisy of their parents are drawn to such music as it gives them and their pain something bigger than themselves with which to join, and in so doing, it temporarily secures the fragile frightened ego. Are we looking at "evil" here, or is it simply the leaf that has lost the connection to its source and is withering on the vine? The destruction that can occur in this isolation is not the wrath of God's anger; it is simply what happens when we are no longer in touch, when we are "out of tune." This Moment *lives*, and your connection to It is essential if you are to be fulfilled. Don't put ego in the way, not yours and certainly not anyone else's.

Music is the connection of souls and a tool of the spirit. Make it a part of each of your days. Lose yourself in it, let it lift your spirits, broaden your horizons, and remind you of our purpose here. Enjoy!!

I Am Music

Servant and master am I; servant of those dead and master of those living. Through me spirits immortal speak the message that makes the world weep, and laugh, and wonder, and worship. I tell the story of love, the story of hate, the story that saves, and the story that damns. I am the incense upon which prayers float to heaven. I am the smoke which palls over the field of battle where men lie dying with me on their lips. I am close to the marriage alter, and when the graves open I stand near by. I call the wanderer home, I rescue the soul from the depths, I open the lips of the lovers, and through me the dead whisper to the living. One I serve as I serve all; and the king I make my slave as easily as I subject his slave. I speak through the birds of the air, the insects of the field, the crash of water on rock-ribbed shores, the sighing of wind in the trees, and I am even heard by the soul that knows me in the clatter of wheels on city streets. I know no brother, yet all men are my brothers; I am the father of the best that is in them, and they are fathers of the best that is in me; I am of them and they are of me. For I am the instrument of God.

—*Author unknown*

Chapter VI
RELATIONSHIPS

Of all the music that reached farthest into heaven
It is the beating of a loving heart.
> —*Droplet henry ward beecher*

Putting all the responsibility for your happiness onto some other Droplet is not fair, practical, or even possible. Only your connection with the Eternal can truly fulfill your deepest longings for love and union, and to think that someone else can is heaped in illusion and the fantasy of Hollywood. Don't misunderstand: learning to love and be loved *is* what Life is all about. It is our most precious experience and should be cherished and practiced often in preparation for our surrender to our Lord and in recognition of our divinity. To love is why we are here! However, for many, placing the onus of fulfilling all that we need onto someone else can create much resentment, anger, frustration, turmoil, disappointment, and pain. ......

> Give your hearts, but not into each other's keeping. And stand together yet not too near together: For the pillars of the temple stand apart, and the oak tree and the cypress grow not in each other's shadow.

These are powerful words from *The Prophet* by Droplet kahil gibran.

Picture two Droplets coming together. The magic that is falling in love happens. There is in both membranes a "window of opportunity" that will allow the Love that *is* our essential nature to surface and be shared. This romantic "forever, till the end of time" love is the first stage of any relationship. The ego is, for a time, overwhelmed and humbled with the acceptance and pleasures of romance, and we are in touch with that eternal presence that is this love and find ourselves vulnerable, mortal, alive, and in *Love!* That love can be shared, as long as there is honesty and trust in the relationship, keeping the window open and the ego at bay. Sooner or later, though, the ego is threatened and/or needs to take control, and the membrane crystallizes again to protect its very vulnerable position, and the flow of love is inhibited and/or conditional. If we were conscious enough to recognize the frailty of the ego and the insecurity that creates this "shutting down" to happen, we could open ourselves to our "higher self" as witness. Instead, most simply blame their partner for not fulfilling their needs or believe they have chosen the wrong partner. And so the "story" of our lives intensifies as our egocentric identity crystallizes.

Truly loving is not a function of ego, and the impulse to love can often be abused and exploited by the ego. The word "love" from the perspective of ego has a very different meaning than it would from the perspective of Soul. Anything or anyone that is of comfort to the ego, or anything or anyone that the ego may lust after for identity or pleasure would be considered a "love object" to the ego and can easily turn into something that is hated or despised if our needs are not met or we have been rejected. It can be accompanied by violence or compulsive behavior as the ego panics or becomes desperate. The word "love" has a completely different connotation when used to describe the meaning of love from the experience of Soul. Here love is a universal, complete, and unconditional acceptance of all that is in a total surrender and union with all that is. It is a joyful "Yes!" to all of life and to God in His fullness. Love radiates from within ourselves, as ourselves, in fulfillment of ourselves and the Life around us.

The experience of "enlightenment" releases the Soul from the bondage of ego and the limitations inherent in an egocentric identity into that unbounded field of Being in an overwhelming experience of completeness and joy that is this "coming home." The Soul, in a total and unlimited experience of Now—that is, in a conscious union with Its eternal nature—is released from the prison of mind and ego. Our relationships are the starting point for this unconditional surrender into Love. Understood as this, our love relationships, our family, our fellow man, and nature can be gateways to the eternal. Silence the mind and feel the eternal presence of this Love within you. Open your heart and let your love flow into every activity you are engaged in. Put the critical, doubting, unhappy, needy, and fearful ego aside and allow Love to happen. "Enlighten up!"

To create an unconditional love affair involves a great deal of faith in and for the process of love and a release of those traumas that created the egoist need for protection. These "blocks" must be identified, recognized, and dealt with so that we can see where the ego's needs end and truly loving begins. This is where the real work that is a relationship comes into play, and believe me; it is not for the faint of heart! As we open to this energy and become more present, the ego will be completely threatened and will hang on desperately to its pitiful identity. In its desperation it will blame and accuse or demand that it is "right." It will demean and find fault in the "other," or at times withdraw and pout. Recognizing these frailties can be difficult introspective work, but if worked through, a *huge* step in the right direction. Look to the enneagram for help through this process, for as we watch the ego interact in relationship much can be learned that can free us from our limiting ego structures and our shallow narcissistic reactions, and allow "love" to truly happen.

In *A Course in Miracles*, we are reminded that "we are not our bodies, we are not our minds," and that we must free ourselves from those concepts for unconditional love to happen. Our essential nature is unconditional perfect Love, as we are an expression of *"That."* If we are to truly love our partners and our children, then we must be prepared to love all children and all other Droplets, to "Love thy neighbor as thyself." These are powerful words that threaten the ego's concepts of "mine" and "yours." But truly loving is an essential aspect of our "higher self" and *It* sees none of the differentiation that the isolated ego makes. Becoming a "lover of life" is to fulfill the desire of the Soul and will bring you to the peace and splendor of Eternal One.

It is all too easy for some and at times absolutely necessary to make themselves "right" by finding faults in others and, through the practice of gossip and reason, reinforcing their sense of superiority. They tend to believe there is only one way and that they know what that way is. In so doing, we boost the ego identity, deepen our isolation, and shut down our love. Spurred by the unconscious fear of death that is inherent in the loss of ego identity, we become addicted to whatever has secured that ego structure, and God help those who would threaten it. Being "right" is not the experience of Soul, for Soul has no need to find identity in the superficial machinations of mind. From the perspective of Soul, loving, acceptance, and forgiveness have unbounded resources that can never be depleted. Here the peace of our Lord is our identity. That does not mean that one has no opinion; it simply means that one's identity is not bound or dependent on that opinion.

With a faith in this "higher knowledge," you can allow yourself to grow beyond the limits of ego, letting go of your fear and insecurity that demands that you be "right." Go beyond your "comfort zone" and find ways to love, indeed, allow love to happen. Freeing yourself of the ego identity means making a continued effort at stilling the mind, becoming a non-judgmental witness of your experience of life and so becoming completely present. Mind can only find its identity in the illusion of past, and hope for its salvation in the illusion of future. Here is why ego has become so lost and so destructive, for it can only use this eternal Moment, the only reality that is, as a stepping stone in an endless and hopeless pursuit of itself in the illusion of mind.

Only this Moment truly exists, and you must become completely present, free from ego, to know *"That"* and to be fulfilled in *"That."* It takes work, it means making a conscious effort to identify

our shared, innate insecurity which necessitates the egocentric processes of identification in those things and experiences of our lives.
It means detaching yourself from the involuntary reactions of mind
and emotions and becoming more aware of yourself as the "witness"—the consciousness—that resides within you, that is truly who
you are. It demands paying equal attention to what is going on inside
you as you react to what is going on around you. The limiting ego
identity can only get in the way of our loving and needs to be
brought into awareness. We need to recognize its "ways" and put
them gently aside with a focus on the miracle of Now. In the end
the more you put aside and/or dissolve in recognition, the more
potential there is for something greater within you to express itself
and the more meaningful your relationship with Life and indeed all
of your relationships will become.

It is essential for your understanding of the dynamics of this
Moment that you come to know that Love and the Eternal are mys-
teriously linked as one and are the same in this glorious play of Consciousness. They live here and now as the essential nature of this
ever-present Holy Spirit, of our Lord and Creator, and cannot be
separated. It is in this atmosphere of eternal nothingness that your
sacred love will blossom and fulfill you. However little sense this
may make, you must know that love and the eternal are inseparable
and one cannot be without the other, and that you hold within you
both. It is, ironically, in your becoming empty that you will be fulfilled by the unimaginable, unconditional Love of our Lord.

It is through this "Art of Loving" (also the name of a wonderful
book by Droplet eric fromm), by which I mean reaching inside oneself and consciously making efforts to bring your love and compassion into every activity in which you are a participant and through
the recognition and opening up to this eternal divine presence—this
sacred *"nothingness"* both within and without—that you will begin
your connection to our Lord. Truly, this is the only relationship that
will inevitably matter and will endure in your life. It should be
nourished and explored through the unconditional loving of others
and through the love, appreciation, and enjoyment of His gifts to

you. Your loving will take you out of your head—the "story" of your life—and into your heart—the essence of your life. Your attention will serve you and this world far better there.

This act of "loving" may need to be a conscious effort made with a focus on that center of love and compassion located in the middle of the chest adjacent to the heart, known as the "heart chakra." This is not so much a physical place but rather an energetic center of the Spirit from which these attributes of love and compassion arise. If you have ever loved, if you have ever cared, then you already know where this center is and you will have no trouble locating it. You may have lost touch with those deeper feelings, though, and will need to "remember"; this world has hardened many hearts. If so, then consciously recall those magical moments, whether as an adult or as a child, when you were filled with the warmth of Love and you melted into Its embrace. Bring that "warmth" back into your heart and remember. Bring to mind your beloved, or remember the love you had for a pet or a film that may have touched you, something or someone who invoked that love in you. Hold it and know that this love is emanating from within you and is a part of who you are. Then let whatever has brought you to this feeling of love go and just bathe in the warmth of an open heart. Let go of all that binds you, and let your awareness be free to explore the eternal presence that is all around you. Fill it with this unconditional love that is your eternal nature, and be free. Practice this "remembering" and bring your awareness of this compassionate, open "heart center" into your daily life. You must be totally present to love, for truly loving can only happen in the Now.

As you encounter each person who comes to you in your day, go within and say to yourself, "God has blessed us both, let me show you how." Then open your heart and let this love and compassion be a part of your exchange, and let it become an integral part of your "relationship" with Life.

There are many who want me to tell them of secret ways of becoming perfect and I can only tell them that the sole secret is a hearty love of God, and the only way of attaining that love is by loving. You learn to speak by speaking, to study by studying, to run by running, to work by working; and just so you

learn to love God and man by loving. Begin as a mere appren-
tice and the very power of love will lead you on to become a
master of the art.

—*Droplet st. francis de sales*

Our relationships are "sounding boards" for our spiritual growth process. If we find ourselves in pain, unable to love or even be loved, or if we expect to be "saved" by another and are compulsive to that end, or if we, in fear, have isolated ourselves and barricaded our hearts from the influence of love or we find ourselves in any other condition that does not allow our essential nature to express itself, then we had better look within and begin the process of removing the "blocks" that are clouding the membrane and isolating our spirit. There can be no blaming someone else; you must be totally responsible. Relationships will not take you where you want or inevitably need to go; however, they can show you why you can't get there and what is in your way. Love and fulfillment can happen only in the Now. Believing that "someday" you will find this love is a denial of this Moment in the illusion of "future" and in ignorance of the eternal love you hold within yourself, Now. It all can only happen Now and is why you must become present, free from the bondage of ego and desire!

Relationships are powerful guides for our spiritual growth, especially when the "buttons" are being pushed and we can witness the squirming and/or outrage of the ego. It's easy to be "holy" sitting in a cave, unchallenged and untempted. But to be "whole" in a relationship is the real challenge to this spiritual journey. Watch and be cautious of those "co-dependent" relationships that seem to complete the needs of both in a false harmony that limits you. Close attention needs to be paid to our programmed reactions, egocentric structures, and to our ability or inability to love and be loved in relationships. Here is our most important work, for as we learn to release ourselves from the ego's need to be loved in a conscious exploration of that need, we come to the realization that we hold within ourselves all the love we seek once the "needs" are removed. We will develop a wholesome reverence and love for all of Life and for all of the relationships that are a part of It as we become present and in touch with our own eternal nature.

Look closely at your relationship with your parents, for what you needed and didn't receive from them can be the keys to the recognition of the drives of the lower self/ego and the blocks that are in your way. Your identification with the pain that may have been a part of your relationship can easily be adopted by the ego in its quest for identity. It may be a subtle part of your personality that only manifests in the intimate moments of your present relationships. Or it may have become the "who you are." I'm sure you have met those who seem to be angry or in pain all of the time. In either case, the ego will stubbornly resist losing even this negative sense of itself due primarily to the powerful emotions that support and give it life. We all have a "story" to tell, and that story may be laced with terrible abuse and the torment and pain of that abuse. To try to define and analyze the what, who, and why can only strengthen the isolation of ego and add substance to the "story." To dwell on the verbiage of this knowledge, seeking someone to blame in an intellectual understanding of the experience, is truly a waste of time and will create yet another addition for the mind/ego to use in its "story" on its hopeless quest for identity. Understanding your need for love and the trauma of loveless or abusive parents is enough. Go to the pain, feel it deeply, and become aware. Becoming an aware witness to the underlying emotions that evoke this pain will free you from identity with the pain and open you to your true self as witness. This stepping away from your "story" can free you from it in consciousness. Your freedom can be found only here and only Now, outside the chatter of mind, and the pain you are holding so desperately onto.

This vast eternal presence is who you are, and your experience of *"That"* will free you from your pain and the limited identity taken in it. Being completely in this Moment is to become aware of the glorious mystery of Life in a consciousness that cannot hold on to the illusion of your "story" and the pain it carries, anymore than darkness can stand in the brilliance of light. You are now truly "Real" as a part of Life that has no boundaries, free from illusion, free from pain.

It is, for the most part, the ego that comes to a relationship with all of its needs and insecurities. It is within this insecure identity, which has been our lot since the dawn of creation and is the impetus for the processes of "self-awareness" and "self-discovery," that we began looking for acceptance and love and a relief from our isolation. But the ego can never be truly satisfied in a relationship, as it can only sustain the *need* for a love that is driving us into relationships. In fact, it can ultimately only stand in the way of a truly loving union in the illusory experience of being separate. That union for which we are longing can be achieved through the recognition of the Love that we all have been privileged to be a part of. We must come to recognize and then deny the superficial egocentric needs and demands that isolate us. Through the awareness and *practice* of that unconditional Love which resides within us all, our connection to the Eternal will be assured. Open yourself to the grace of His Love and forgiveness. Become present in the stillness of Being and practice loving that is done for Its own sake, with no motive, desire, or expectation. This is truly Loving and has the power to heal and make whole—that is, to make Holy your experience of Life. It is in and through your connection with the Eternal that His "second coming" will be truly realized. You have within you all that is necessary to be a mirror of His eternal Love. You need only to clean the mirror.

Relationships do take work, sometimes lots of work, but nothing will happen by just wishing for it, and what point is there in suffering? Believing that you will be fulfilled by your relationship is a foolish and fanciful belief. Yes, there can be moments of happiness and joyful times shared and cherished together; however, no one or no thing can truly fulfill you. As long as you are searching for or are dependent on anything outside yourself for happiness, you are playing a dangerous game. Only what *you* bring to this Moment determines your success or failure in relationship. In case you haven't noticed, your relationships are not meant to make you happy beyond the first few weeks or, if you are lucky, months. However, the partner you have chosen is never a mistake. They are what you need to see who you are and what is in your way. Explore deeply the issues that drive you nuts in your relationship. They are vital keys for your awakening. Moving on to another relationship as so many of us do may simply end up as a temporary avoidance of the inevitable failings of the ego and is a terribly selfish act if children are involved. The shallow needs of an insecure, ignorant ego can take us so very far from ourselves and create so much suffering.

Take the time to find out who you are outside the relative influences of family and work so that co-dependent relationships don't develop. It is very important to have time alone and to become comfortable with nothing to do and no one to see. Allow yourself to be just you as your awareness. Let go into that core of your existence and come to *know* who you are as an undefended, egoless expression of the Holy Spirit. When you come to that *knowledge*, you will no longer be consumed by the egocentric (lower self) need to take all you can from Life in an attempt to secure the ego's vulnerable position; rather, you will experience Life from the perspective of the Soul, your higher self. From that perspective, Life is complete as it is; there is no more need, and every Moment is a perfect offering of Love from our Lord. You will be fulfilled as you realize that you, too, are an experssion of and are in union with our Lord. You will have found and will become the Love you were seeking. Your Soul, unbounded and eternal, will be free from the illusions of mind. You will truly be a lover of Life, your heart joyously open and radiating an unbounded Love, in reverence to and with eternal gratitude for the Creator and all of His creation.

Your relationships will be your guide on this journey. With love and forgiveness as the vehicles, you will begin to humble the ego and relinquish the need to control that can be so much a part of your egocentric, needy identity. You will raise your awareness to the sanctity of Soul and come to know your eternal birthright.

Listen to more words of wisdom from *The Prophet*.

When love beckons to you, follow him, though his ways are hard and steep.

And when his wings enfold you, yield to him, though the sword hidden among his pinions may wound you. And when he speaks to you, believe in him, though his voice may shatter your dreams and the north wind lays waste the garden.

For even as love crowns you, so shall he crucify you. Even as he is for your growth, so is he for your pruning. Even as he ascends to your height and caresses your tender branches that quiver in the sun, so shall he descend to your roots and shake them in their clinging to the earth.

Like sheaves of corn he gathers you unto himself. He threshes you to make you naked. He sifts you to free you from husks. He grinds you to whiteness. He kneads you until you are pliant; And then he assigns you to his sacred fire, that you may become sacred bread for God's sacred feast.

Chapter VII

SEX ON THE MIND

Our lives are songs; God writes the words
And we set them to music at pleasure;
And the song grows glad, or sweet or sad
As we choose to fashion the measure.

—Droplet ella wheeler wilcox

Our Lord is very wise. By putting so many good feelings and so much energy into the act of procreation, He has insured the growth of consciousness and our need to be more than we are, a need that will and is bringing us closer to Him. Through sex, He has secured and continues to secure the survival of consciousness on this majestic blue planet Earth and the evolving life forms on it. There is no doubt in my mind that our orgasmic ecstasy is a mini recreation of the ecstasy that was the impetus for God's creation of this glorious universe! Being made in His image, we are all born with the desire to create and to become. In maturity, that desire can be enjoyed through the sex act, a most natural and delightful experience! Performed as the natural and intimate climax to being in love, we would be in tune with God's will and our children the product of God's love. ...... Alas, enter stage left, the mind.

Once the ego found identity in this pleasure of procreation, it was taken from the domain of God's will and His gift to us to something to think about and examine, for which to feel guilt and shame, something to identify oneself as, something to desire and lust after, something to manipulate and abuse. What was once the natural expression of physical love for one another and the means for our survival as a race is now big business. Love was removed and the quest for bigger and better orgasm has replaced it. The huge industry of sex, with "how-to" books, sex paraphernalia, pornography, prostitution, and the obsessive need to stay young and sexually attractive, has taken the sexual energy into the mind and twisted it into something ...... else. What was once the impulse of the Life force energy within us to procreate is now the obsession for "turn-on" and orgasm.

God's will be done, and although we may be looking for the ultimate orgasm, when sperm meets egg the miracle that is conception has begun. To abuse this energy in egocentric pursuits defiles this most sacred ground and denies God's will, and too often this results in the most horrific act of egoistic ignorance and indifference, aborting the "accident" that is God's most precious gift to us, demeaning the whole of Life itself. If we cannot hold as sacred this miraculous act of creating a new life, how then are we to hold any part of Life as sacred?

My son asked me recently why Droplet joseph was not an important figure in the life of Christ. After all, he was His father. I realized in answering him what a terrible injustice the Church has done, not just to the memory of Droplet joseph and his humanity, but also to the miracle and joy that is procreation. I tried to share with my son my sense of wonder and the gratefulness I hold for being a part of this Life. I tried to make clear to him that our Lord is all around us in all that is as the miracle of Life, and He is made joyful in that recognition through our heightened awareness and role as witness. Anyone who has witnessed the documentaries that provide an in-depth look at the process of fertilization and the growth of a fetus knows how incredibly miraculous this process is, enlightened or not! All of my sons were birthed at home with the help of midwives, and I "caught" and gave them all their first bath. I know, and anyone who has taken an active part in the birthing of their children knows, what an incredible, life-altering experience it can be! It is no less a miracle, it is no less a mystery, no less an act of the Divine than the "virgin birth"! God's hand is so blatantly obvious here in this awesome display of miracles and magic that one is left speechless. Had we promoted the knowledge that Jesus had been conceived through and by the sacred love shared by Joseph and Mary, I can only gape in wonder as to what miracle would have been lost, what part of the life of Christ would have been defiled! With this in mind, perhaps the act of bringing and taking human life into and out of this world would not be taken so lightly and we would hold more reverence for the process and its potential. Here, too, our heightened awareness must be brought to bear on this act of procreation. In so doing, the miracle that surrounds us, in this act of Love as in *all* things, will prevail and "love making" will be elevated beyond the superficial, perverse needs of the ego to an expression of His eternal joy.

Sometimes sex is just sex, and sometimes enjoying the "flesh" in the tantric tradition of acceptance of all that life is offering is just fine. However, if only the mind/ego has made the connection with the genitals, then we abuse this energy in the assorted perversions of the ego, which are all too prevalent in our time. But sometimes, with love and the right person, with the heart and the genitals in touch, the ego set aside and humbled by Love, it would be then that sex is divine and it is in that divinity our children should be brought into this world.

The more we become aware, the more we learn to love, the more the miracle that is Life will manifest itself before us in every aspect of our lives, including procreation. But beware, for leaving the limited mind/ego alone in charge of this sexual energy can be very hazardous to your health and a difficult "block" to overcome. Orgasm is a powerful and desirable experience under any circumstance. Beware of the ego finding its identity in the sex act, and rather, open your heart to this energy and gratefully *allow* it to happen with reverence, humility, and your love.

Droplet d. h. lawrence reflected his awareness of the sacred nature of love making and elevated it in beautifully inspirational stories like "The Man Who Died," which brought the Christ Consciousness, indeed Jesus Himself, into this sacred act of Loving. Although it is not a historic account to be taken literally, it does bring with it an opening to the divine potential of "love making" and the sacred role the physical body holds in our awakening.

So much more awaits our patience and discrimination as it concerns the process of taking a mate and the giving of ourselves sexually. Being conservative in this regard is in effect putting superficial egoistic needs aside, practicing discipline and delayed gratification, and looking to something more in "tune" with God's will and in keeping with our own essential nature. The term "yoga" means union and is a disciplined approach to life that attempts to unite us with our "higher selves" through spiritual, mental, and physical techniques that raise our awareness beyond the limitations of egocentric pursuits. Life is this process of "yoga" that is leading us to a union with our Creator through that uniquely human experience we have come to know as Loving. In your relationship with Life, as in your relationship with your beloved, you must choose to develop a focus in that "heart center" mentioned earlier and begin your relationship there. Let it grow and be nourished in His love before you plant the "seed" of love and bring the expression of your love, commitment, and union with one another into being. With a selfish, greedy ego in charge, it is so easy to ignore what is sacred and of value in the superficial quest for immediate pleasure in an abuse of this sacred energy. It is from an enlightened heart-centered *you*—your "higher self"—that your choices should be made and your reverence for Life and Its processes maintained.

The "sexual revolution" was indeed a necessary revolt against our repressed, Victorian attitudes toward sex. It was time to acknowledge the "weakness of the flesh" and elevate that energy to something higher than the "work of the devil." Our religious leaders were not comfortable with this notion of the human *animal*, even though we survive by taking from this earth just as surely as do all the animals with whom we share it. Their own insecurity with that perception, and the need to control inherent in religious dogma, made it necessary to create the concept of divine intervention that would elevate humanity beyond the animal kingdom and the evolutionary process in which we, like it or not, are engaged.

Regardless of theory and our beliefs, the act of procreation we perform differs very little from the other creatures with whom we share this planet, and was an embarrassment to our religious leaders; these base instincts seemed a contradiction to the new divine image of ourselves these leaders imposed, which suggested that we were above and apart from the natural world. The limited awareness of ego and the insecurity of that limited awareness blinded us to the glorious presence of our Lord in this Moment as this Moment. It looked for and found identity in mind as we fell from grace and exiled ourselves from this, the Garden of Eden.

We do, however, in this animal body, have the potential of an awareness of our divine heritage and the gift of loving that has set us apart from our more natural brothers and sisters who live unconsciously yet in perfect union with our Lord. And too, we had the need to free ourselves from the mind-induced guilt and shame of being a part of this "animal" existence, one whose sanctity had been lost in the isolation of egocentric religious concepts in our misguided quest for fulfillment. Lost in the illusions of ego, ignorant and isolated from our spiritual heritage, we attempted to raise ourselves above the natural world. The miraculous source of our physical existence was lost to the illusion of ego and its false, narcissistic identity. In our need and desire to know God and ourselves, we created concepts and beliefs that obscured His glorious presence in all that this very Moment offers, right before our eyes!

Limited and guilt-ridden by these doctrines, we rebelled in a desire to truly enjoy this intimate sharing of physical love. And so we have! However, ego did not include in this quest for freedom the consequences that accompany the irresponsible behavior that undisciplined freedom can bring, but conveniently found ways to circumvent responsibility with technology. We still are playing with egocentric concepts as to whom we think we are and remain ignorant of our glorious potential. In the arrogance of ego, isolated from the sanctity and fulfillment of this magnificent Moment of miracles, we flounder about in exile and suffer the "sins" of our ignorance.

How many more of the innocent need be aborted by our arrogance and ignorance? How much longer need the Soul suffer in the exile of ego? We continue to suffer in this isolation the ego has created, leaving us out of touch with the most fundamental laws of Life, and have taken this most precious energy and perverted it to satisfy our own hedonistic desires and shallow narcissistic needs, creating more pain and deeper isolation. How much more pain need be inflicted? Isn't it time to listen to the heart, not the head, and become a part of something more than we are and be fulfilled by it? Let God's will be done and ignore the ranting of those lost in the illusion of their separateness to Life. Our "rights" should not supersede the responsibility we hold to Life, to God, and ultimately to ourselves. If "unwanted" children are the result of our behavior, then how much clearer does it have to get in order for us to modify our behavior?! Finding and using methods and technologies that make adjustments for and allow for irresponsible and undisciplined behavior—which ultimately demeans and defiles Life itself—is not the solution! And please, let's end the moronic debate as to "When does life begin?" Life *began* with the Creation. It is, It was, and It always will be. We Droplets have only recently begun the "manipulation" of that which we have barely begun to understand. We are this Life in search of Itself! The real question should be "When will we truly realize the miracle that is this Life in the Now, and not be so easily influenced by the shallow, transient needs of the isolated, ignorant ego whose knowledge can only come from the limited past and whose fulfillment is seen only in the illusion of future?"

Is it any wonder that ego would lust so for that delightful moment of orgasm? For that brief instant, we enter that glorious state of "no mind" as we leave thought behind and enter into the ecstasy of the body. For a moment we no longer exist and have surrendered ourselves to more then we are as we experience the joyous mystery of the body. A body, I would remind you, that *you* cannot claim as anything more than a gift from our Lord and as a vehicle for your soul on its quest for Love. Whenever you have a moment, consciously experience the life energy of the body. Feel your breath as it involuntarily flows in and flows out. Listen to the heart as it steadily, relentlessly pumps your blood and life to the body. Become aware of this sacred gift that *you* as an egocentric identity can only manipulate and will forever remain a stranger to in that identity. As ego takes its identity in the body, it is often frustrated, frightened, and angered when things go wrong. This would be the time to let go of ego and come to "That" which has given Life to the body and the senses. As you come to "That," the unseen essence of Life at its core and the truth behind your being, you would leave ego behind and the limited identity it falsely took in the body. This experiencing of who we truly are can only happen in the Now Moment, for it is only here, free from mind, that you can realize that you too are "That" and can be fulfilled by the presence of our Lord as yourself.

This of course is an evolutionary process we are following and as I see it, we are in the "adolescent" stage of that process. And like an adolescent, we have been given most of the power of being an adult but without the wisdom of experience to use it wisely. The abuse of this power, the obsession over sex, the ignorance and insecurity of our limited experience, and the results of our irresponsible behavior can be overwhelming and confusing in this "modern world." Droplet audous huxley's vision in *Brave New World* is one where ego runs amuck and our greatest fears of dehumanization are realized. In his vision, abortions could be done before lunch as easily as getting a haircut. Sex had become indiscriminate and without emotion. Family was non-existent, and children were created and raised in institutions. Our relationship to the natural world was completely severed in city life and egocentric pursuits. Periodic "soma holidays" were taken, which were little more than drug-induced comas that offered a complete escape from this sterile world in fantasy. Are we headed in that direction? Certainly Droplet huxley thought so. Let's hope we never see his vision completely realized. We need to stop for a moment, take a measure of our pain, and look to the wisdom of the ages as guides.

The lights of Love, compassion, and understanding need to be shown on this natural process of taking a mate and procreating. The disciplines of delayed gratification and patience and the building of Love can hold a lifetime of happiness for the practitioner in a spiritual approach to life. I cringe at the blatant promiscuity and the glorification of "looking good" so prevalent in film and television, and the influence it is having on young people searching for identity. The proliferation of single-parent homes is staggering, and although it may be considered "politically correct," the toll it is having on our children can only be considered tragic. *Both* parents are necessary to produce a whole child. Both parents hold their own specific qualities that are passed on to their children as they develop in a loving family structure, even one that may be troubled in the process of working out egocentric conflicts. If that loving family structure is not in place, then we are sacrificing our children to the shallow and selfish needs of the ego in a hedonistic approach to Life that glorifies power and the pursuit of pleasure.

Jumping into bed when the first sign of mutual attraction is displayed may be considered being "with it" and sexually "free," and I would not want to be put in the position of putting Droplets down for "loving" one another. However, look at this world and tell me what good has come from this kind of lustful, undisciplined behavior. When life is lived from one orgasm to the next in a wanton and shallow pursuit of pleasure, a tremendous amount of life energy is being wasted in the superficial egocentric abuse of the ecstasy that is orgasm and it becomes difficult to go very deeply into the *total* Life experience as a result.

The use or abuse of the momentary pleasures of sex, food, drugs, or anything else that can be applied as a means of escaping or for relieving the state of isolation we are in, is all too common and has created "mega" industries that have profited handsomely from the pain of our exile. There is a group of African monkeys that fornicate almost constantly. Any anxiety-laden event encountered (i.e., violent conflict between rival males, the presence of a predator, intruders from other groups, squabbles over food or children) can easily lead the entire group to fornication as a means of releasing the tension created by the event. It is somewhat comical to witness but does present insight into the nature of sex and the momentary release it can offer from anxiety and fear. In our own culture, a significant rise in child birth is noted nine months after any catastrophic national event. The "baby boomer" generation owes its status to the events of WWII. The egocentric influences of insecurity and the anxiety of life lived superficially can easily lead those who have not discovered a deeper meaning for their lives to a wide and incredibly creative variety of escape mechanisms, including but not limited to sex and orgasm, as a temporary means of relieving themselves of the anxiety and pain of their ignorance.

With the limited ego in control, partners become objects and love is a dirty word, as the ego ultimately cannot love, it can only take, demand, and need to be loved. Love becomes a head trip and not a heart-felt passion. The bigger the ego, the further the detachment, the greater the fear, and the greater the need. Love making is done out of the necessity of the ego and children are brought into this world to fulfill the needs of the ego rather than as a celebration of Life in the process of fulfilling Itself.

Droplet george leonard's book *The End of Sex* is a highly recommended and insightful look at the obsession we have developed for "sex." In it he emphasizes the need and necessity to bring love back into our experience of sexual communion as a means for our fulfillment and to put an end to the abuse of this sacred energy.

Much attention has been directed toward the Catholic church and the problems it is having with sexually deviant priests. My experience has shown that this phenomenon is not limited to the Catholic church and that sexually deviant behavior is indeed a part of most monastic environments. Celibacy is simply unnatural and is a denial of a powerful and fundamental aspect of being human. We carry with us a physical, emotional, and intellectual body that is meant to serve the soul as we use our free will to develop it to its full potential. Imagine taking vows that would deny and repress some aspect of our emotional body—that is, to never feel such and such again or to only feel a certain way! What would happen if we vowed to never inquire into specific concepts as a denial of our intellect? Can you begin to imagine the perverse expressions that would arise from such vows and the limits we would have placed on our personal growth!?

These institutions have, it seems, put the cart before the horse and have created an atmosphere that would indeed attract and foster deviant behavior. Celibacy may have been the experience of those saintly Droplets who have graced this earth, but it was not necessarily the methodology that brought them to their heightened awareness. Because an enlightened being may have been celibate, it does not necessarily follow that you must be celibate to be an enlightened being; indeed it may be just the opposite. By embracing *all* the gifts with which Life has blessed us, we acknowledge that this is *all* an expression of our Lord's love for us. By letting go of egocentric identity and the "relative" values it would apply to Life, we would open ourselves to *all* that this Moment is offering. Within that opening and in our total surrender is the realization of the perfection that is our Lord and the sacred role we play in His creation. To be grateful for this gift of procreation and to use it consciously and lovingly is to be in tune with His will. The denial and/or mind-oriented, egocentric manipulation of this powerful energy, for any other purpose, is creating the deviant behavior so prevalent in our time. The desire to have sex with someone can be a natural extension of our love for them. However, if only our egocentric desires are served, then this is not love, it is lust. Lust is wanton, short-lived, and can be violent and cruel. It is not a vehicle to heightened awareness, but indeed a powerful barrier to it as here only ego is served.

Becoming conscious of the Love that created this universe can be an experience that would make even the sexual experience pale in comparison, and it may indeed become secondary or even unnecessary for our fulfillment in the light of this Love. Celibacy may be the experience of those who have become enamored by this Love and who may even have elevated their awareness through the practice of celibacy. This is all *energy*, after all! However, redirecting this powerful sexual energy in a quest for enlightenment is most certainly an egoistic impulse for achievement. Desire for enlightenment is a barrier to enlightenment, and thwarting natural impulses is certainly not in tune with God's will. You will remain bonded to ego and suffer the consequences of desire, even the desire to come to our Lord. Be an expression of our Lord and accept all He has blessed us with. Who you are cannot be denied, and love making performed as a commitment to Love and the creation of another is a sacred act that is to be enjoyed and cherished.

Take responsibility for and bring awareness to your actions and their consequences; you have far more to give and much more to receive. Unless the sexual experience is coming from or is in fulfillment of an egocentric need or identity, it cannot be a detriment to our spiritual growth; indeed it may be what makes us whole, what makes us holy. Its denial, its repression, its manipulation, and its association with sin and the guilt that follows is the source of "evil" here and not the longings of the body to experience the ecstasy of orgasm in union with our beloved in the act of procreation. So choose your partner well. The passion that comes with that initial "falling in love" will be cherished forever as a part of your relationship. This should not be something that is sought-after to be infinitely repeated with new partners once the fire has faded and the ego becomes "needy" again. Your love will grow in commitment to one another as long as you are open and truthful, willing to face the ego and its shortcomings, and you are committed to a spiritual life of higher consciousness and deeper awareness. Your children will be products of that love and witnesses to its power and security. Your family will be a celebration of Life fulfilling Itself, and your devotion and unconditional Love to it a guide back to Him.

Too many of us have taken the easy way out and let the ego and its shallow needs take our lives in an endless pursuit of desire. We have "insecured" our children in the superficiality of the ego/mind by destroying the structure of love the family represents. But it simply isn't enough to "keep the family together for the kids." A family is created by the innate longings for love and union. Our children are the product of that gift of Love. Once created, it *must* remain sacrosanct, not just for the children, but as a temple dedicated to our growth and spiritual maturity. And I repeat: *the partner that you have chosen is not a mistake.* The conflicts that may be so much a part of your relationship are directional signals as to where your work must begin. It may not be easy and there may be many temptations, but it can be within this intimate structure of family and your relationship to it that you will come to understand the meaning of your life. Only an extremely abusive relationship cannot be tolerated and should be terminated if it cannot be changed. You must hold and respect the same love and compassion for yourself as you would for the world around you, and your children can only suffer and be traumatized by violence and abuse.

For those who now look back with pain and sorrow in their hearts and who feel it is too late to undo what has been done, I would say to take another look. Your pain, your fear, and your sorrow are the perfect expressions of having experienced His loss. Don't let your suffering and the suffering of all you have loved be in vain. Now more than ever, you can be a witness to your purpose and to your role as "lover," and to the absolute necessity of living a life that embraces Loving in the Now.

As a misguided parent, He will forgive you. As an unloved, forgotten child, He will embrace you. As a rejected partner, you will come to understand your need for love and your role as lover. Your bitterness, your anger, your shame and regret will serve no one. Understand your error, know where and when you were lost, open your heart, forgive those who have hurt you, and forgive yourself. You will find your way back to Him as you find your fulfillment in this Moment.

I was taken by the Zen Buddist practice of *metta*, or practicing prayer for loving kindness. In it, we pray to our Lord to: "Free me from fear; free me from pain; may I be happy; may I be filled with loving kindness." We say this prayer for ourselves, then for one whom we love, and finally for one we may hate or have rejected. As you will see, it is a powerful experience of forgiveness and an opening of the heart to your "higher self" and to the unconditional love within you.

If your sexual desire is acted upon without a loving and grateful heart, then you are limiting your awareness to egocentric needs. With so many books, theories, and traditions related to the enhancement of sex through more intense orgasms, the experience of ecstasy, and even the promise of spiritual awakening, it can be difficult to understand who we are as sexual beings as we become more alienated from the process in the pursuit of its fulfillment. Don't complicate your life in egocentric pursuits and the manipulation of these gifts of life. The simplicity of being present with an open and loving heart will fulfill not only your sex life but the whole of your life as you enter it in a state of wonder and gratitude.

It is my suggestion that we consider our sexual encounters as spiritual encounters, that we take thought as we embark on them, and that we enter into them as we enter a temple, with awe and reverence. Perhaps then we can journey from the era of Sexual Revolution to the era of Sexual Enlightenment.
—From Droplet jean lanier's book
From Having to Being: Toward Sexual Enlightenment

Chapter VIII
SPONTANEOUS KUNDALINI

If God shuts one door, He opens another.

—*Irish Proverb*

Now that you have the concepts of Droplet, membrane, the "ocean," and our *Source* well in hand, I can attempt to explain what a "spontaneous Kundalini rising" is all about. In the Indian mythology, Kundalini is described as a serpent coiled at the base of the spine in what we call the sacrum, or "sacred ground," waiting to uncoil and rise. It is curious that the metaphor of the serpent is used in the Christian mythology as well. In both instances, the serpent is used as an impetus for opening our awareness from an *unconscious* union with our Lord, in ignorance of our relationship to Him, into a dynamic quest for knowledge and to a far more "enlightened" relationship. Kundalini yoga is dedicated to making this "opening" happen with much in the way of preparation and guidance for the student over a substantial period of time. Releasing this extraordinary energy and enlivening the "chakras," or energy centers, in the body as it rises is considered essential to enlightenment, but there must be considerable preparation, for all that we knew and how we once "vibrated" will be altered. In preparation, that "silent witness" we all hold within ourselves must be nurtured, and that center of awareness developed over time so we can remain "centered" within the chaos that will ensue. Life will no longer be witnessed from the illusionary, relative identity of ego, but rather awareness will radiate from the universal center of "Soul." For me, though, at the time, the Droplet "yogi" berra was as far as I had researched into eastern philosophy. The concept of "Soul," as I understood it within the Christian doctrine, was something that developed black spots on it as we sinned and could only be cleansed in confession. If the timing was right and you had a "clean" soul when you died, you went to heaven—whatever that was.

I was young—just twenty-three—and completely unprepared for this extraordinary Kundalini event. I was nearly driven of the edge by the effects of this powerful energy, with the trauma, extreme loneliness, and disorientation that were so much a part of it. Why it happened just then was karmically ordained and certainly not willful on my part, for all that was my life was taken in that instant, and I was left completely alone, overwhelmed and frightened. Imagine your domesticated cat, which has never left the house, a lazy, fat, old cat, suddenly taken for a 100 mile per hour joyride on the handle bars of a motorcycle without warning or preparation, and you'll begin to understand what I was going through. I was no longer Steve Pfister. I no longer had a family or a home. My identity could no longer be defined by any mental concept or memory of what was, for what I was experiencing left my mind and memory insignificant in comparison to the spectacle to which I had been opened. It was not as if I had been taken into amnesia, for I still remembered the "dream." Rather, it was more the experience of a candle being exposed to the sun for the first time. Although its light was shining still, it had become overwhelmed and made insignificant by the sun, the source of all light. From the perspective of egocentric identity—the candle—I no longer knew who I was or from where I had come. Time and the illusion I had of myself no longer existed in the eternal presence of this Moment. This was "It," and I could no longer be defined by the illusion of mind. I was taken out of time and "out of my mind" and brought to this Moment of miracles, frightened and confused. My mind still functioned, but the false identity I had taken from it had been exposed, and I floundered with the truth of my being.

The circumstances that proceeded the "event" were normal by any standard and certainly not that unusual for me at that time. I had taken a weekend pass from my tour of duty in the army. I had only seven months left before I would be released from the service and had made the trip many times. Being stationed at Fort Belvoir, Virginia, it was about a four-and-a-half hour drive to my family's home on Long Island. On this particular weekend pass, I had decided to visit my older sister who lived an hour or so from my home. When I arrived, we sat for dinner, had a few drinks, and proceeded to chat well into the early hours of the morning, catching up on lost time. Tired and talk out, we finally said goodnight and I was given my niece's room to sleep in.

I was laying in bed, waiting to be taken into sleep when I felt something quite tangible begin to move up my spine. This Kundalini energy reached the base of my skull before I could react to its presence. At that moment, as it entered my head, what can only be described as an explosion occurred. It was as if the lid had been blown off and everything that was familiar and intact removed. I became terrified and disoriented by the unfolding cosmic spectacle now revealing itself to me. No familiar frame of reference had survived this "explosion." I was terribly frightened and totally confused. I had become a witness to my life from a place deep within myself. I had become detached from all I had known and could no longer feel a part of or participate in a life that had become insignificant in this very intense experience of Now. I was referencing life from a place I had never been, outside mind and the memories and perceptions taken from it. As I made my way to the bathroom and peered into the bathroom mirror, I was stunned to find that even my own self-image seemed unfamiliar and no longer had meaning.

As I wandered into the kitchen, feeling lost and totally alone, a most significant event occurred. From her bedroom, my sister called out to me "Are you all right?" In spite of the terror and confusion I was experiencing, a compassionate "silent witness" that did not want to pass this terrible fear and confusion on to anyone else simply replied, "Yeah." Some compassionate point of reference had remained, and although it had become totally isolated from the familiar life I once knew and could not begin to understand what was happening, it would, by its presence, be my salvation. For what had remained would rise to a new awareness of itself and would begin to incorporate "higher knowledge" into its relationship with

Life—not as an identity, but as a means to communicate what I was experiencing and ease my own inner turmoil and isolation.

I had suddenly become a witness to the majesty and mystery of this incredible Moment without the limitations or comforts of a remembering mind and secured ego. I had been given an unbiased glimpse at our Lord as this Creation and I trembled in awe. In effect, the "membrane" had been cleared and all the illusions of life that I had built into it were removed. This veil of illusion had been suddenly and unceremoniously lifted, and I was lifted, some would say "vibrated," beyond my mind's ability to comprehend. With God's grace alone, I had been given the opportunity to experience this Moment as It truly is and had come face to face with the Almighty. This is initially a "God-fearing" event, as I was opened to the vastness of this universe and to the Mystery that is this Moment, and was completely humbled by our Lord. I had become a witness to the void, the emptiness, the great abyss that is this Moment, out of which has come this endless universe, ... ever growing, ... ever creating, ... ever becoming. Through it all, I was allowed to maintain some identity, however fragile, leaving me not fully in the world of illusion nor fully in the "Real" world.

The relative world gave me small comfort, as I could see little or no difference between a psychotic walking down the street, engrossed in conversation with an imaginary companion, and the "normal" man walking down the street, lost in the membrane of his making. Both were disconnected and oblivious to this mysterious and most miraculous Moment, one in which I had become so intensely aware and immersed. Both were lost in a fog of mind-stuff, unable to be truly present.

The *Real* world, although intuitively recognizable as the only world, was too overwhelming and difficult to incorporate into the everyday life of "mind-stuff" without looking psychotic myself. I was not granted the peace and serenity that is enlightenment, and had most everything that was familiar and of comfort to the ego removed. I was still enlisted in the army, and found it impossible to function as the disorientation, isolation, and loneliness of this event had become unbearable.

A compassionate commanding officer directed me to a therapist on base, and once we established that this was not a ploy to be removed from the service, we proceeded with his brand of the Droplet freud's analysis. I saw the therapist frequently; however, it soon became apparent that this was not going to fit into his scope of knowledge, nor for that matter Freud's, and that trying to tie all of this to something sexual was going to be a stretch. As I came closer to verbalizing what I was experiencing, I became more and more uneasy with the prospect of passing the experience on to yet another unprepared soul whose reaction could not be anticipated. I stopped therapy and struck out on my own. I was extremely vulnerable and open to almost any suggestion.

As stated, my experience was not one of unity and peace but rather an encounter with this Moment that is at once an empty, vast abyss, the great void that we all unconsciously fear as the annihilation of death, and this incomprehensible miracle that is God's work in progress. My fear was great, as I simply could not fathom what was going on or even begin to know why! There are no words that can truly begin to describe what I was going through. I felt as if I were in some incredible dream and yet I knew there was nothing more to wake up to ...... yet I had the unrelenting sense that I could. But how and to what? My isolation and the loneliness I was experiencing brought me at times to great despair. I clearly remember the moment of my final decision not to surrender to my despair and give up. I knew with certainty that what was before me was the true nature of reality, and though I was frightened and felt totally alone in the experience, I was determined to see it through.

A big step in the right direction came in the form of a rather ordinary event. As I was walking back to my barracks one evening, a car had gotten stuck in the snow. I stopped and gave those in need a hand pushing their car out. As they drove away, I recognized a profound change in my perspective. That physical activity seemed to have taken me out of my isolation to some degree. I consciously returned to sports and spent the remainder of my tour of duty participating on a physical level with Life again. It was simple and direct, and although it did not relieve my anxiety and was not the answer to my overall dilemma, it would be the first step toward an integration of this powerful "energy."

About eleven months after the "Kundalini event," and having by then finished my tour of duty, I found myself in a bookstore one day, and the Droplet alan watts's book *This Is It* jumped out at me. (Thank you, Great Spirit!) He became my mentor for many years. I simply *loved* reading and listening to his work. A balance was struck as more and more knowledge arrived, and I was able to let go of my fear and begin to integrate mentally what I was experiencing into everyday life. For me, the cart had come before the horse, and I struggled to find the words that could explain the how, what, and why of the spiritual awakening I was going through. Normally, the words and the wisdom taken from spiritual texts would plant the seeds of the "higher knowledge" that would hopefully blossom into a spiritual awakening. With the contemplation of this new knowledge and the application of *words*, Life was becoming a "look at what God is doing now," and I was eased somewhat from the pain of isolation.

I returned to college in the fall of 1968 in search of a deeper understanding of my life. I majored in philosophy and minored in psychology. I was not your ideal student and was soon at odds with my professors. The presence of multiple-choice philosophy tests outraged my sensibilities. I had a need to *know*! The "New Age" was all around me with icons like Alan Watts, Krishna Murti, Timothy Leary, Richard Albert, and Maharish Mahesh Yogi, who were exploring Life in relatively radical ways, and I could not be satisfied with mundane exercises in memorization.

I had become fascinated with the concept of meditation and began to explore it more through direct experience. Zen meditation was too rigid a practice for me and seemed a contradiction with its emphasis on concentration, denial, and the importance of ritual. Too much "mind-stuff," I thought. Maharishi Mahesh Yogi and his method of Transcendental Meditation was getting an enormous amount of publicity through his involvement with the Beatles, and I followed it closely. It was a simple meditation that was non-invasive and non-secular with very little "fanfare." I was finally initiated into the practice of Transcendental Meditation in the winter of 1968 and absolutely loved it. It had given me a way of letting go of my fear and allowed me to open further into my experience of Life.

I began spending most of my free time doing volunteer work at the "center," then a townhouse on the upper-east side of Manhattan. Because of what I was going through, it seemed I had much to offer this "movement," and I felt I had found my "niche." I was soon giving introductory lectures and was playing a significant role in the advancement of TM. At the time, the student and adult branches of the movement were together in that townhouse, but it was not long before a move was in order. The practice was becoming very popular, and space had become an issue, especially on "initiation day." And so, about a year after my initiation, the "Student International Meditation Society" moved to the west village and the "Spiritual Regeneration Movement" moved to West Seventy-Third Street.

It was with that move that I was offered the directorship of the Manhattan chapter of the Spiritual Regeneration Movement. I was pleased and excited to accept the position, and I quit college at once to take it. Amazing people from all over the world would come to the center, and we would spend hours talking about life. I was responsible for all that went on, and did most of the introductory lectures, both at the center and as an invited guest elsewhere. Initiation day was always exciting, and I looked forward to becoming qualified as a teacher. It was a wonderful time in my life, for I had found an activity that reflected and was in tune with my overall experience of Life, and I truly could not wait to go to "work."

It was during that time I came to know Droplet charlie lutes. I had first read about Charlie in the now defunct *Look* magazine. In an interview, he told of how he had come to Transcendental Meditation. Apparently, Charlie had become gravely ill and while literally on his deathbed he had been visited by an angel. He was given something of a choice; he could either help this "man" who was coming to this country from India, or he could die. Naturally, Charlie took the first choice, and so the Spiritual Regeneration Movement was formed, and I would one day be director of the New York City chapter.

Charlie was a charismatic "man's man" who earned his living in the corporate world. I relished his lectures in his three-piece pinstriped suit, wherein he would refer matter-of-factly to his experiences with angels, astral travel, and other mystical wonders. It was from Charlie that I learned about this phenomenon called "Kundalini" and how it manifested in people. I had eavesdropped on a conversation he was having with a fellow meditator as he described how this powerful energy rose in people and the extraordinary effect it had on consciousness. It was obviously a major piece of information for me, as I had finally found a word that gave meaning to an experience that had altered the course of my entire life. However, I kept the knowledge of this experience to myself, and no one would know of it until I married and confided in my wife. The experience that so many were hoping for had already happened to me, and it was not, at least for me at that time, something I would have wished on anyone.

Charlie was loved by all, and his visits to New York were looked forward to intensely. However, as those more influential members of the movement decided the movement needed to take on a more scientific, down-to-earth persona, Charlie and his "far out" spiritual approach were unfortunately eased away from the public eye, and for me at least, the movement would never be the same.

In the winter of 1971, I had saved enough to complete my training as an instructor and flew off to Majorca, Spain, to join Mahareshi for a six-month course in the practice and teaching of Transcendental Meditation. It was a joyful time, filled with wonderful new friends and extraordinary experiences. My "silent witness" status intensified during that time but was becoming more comfortable with the acquisition of new knowledge and deeper experience. There will be more said about those experiences later on in the chapter entitled "Meditation."

When I returned to the states, my directorship position had been filled, and the "movement" had taken on qualities I found difficult to reconcile. It had become big, and the "ego trips" of many vying for positions in the movement and the squabbles over initiation fees were discouraging. In my heart I knew it had become dishonest, and although I continued to believe that meditation was the key to our salvation and I still taught, I went back to construction and to the more honest, unpretentious, and hardworking atmosphere of men whose concerns centered more around taking care of their families rather than what now appeared to me to be the self-serving prospects of "bliss ninnies" in a movement that was becoming more bizarre as the days passed. Promises of flying, invisibility, and superhuman strength closed the door on my participation in that movement. However, I still recall with pleasure the fond memories of the "good old days," and have no regrets. Having spent time with Mahareshi and his movement, I know what a very special being he is and how many souls he has brought out of darkness.

The next few years were marked with a hasty and short-lived marriage, a return to college at NYU film school, a move back to Long Island, and the adoption of my now ex-wife's daughter. I had started my own business and was working again as a carpentry contractor in Manhattan, and while commuting to work on the Long Island railroad, I had been taken by the repeated eye contact of a young lady who seemed to have the same work schedule as mine. After weeks of electrifying stares, I finally got the opportunity to sit next to her, and we marveled at the similarity in books we were both reading, books, as it turned out, about higher consciousness. We immediately "hit it off" and could talk for hours about spirituality and the importance of raising children.

It wasn't long before we married, and not long after that our first son would be born at home with the help of a midwife. The birth was incredible, as I truly watched and became a participant in "what God was doing now." (I was there to "catch" my son and give him his first bath.) I was now a father, and my whole perception of life had changed. I became responsible for someone else, a son! I became "grounded" in the daily activities of making a living and supporting a family. The insidious aspects of ego were ever so slowly creeping back into my experience. The insanity and demands of the "relative world" would have to be dealt with.

My wife and I shared the dream of living in the country, and before long we headed north and bought our first farm. I knocked down the existing farmhouse that was sorely in need of repair and joyfully built our first country home. My twin sons were born in that home a few years later, and once again I "caught" them both and gave them each their first bath. I was bathing in the joy of family and country life and was deeply committed to it.

My wife has been my greatest teacher, and we have grown in ways we could never have done alone. Our marriage has not been without its difficulties, but we have learned to go deeply into them and have come out with a richer understanding of ourselves and our relationship—not just our relationship to each other, but also to the eternal spirit that guides our lives. A commitment to marriage is a commitment to understanding who we are on this "relative plane." It brings with it an integration of this "higher knowledge" through an exploration of our relationships and the difficulties they may hold for us. What I had been as a personality before the Kundalini event—a Number Five for those who follow the enneagram—had returned, although "I" would still remain, for the most part, a "silent witness" to it. I had my work cut out for me and struggled with many unresolved egocentric issues. My difficulties were compounded, as in my isolation I had expected far too much from my wife to fulfill longings that could only have been fulfilled by a deeper understanding of this Moment and my immediate relationship to *"That."*

Beneath ego identity there is a sadness, a deep sorrow, a longing for fulfillment, as the ego, on some level of consciousness, knows of the deception that is its nature. In my desire for a love that would "complete" me and end my isolation, I had gone outside myself. The demands and frustration were a terrible strain on my wife and on our marriage until that truth had been realized. My marriage and my children were not the answers to life; they were the gifts of life. I had to learn to recognize and let go of the egocentric needs that had begun to slowly develop and intensify in my isolation. I had to become the "Lover" in a realization that there was nothing I could take from this world of form that could finally and completely satisfy my longings to be free from isolation. Within me was the Love I was searching for, beyond the needs of ego and the world of form into that field of Being that lies at the core of our humanity, our *Source* and our Lord. My family and my part in it would be the impetus for that glorious realization.

On that faithful night when the Kundalini energy spontaneously awoke within me, I became aware of this incredible expansiveness of Being and the ineffable *Source* of all that is. As the Kundalini energy rose, It completely altered and expanded my limited perception of Life. However, it was an experience that I could not, at the time, readily integrate into "relative life." I would in time come to realize that it is within this immense, silent stillness, which is the eternal presence of our Lord and the essence of our Soul, that our fulfillment truly lies. As we become aware of and identify with the silent witness within, in a state of "no mind," we are able to merge with this ineffable presence. Free of the limitations of mind, we can now truly experience and totally enjoy events, yet not be identified with them. Our lives become open to the full potential of truly living, free and IN Love.

And so I have spent the last thirty-odd years observing, listening, exploring, and surrendering to Life, ever mindful of the illusion of mind and ego—the coyote "trickster" of American Indian lore—and to the majesty and mystery that is this Moment as I truly observe what "God is doing now" as "consciousness" in form. My fear is gone, and the knowledge, faith, and experience that this eternal Love can dismiss, even the great abyss, has replaced it. Once I embraced my fear and no longer turned from it, once I found the courage to let go and fall into the great abyss, and through it come to His eternal presence in *"That,"* it was then I found that there is truly nothing to fear and that underlying all of this existence is His eternal Love.

The illusion of the ego cannot survive in His presence, so the experience of fear and insecurity is certain as we draw closer to truth and expose the ego's deception. It was within this "dark night of the soul" that I came to know that no illusion of a separate self can stand before our Lord any more than night can stand before the sun. I have come to know that we are not our bodies and we are not our minds, and that we are all a part of and swimming in this eternal sea of Love, and that we are never alone. I have come to recognize that this "silent witness," at the very core of our existence, is the "soul" we carry with us from life to life. Its experience of "cosmic consciousness" that came to me in that initial "explosion" and which lies outside the illusion of ego and mind, is a state of consciousness that proceeds "God consciousness," and it is within that state of "God consciousness" that union with our Lord is assured. It will happen not through wanting, not through grasping, nor through knowing. It will happen simply and miraculously through your loving, not in the pick-and-choose love of the ego, but rather the all-embracing, unconditional, wholesome love of a Soul that has become conscious and aware of the silent beauty and presence of our Lord in all that is, as this Moment. It is a Soul that is free, a Soul at peace.

I consider myself very fortunate, for many other unprepared souls did not fare as well in the face of this powerful energy. That fragile "I" which had given me at least some point of reference and which had kept me somehow "centered," however painful, was in some way either unavailable or had become too distorted by trauma and/or perversion, and was of little use to those poor souls. Even the Droplet gopi krishna, considered by many the world's leading authority on Kundalini and to whom I owe a great debt for his work, was unable to function properly for months after his traumatic and sudden awakening. His insightful book *Kundalini, The Evolutionary Energy in Man* is an autobiographical account of his awakening and, I believe, the first of its kind and certainly a worthwhile read.

It was my wife who introduced me to Droplet richard moss. He has been blessed with a deep and powerful insight into our predicament. Richard's "awakening" had come to him suddenly and without warning as well. Although already deeply spiritually connected to life, having had insights and experience into the nature of consciousness and the healing power of love in his practice as a physician, he too found himself completely unprepared for this event. On his way to meet a friend, he was suddenly opened to this Moment and everything that was his life was taken from him. He had become a witness to a life he could no longer recognize or participate in. He anxiously met with his friend and tried to relay his dilemma. He was obviously in great distress. This "dark night of the soul" lasted many months for Richard, and he was fortunate to have had souls around him that could sympathize and support him during that terrible time. It is an experience not many souls have had to endure, and in it he and I and all who have gone through it share an unspoken comraderie.

This "dark night of the soul" contains a sorrow beyond anything that can be put into words. And yet, Richard has labeled it the first step to divine Love, and it is one of God's greatest gifts. Within its hold, the true mystic is born, as we enter into a state of consciousness that allows us to witness our Lord in all that is.

Richard has and continues to guide many back onto the path of the spirit. He is an eloquent speaker, a thoughtful and powerful writer, and a deeply sensitive and aware Droplet whose insights into our predicament can be inspirational and a true perturbation. His books, *The Black Butterfly*, *The "I" That is We*, and *How Shall I Live* are poetic journeys into the human experience and a must-read for those who would open themselves to Life.

In his book *Kundalini—Psychosis or Transcendence?*, Dr. Lee Sannella describes the effects the Kundalini energy can have on those who have awakened it either purposefully or accidentally. As an unknown, "uncentered," and without a faith in and knowledge of this process of *becoming*, this event can easily seem like a psychotic episode often marked with great physical pain, delusional thinking, and with an apparent "detachment from *reality*." As a psychiatrist, Dr. Sannella recognizes the difference between a psychotic episode and a Kundalini awakening, even though they hold many similar symptoms.

Kundalini in the Physical World, by Droplet mary scott, also offers an extraordinarily well researched account of the experience of the Kundalini energy and the effects it can have on those prepared and unprepared for the event. She has synthesized concepts from many esoteric disciplines and integrated them with science and contemporary thought. The Kundalini energy is an awesome force of nature whose transformative powers are without equal. This life force, as Mary notes, can be accessed through certain yoga techniques but can, as in my case, arise spontaneously with both enlightening and painful effects. The frequency of these spontaneous events seems to be on the rise and should be looked for by the medical community even though, at least for now, most are not properly prepared to deal with it.

As you can see, this "Kundalini" is not some obscure, esoteric phenomenon or some ancient myth of a lost culture, but rather the fundamental essence of the human experience that will have Its day in all of us in this process of becoming. In the evolution of man, Kundalini is the energy of growth and the source of higher states of consciousness. We know so little about this powerful energy of transformation. It behooves us to explore, come to understand, and prepare for this extraordinary phenomenon. It is nothing less than the "fire" that would destroy all that is in the way of our fulfillment, and is the gateway that would open you to the glorious mystery and beauty of this Moment. It is, if I may be poetic, the orgasmic impulse of life which must suddenly rise and explode in a creative display that is in fulfillment of Itself.

Obviously, if the "higher knowledge" of this process of becoming is part of your reference library, and if your faith is unconditional, then coming to our Lord in this Moment and so to "the fire" will not hold the fear and disorientation that would be found in ignorance of this powerful energy. I have often wondered what my experience would have been had I been prepared and had a knowledgeable teacher guiding me through this time of awakening. It is, however, very difficult for me to believe that anything outside myself would have brought me comfort. I remind myself of the saying, "Strong souls are forged on the anvil of suffering," and realize there are no mistakes and this is how it was meant to be for me. What would this book be, or, I wonder, would this book even *be* otherwise? I accept and remain in awe of the process, grateful for this miracle of Life.

During the event, I experienced the full range of mental disease, from extreme anxiety to deep depression—anxiety in the face of this overwhelming cosmic display now before me, and depression from the loss of any significant personal identity on this relative plane. I would ask you now to take a *good* look at what it is you fear, what you are anxious about, what has caused your depression and what it is you crave. You will come to know the power of the Kundalini energy within you as it awakens you to who you are and to whom you are not. You are surrounded by mystery; you are a miracle of creation. To raise your awareness to an appreciation of this is to live a spiritual life. To remain in ignorance of this is to live superficially, and you will suffer the anxiety and fear of your ignorance. This is the energy of growth, whether desired or not. Its effect can be felt consciously or may be experienced unconsciously with anxiety as an aspect of your personality.

This growth of awareness is happening within all of us and may be painful if we are unwilling or unaware of the need to let go of our fear and allow it to happen. We are creating so much more pain by trying to "fix" our pain and cover up our anxiety with the random use of drugs that repress this need for change and growth. Go to whatever is giving you pain and go deeply into its cause. Do not make any attempt to avoid or resist these issues, for they will bring you to the peace of self-knowledge.

We are all Droplets of this great ocean of Love, and suffer in the same syndrome of isolation and pain that is inherent in the unconscious separation from our *Source*. In our perfect "forgetfulness" we don't even know why we suffer, leaving us with the anxiety, depression, loneliness, fear, and insecurity that are so much a part of relative life lived in ignorance of our Lord. As long as you find your identity in mind, fear and anxiety will always be with you, for it is the mind that isolates you from this Moment and your eternal nature. No lasting peace can be found in egocentric identity as you live each day trying to fill the void of your isolation. Moments of happiness may be achieved and will keep you in the mode; however, the chaos and fear of your ignorance will necessarily and obsessively have you cling to your false identity formed in mind, which can only perpetuate your suffering and the anxiety of your isolation. It is mind that separates you from this Moment and your eternal nature in the illusion of ego, which necessarily gives you a sense of identity in the chaos of ignorance.

I became *consciously* aware of this isolation we are in, I *know* this pain, and I have seen you suffer in it. I know your experience of life. I have shared your dreams, had your fears, and hoped your hopes. I know how difficult it is for you to have your experience of Life be any other way and why you fill each day with as much as is needed so you can forget your loneliness, hold back your fears, and calm your anxiety. We are all in exile; we have all suffered the loss of a Love too great to bear and have built defenses to protect ourselves against further loss. We are, however, constantly reminded of our loss, for each time we must "move on" in our lives and leave the relative comfort and security we have come to know and enjoy, every time we are rejected by a lover, a friend, or a family member, each time we leave those we love or a home that was dear to us, we suffer that great loss again and open the wounds of our exile that the illusion of ego had managed, for a time, to bandage.

Be comforted though, for truly, "Blessed are those who suffer." It is from within this pain that would awaken us to our loss that our Lord beckons to us to return to Him and come to the Love we seek, and end our suffering in the illusion of ego. Our pain can be a powerful "gateway" to our Lord. Do not resist or avoid it, but go deeply into your pain and know its source.

The illusion of ego and the identity we take from it is a formidable one, and all too often, the ego will fearfully cling to the memories, wallow in the nostalgia of the past or desperately try to recapture the lost loves and the good feelings of our yesterdays. We continue to live in the illusion of past and fear for our future. It is here that the irony of our lives is so blatantly clear, for the spirit of our Lord is here and now, as this Moment, as the essence of your life. Here, in His presence, time does not exist, and the illusion of your life as a problem disappears as all of your difficulties have been created by the limited perception of your mind as you live in the illusion of time. You suffer because you have not been able to let go of that illusion as you live outside the perfection of this Moment in your "story," your relative identity. That does not mean that your suffering is an illusion, for He suffers as surely as you suffer in that ignorance. But all the love we seek, all the love we are capable of giving, is clouded by what we are so desperately holding on to in an identity that stands as the barrier to the glorious realization of our true nature ...... Now. Still your mind and come to this eternal presence. ...... Know thyself.

The suffering of the Soul isolated by ego is reflected in the ego, and we all too often find our identity in the pain and live a life that attracts further pain in an endless unhappy cycle of suffering. For us to know who we are, the ego must be surrendered and the illusion of time dispelled. An ego identity filled with pain can be even more difficult to let go of because of the emotional energy attached to it as we lament our past and fear for our future. But truly, our Lord wants you to know, needs you to know, and you will suffer as long as you live in ignorance of this great Love. We have reached a point in our evolutionary process where we can no longer continue in the egocentric state of consciousness as we continue to find our identity in mind and suffer the illusion of time. Our fear, our pain, our longing for fulfillment in a quest outside ourselves is killing this planet, and we will destroy ourselves in the narcissism of ego and in the darkness of our self-serving ignorance. We continue to perpetuate needless pain as we reap the destructive consequences of our ignorance in a consciousness that is oblivious to the glorious presence of this Moment.

As much as the ego is in the way, we must, it seems, have something of value to "bring to the table" for us to surrender, and that something must be instilled with the light of "higher knowledge" and with the humility and grace of wonder taken from our sincere exploration of Life. We have reincarnated into this body and into this life for a reason that must be looked to and explored. It is essential that we do not become totally identified by this relative ego identity. An ego identity that has become lost in the turmoil of a traumatic life and in the fear and neurosis that can claim *you*, needs to be understood, and your direction re-established, if anything of value is to be "brought to the table" and surrendered. You must at least begin to question your life and open yourself to all you *don't* know so you can begin your inner quest. Your searching and your pain may take you in many directions. Psychotherapy and the promises of the ego-boosting "self-help" movements may have some merit in securing the ego in this ego-oriented world, and may even be a start to clearing the membrane of the trauma and blocks that can terribly distort even our "relative" view of life, but they remain woefully inadequate as a measure of this incredible journey.

Pretend for a moment you have suddenly found yourself walking on an unknown highway and a stranger stops to pick you up. Would you, in your wildest dreams, at least not wonder where you were or how you got there? Would you not ask the driver where he was going, who he was, and where this highway led before you got in? If there were other passengers in the car and you did take the ride, how long would it be, had you remained estranged from them, before your anxiety would lead to paranoia as to their motives and intents, and you began to fear for your safety? Who is this driver, where is he taking me, why am I going, what is the purpose, who are these people, how did they get here? These are just a few of the questions that would enter any reasonable person's mind, yet very few of us give any serious consideration as to the purpose and meaning of our lives. We avoid real exploration into the mental anguish that comes from a life lived in isolation and ignorance. We merely exist and flounder about with the many "others" in a relative identity that has no real direction, or knowledge of this journey we are on and of the circumstances that have allowed it to happen.

Perhaps on this hypothetical journey you put some trust into one of the "others" who claims knowledge of this journey and offers you help and guidance. However, all too often this "therapy" is little more than adjusting your behavior within the vehicle so you can feel okay and "fit in." The driver is ignored, the how and why you are there unexplored, the vehicle and its reliability unquestioned, and the destination still unknown. We become limited to an identity within the vehicle only (albeit all-consuming in the confines of this vehicle) and "lose the forest for the trees." We still suffer, regardless of what game we choose to play, from the anxiety and fear of our greater ignorance.

Too often, the "therapist" becomes our anchor and we develop a dependency on them, adjusting our lives around "therapy." Until we become "aware" again of the mystery that is this journey and generate in ourselves a desire to solve the riddle of our existence and explore further the miracle of how we got here and where we are going, how can we come to feel at ease? Until we question the true nature of the "driver" that is making this journey happen and consider what our destination may be, how can we truly enjoy the journey? Until we have a clear understanding of the circumstances that have brought us to where we are and feel comfortable with the "others" with whom we are sharing this journey, how can we possibly find a deeper meaning and purpose for our life? How can we truly live?!

Fortunately, the Kundalini energy is one of transformation and growth and cannot be denied. Like the life force that creates change and growth in flowers, we are being forced out of the darkness of separation and ignorance, sometimes kicking and screaming, but nonetheless it is happening. We are being confronted by our fear and anxiety that are both so much a part of this superficial world of ego/membrane. We will need to let go of much that is holding us back so we can continue to grow. We will have to confront our shortfalls and our fears, however painful they may be, and go beyond the limits of the ego and the traumas of a life caught up in the illusion of time. We will need to let go of the "helpless, needy passenger" identity, take a step back, and examine our life. We must look to and evaluate the "co-dependent" relationships we've developed that keep us pacified and comfortable, yet unconscious of our true nature.

In faith and with love in your heart you can surrender the ego structure that tries to protect your transient, limited identity but only serves to isolate your eternal spirit. The ego identity is a false identity, and at the level of Soul we unconsciously know of the deception and long to be free of it. It is the Soul—that part of our Lord that is truly who we are in this Moment—that suffers the falsehood of the ego. It is at best a relative identity, which holds no real meaning as we consider the true reality of our situation.

These, then, are the words that describe who we are not and why we suffer. But they can never convey to you the experience that lies beyond your fear and your pain. Go to them, become conscious of your anxiety, which ego has created, and go deeply into the "energy." Become the witness and then let go in faith and in Love. It will be then that you will come to Him—your higher self—and you will know that all you suffer from can be relieved in the presence of your inner essence. *All* of this is a spiritual journey and must be acknowledged as such if you are to come to know who you are, why you are, or for that matter, why there is anything.

You do not have to travel across the planet to find what it is you are looking for; it is in the very room you are sitting in, embodied by you. Yes, the ego must be surrendered to something more than we are in order to know who we are, and that is a task we must face daily. Practice silencing the mind and becoming aware of the "witness," aware of awareness. For within *you* lies the secret to this Life, and your work must begin there. Through expanded awareness in a release of the limits the ego has placed upon you, and in reverence for the silence that surrounds you, you will come to the "Mystery," that something whose presence can be sensed but has no name— that which is bigger than who we believe ourselves to be, yet is ironically who we are once we are emptied. Once found, you will have all you will need to surrender your egocentric identity to.

Jesus offers you this same mystery, this same miracle, this same wonder to surrender your heart to, for He knew and embodied "*That,*" indeed was "*That.*" Beware of those who would peddle His name and stand in His place and whose motives may not be so pure. Having your own limited ego in the way is more than enough to overcome; you don't need someone else's fear and ignorance. Avoid anyone whose view of life contains something or someone to fear, or one that would hold you in that fear as a means of control and as a power over you. There is truly nothing to fear here but fear itself, and fear is the product of the mind unconscious of this Moment, lost in the illusion of time. Know that life at Its core is good and that the spirit of Christ is the source of that goodness. Do not take His name in vain or believe you can know him through it. He is the ineffable spirit of this Moment, the miraculous source of Love whose name is simply a sign post that will point you to the Eternal.

Of course, there are those Droplets who still live in the body and have made the journey beyond the confines of ego and have come to that transcendental field of Spirit with much to offer you. Seek them out if you need reassurance, but keep in mind that your family and your friends can offer deep insight into this journey if you are willing to open up, let go of ego, be truthful, pay attention, be forgiving, and love. You have been placed here for a purpose, and that purpose has structure in your relationships. How you deal with the karmic debt you owe to those around you and to the debt they owe you will be a measure of your spiritual growth. Remember, we are all a part of the same spirit in Him, and your actions will express that "higher knowledge" as you come to know who you are. Do not be fooled by the illusions of ego and time and the limits of your senses; your life holds more than you know. The charity, love, and guidance you give to others will have a direct and positive effect on your life. Your wisdom and your connection to this Great Spirit of Life will grow as your love grows.

Practice your loving every day. Find something or someone to show your love to. Open yourself to this wonderful experience that is your life and learn to love every aspect of it. Love the clouds, the trees, the never-ending presence of this incredible universe. Love the beauty, grace, and mystery of everything that grows and every-thing that does not. Love your desire and your ability to Love.

Love is something eternal—the aspect may change, but not the essence. There is the same difference in a person before and after he is in love as there is in an unlighted lamp and one that is burning. The lamp was there and it was a good lamp, but now it is shedding light too, and that is its real function."
—Droplet vincent van gogh

The Kundalini event totally changed my life. I was in no uncer-tain terms "born again." The "veil of illusion" that shrouded my per-ception was suddenly lifted, and I was given a glimpse at the miracle and mystery that is this Life—that is this Moment. I have come to know that this "silent witness" that suffered so during that "dark night" was in truth our Lord, the essence of Life, the core of our existence in search of Itself, and that through you and through me He will be revealed. It is from within this light of pure consciousness that each of us holds, that field of Being which is *"That,"* the cause and purpose of this Creation, the knower and the lover of Life, where we will find our fulfillment. I cannot give this experience to you with words, I can only assure you that what you hold is more than you could have dreamt of in your philosophies, and that you hold within you the potential of taking the experience of a simple blade of grass to unbelievable heights of beauty, grace, and wonder in a love too profound for words.

It has been from within this "silent witness" that this book has been written. It has served as a bridge between my experience of the Eternal and my experience of "relative life" and the illusions of mind. I have come to know the Eternal and feel Its presence as the *Source* of all that is outside of those illusions. This book hopes to provide a glimpse of the magical effect "present Moment" awareness can have your "ordinary" life as it becomes one filled with the mystery, beauty, and peace that are His eternal nature, now no longer a *belief* locked in mind but rather as a direct and immediate experience of the Now Moment. This, then, is the "higher knowledge" of the Soul that serves as a universal guide and as direction for all who seek. There is a time and place for certain things, and this is a knowledge that is best absorbed during those quiet moments of reflection for which few of us take the time anymore. Once it is understood, however, it is a knowledge that will enrich your experience of your everyday "relative life" as it takes on the presence of the Eternal One and you become aware that you are an expression of His love. He is here, He is now, in all that there is, as who you are, ... joyfully, lovingly!

Understandably, there are still moments when I simply "space out," and I do revel in those times. They are a necessary shift in focus that brings the Eternal into my awareness and dwarfs relative life and the importance we put on so many silly things. Don't be afraid or reluctant to do the same. It is all too easy to become lost in an identity that is defined by the body with all of its sensations and desires. It is equally as easy to get lost in the identity of mind and emotions with the memories, traumas, longings, nuttiness, and need for security. Opening ourselves to the mystery that is this Moment allows us to become a witness, a witness bathing in consciousness who is free of the identities of mind and body, yet grateful for those gifts and awed by this ineffable spectacle of Life.

And so, I have become the "mystic," for I have seen the "Mystery" and have been humbled by It. Yet, I am no different than you, for if you have ever been awed by the majesty of the night sky or left speechless at the sight of a newborn or humbled by some profound beauty, if you have ever feared or wondered what will happen at your death or where you were before your birth, then you, too, are the mystic and hold a sense of the world of mystery and have it as a part of your life. Now open your heart to It and become the lover. Bring your faith and trust to this Moment and leave your fear behind. There is nothing that can exist outside this Moment, beyond the loving embrace of our Lord, and once you have come to It completely present, you will never have anything to fear again. Resist nothing!

As I continue on my journey, I remain grateful, humbled, and in awe of this process of Becoming with a deep faith and trust in His wisdom and His Love. My prayer is that you will take something from my journey that will bring you closer to our Lord and to the Love that resides within and around us all.

The person who has a firm trust in the Supreme Being is powerful in his power, wise by his wisdom, happy by his happiness.
—Droplet joseph addison

Chapter IX

JESUS

For God so loved the world...

—John 3:16

No Droplet has had more of an impact on the rest of us Droplets than Jesus, the Christ. Actually, the Droplet analogy doesn't really apply here. Picture instead a column or wave rising out of the limitless ocean, among us and in form, yet completely connected to the Source, indeed the *Source.* "I and the Father are one" (John 10:30)were His words and His experience. Although we may not hold this same experience, we are nonetheless one with the Father; only ego and the constant chatter of mind keeps us from that knowing. It is through a loving union with Christ that we can come to that realization of unity.

The how and why He came to us can only be considered another of God's graces and an expression of God's love, for what God did was give us a way to end our suffering in exile through belief and faith in Christ.

For God did not send his son into the world to condemn the world, but to save the world through him.

—John 3:17

With faith, love, and in devotion to Christ, that is the eternal *Source* and Spirit of this Moment, we can fearlessly drop the ego's defenses and clear the membrane that is keeping us isolated and in darkness, allowing "salvation" through a union with Him, a union that can only come in a loving surrender. "Understanding" this, knowing this intellectually, or even wanting this desperately can only take you so far, as these are ego functions. It will come only after you have opened your heart to Him and to all of Life in what we know as Loving. The commandment to "love the Lord your God with all your heart and with all your soul" (Matthew 22:37) leaves no room for an isolated ego in a state of desire. You must become Love, and in so doing, you are denying the isolation in which the ego would keep you by actualizing the one function that ego is not capable of—unconditional Loving.

Truly loving can only happen in the Now, and in it we would be making that direct connection with our inner *Source*, and it would be there that you would find our Lord—that you would join with and become Him in the Now. With a *sincere* acknowledgement and in an acute awareness of this "higher power" that surrounds and permeates us and all of life in this Moment, we can humble the mind/ego and open ourselves up to this Moment and to the beauty and "Mystery" that is our lives. Faith and trust are key words here; faith in the *letting go* of the securities the ego has built that would in turn open you to the infinite possibilities outside that security. And trust in His love for us and in what is so much more than what we *think* we are.

In a faithful and loving surrender to Him, the illusion of isolation would be dispelled. Through Him we would gain eternal life in His Kingdom, although in reality that Kingdom is truly *our* lost Kingdom—that which is our *Source* and our essence—which was actually never lost, but rather only temporarily obscured by a veil of illusion the ego had built and by the darkness of ignorance inherent in it. We are the Droplets falling back into the ocean, losing the appearance of separateness and seemingly everything that the membrane had defined as *our* life. In that process of reunion, we would inherit *everything* that is the glory of heaven, everything that we could have ever hoped for or possibly have imagined.

"I am the way and the truth and the life" (John 14:6). So said the Christ and so He is. Through the experience of and in surrender to Him lies the gateway to heaven, should we find the faith and courage to let go in Love. It is so much more than the ego shouting, "I Love Jesus," slapping a bumper sticker on your car and going to church every Sunday. It is in a *total* surrender to Life and a commitment to bringing your awareness of Him and your Loving into every moment of It. He is the light that shines within you. ...... Be still. ...... Let Him out. ...... Let Him shine.

The Christ Consciousness is in the Moment that you are reading this; It is in the moment that I am writing this; It is now, always was, and will always be here for you. This Moment is eternal, everlasting, life without end. You need only "Seek first the Kingdom of Heaven and all else will be added on to thee," and that Kingdom is the *"That"* which is our essential yet unrealized nature and the essence of this miraculous, Holy Moment. Be *"That"* and be with Him eternally. ...... When He was asked who he was, He replied "I am *That* which I am." ...... Indeed!

Jesus told us that he had come not to make peace but to weld a sword dividing father from son. He had come, in essence, not to give comfort to the ego but to destroy the illusions that separate you from Him. Your father or your son, your wife or your lover, and all of the "yours" you can think of are all part of the same Spirit in Him. Keep the illusion that you are separate from what is "yours" and you perpetuate your exile and your suffering. His message is one of love and union, not the division that is inherent in the ego/mind. When you surrender what is "yours," you lose nothing but your isolation, nothing but your fear, nothing but your sorrow and pain. You will come to this Moment with only the Love that had been masked by all you were so desperately holding on to. In that Love you will have come to Christ and to His compassion, and you will be His light in the world.

Christ's commandments, "If someone strikes you on one cheek, turn to him the other also" (Luke 6:29), and "Love your neighbor as yourself" (Matthew 22:39), are clearly a denial of the ego, its superficial reactions, and restricted structure, allowing for something more to enter—much more. By creating an atmosphere that embraces love and forgiveness, we are denying the relative ego identity, which can only react from a mindset of fear and insecurity. By letting go of this limited identity, we are opening ourselves to the essence of Life, to that unconditional love that is His essence and His strength within us. As we let go of ego, we would allow that which is His presence to rise within us and join Him in the world of spirit outside the illusion of time.

"When you are near to me, you are near to the fire." What else can He mean but that coming closer to Him—that is, raising your awareness to His presence—is tantamount to the destruction of the ego? In order to embrace Him totally, to join with Him and become a clear witness to His essence, no illusion of the separate ego can survive. The experience of Christ is an "undoing" of the ego and the mind's very limited experience that would have us appear separate and alone. Beyond the ego and its limits on you lies a Love so great as to fill this unending universe and end the illusions of time and space. Practice leaving ego behind and saying yes to life and to all this Moment is offering. Let go of your fear, let go of your desire, and come to Him as an empty vessel in a total acceptance of what Is and be filled with His love. This could not have happened yesterday, nor can it be your fulfillment in tomorrow. This can only happen NOW!

You must not let the words, images, and idols of religion give your ego yet another identity trap; they, too, must be left behind. Jesus has far more to give you than the sentiments of words and the superficial security of idols. But you must first let go of the relative ego identity, and that is not easily done. It is likened to climbing to some great precipice and finding yourself holding on for dear life at the summit. What you fear letting go of is the ego identity, as it would seem to be your certain death and total annihilation in the face of this great height. But fear serves no man here, and as fear is the antithesis of Love; it is in your faith, Love, and trust in Him that it will be replaced. Let go, with Love in your heart! This is not a suicide, as suicide is a function of a disturbed ego and would leave you with a huge karmic burden to undo. This is surrender that can only happen consciously with the grace of humility, in the joy of heightened awareness and with Love in your heart. But first you must make the climb to that height, leaving all that you have known, all you are holding onto behind, and travel to where you have never been. And when you have seen It, when you have experienced the vertigo at this great height and are swooning and dizzy and afraid, open your heart, empty your mind, and simply be with Him completely. He will fill the void you fear with His Love, and once you have let go of your fear in love, you will find that you have wings!

It is all too easy to take the *words* of those who have made the climb and experienced His presence, then create a cozy ego identity with words that match, and never make the climb for yourself—in other words, take up religion. There are those who have completely rejected the words of this "higher knowledge" as being fanciful and not reflective of their experience at the base of this "mountain" or, in a word, become atheists. This *realization* of His ever-present love can *only* come in your direct and immediate *experience* of the "summit" that is manifested in a pure experience of this Moment, unencumbered by mind and ego.

Your climb does not have to be riddled with the pain and sorrow of leaving all that was dear to you forever behind. Take the time to cherish the view as you make the climb. Open your heart and embrace all that was and all that is now. Be grateful for what was, as it has given you "footholds" to help you make the climb. Now open yourself completely to what is and become a witness to His presence. Be prepared though, for if you are to climb higher, all of your relationships will necessarily change and what was once your life as an isolated ego, limited by insecurity and need, will become a life driven by charity in the experience of His abundance. Your compassion and love will naturally flow to those who may be suffering outside that Love. You will help them see the new vistas gained in your efforts, and impart your faith onto them. Your love will dispel their fears and bring them knowledge of His eternal presence. Your selflessness will ease the burden you carry and make your ascent less difficult, as the more you surrender, the "lighter" you'll become, and the easier and higher you will rise.

The suffering of humanity is real and cannot nor should not be glossed over with words that would deny the experience. The Christ and those kindred souls like the Buddha who have joined Him in this Moment and expressed the Christ Consciousness in their teachings have, as have all enlightened Droplets throughout the ages, spoken with compassion for those who are suffering, for as you suffer, He suffers. It is through this suffering that we will be led back to Him through an awareness of our true nature as we explore our pain. In our suffering, the membrane, thickened and darkened by the ego structure, can begin to soften and become more transparent as the ego dissolves in its own misery—truly "blessed are those who suffer." We may be forced to let go of that transient, limited identity due to some great tragedy or terrible loss. If we can go beyond our pain, through our pain, we will come to that silent presence that resides within us all. Our Inner Light can begin to shine as we realize the eternal nature of Life at its core. It is in and through our suffering that we can become more aware of that "silent witness" as the false ego structure dissolves. The true and lasting essence of who we are stands peacefully outside the pain, yet can embrace and ease the pain with a boundless love and compassion. Relative life can bring you only so much fulfillment. Unfortunately, that "so much" can be a life-long quest of superficial pursuits and desires that will sooner or later create the suffering of an isolated ego in the passing of form. Whether we suffer or not, we will need to go deeply into this experience of Life if we are to know who we are. Suffering has often been a catalyst for this inner search, a means for our surrender, and can cause the awakening of our true nature in the total surrender required for enlightenment.

Life is said to be suffering, and that suffering is the result of the need for, the attachment to, and the eventual loss of those "things" with which we have come to identify ourselves. The natural tendency of the mind, the God-given impulse at the core of our being, is to seek happiness and fulfillment. It is also the impetus that will eventually bring us home should we choose the path of Love and of higher knowledge. But beware, for if this desire for happiness is not understood as the impulse that is leading you to your fulfillment in *Source* and only the ego is charged with this desire for happiness, then it can be the impetus that will lead you far from the path and create the suffering that is inherent in His absence in the unending superficial pursuits of the ego lost in the illusion of time. It is here that you will find the suffering and, ironically, a "Gateway" into Now. But this "Gateway" need not be through suffering alone. Your Love for Life in the Now also offers fulfillment in self-knowledge. Through suffering and loss, your ego is shattered and your pain can allow you to open to your true nature. But it can also come through your gaining of this "higher knowledge" and in an unconditional Love of Life as you surrender to It. The ego is overwhelmed, humbled, and finally abandoned as you join with Him in a love that ego is simply not capable of in this Moment where time does not exist.

And so, now you know, ... now you can choose. It is a choice you must make every day in every action you take. Choose to love in spite of ego or choose to suffer the loss of that love in egocentric pursuits. Step back from your life and become a witness to the miracle of it. Realize yourself in and as this eternal silence of Being and be filled with this unending Love.

"Blessed are the poor in spirit, for theirs is the kingdom of heaven" (Matthew 5:3). Indeed, ours is a time of great suffering. Look to your Scriptures as guides and bring awareness to your pain. Your pain can be your strongest guide and should be felt deeply, not to be avoided but rather looked to as a powerful beacon that can lead to His embrace. Once it is understood and its source revealed, you will transcend it by becoming a witness to it. As you become aware in the silence of your own being, you will come to Source, the who you ARE.

Droplet pema chodron is an American Buddhist nun and director of the first Tibetan monastery in North America. Her books bring her deep insight into the struggles we all face. Her Buddhist approach is rich with wise and practical advice taken from many years of study and practice. Here is a small sampling of her wisdom:

The underlying point of all our study and practice is that the happiness we seek is here to connect with at any time. The happiness we seek is our birthright. To discover it, we need to be gentler with ourselves, more compassionate toward ourselves and our universe. The happiness we seek cannot be found through grasping, trying to hold onto things. It cannot be found through getting serious and uptight about wanting things to go in the direction that we think will bring happiness. We are always taking hold of the wrong end of the stick. The point is that the happiness we seek is already here, and it will be found through relaxation and letting go, rather than through struggle.

Do get hold of one of her many books. Droplet pema chodron's work reflects a clear and compassionate understanding of our suffering. Her "scriptures" are a potent and useful guide filled with the love and insight of a soul so very close to our Lord.

In truth, your level of suffering can be measured and is dependent on the level of attachment you have to those transient "things" of Life, as truly "*all* things must pass." However, not enjoying or holding back your love for fear of the inevitable loss and the associated pain of that loss is a denial of the gifts our Lord has created and placed before us, and is a denial of our purpose here. Certainly, we are not here to take as much as we can and hold onto it for as long as we can in the unending quests of the ego; however, we are here to enjoy and bring our awareness to and be grateful for these gifts of Life. We are here to Love and enjoy our lives! Truly, all "things" do come and go on this relative plane, but we must keep our awareness open to their *Source*. "The Lord gave and the Lord has taken away" (Job 1:21). Know this and know we are all part of this perfect Love, and your pain will be no more as you become aware of His eternal presence. "Yours" does not exist here, as we are all a part of the same spirit in Him. In your surrender and in your letting go of the false ego identity, there can be no real loss. The pain of loss can only come in the isolation and the ignorance of the ego. It is in your loving surrender to Him that you will flow into this great sea of Love and end your suffering.

"Father, forgive them, for they do not know what they are doing" (Luke 23:34). For me, these are the most profound words that

Jesus was recorded as saying. At the peak of His pain from torture and crucifixion, He looked down upon us with love and compassion from a place deeply connected to our Lord and forgave us for our ignorance. He knew the isolation we are in; He knew the ignorance that is inherent in separation and the "sins" that are so much a part of that state of being. He went beyond His own suffering and felt enough to forgive us because He knew the high purpose that each and every one of us plays in this Creation. And now you know. It is your birthright and your destiny to open to His love within you; there can be no more excuses. Look to your fears and to your needs. If you believe that anything other than His love will fulfill your desire for happiness, then you have missed It. If you have not found the Eternal as the essence of your spirit, then you will fear your death, for you have limited your identity to the illusion of ego and mind. Let go, not just to "save your soul" but to live and enjoy this Life completely as Its Lover. Forgive yourself and forgive those "others," for they are no different than you in His eyes. Their mistakes and your mistakes can be powerful learning experiences once understood. You will suffer in ignorance, and your pain will lead you back if you can embrace it. Do not judge, for only ego would judge. Learn to Love.

The spirit of Jesus Christ lives within us all. As we raise our awareness to "*That*," we are automatically removing the clutter of the mind as we come closer to "the fire." In so doing, you are essentially putting an end to His suffering and taking Him down from the cross. His love and compassion will live again in your heart and His physical return will become possible in the perfection of any one of us. This goes beyond your beliefs, beyond your religion, beyond the limits of the five senses. This goes to the very heart of what it is to be human, to the core of our existence. All that we see, hear, feel and smell comes to us from the world of spirit. Nothing could exist outside of "*That*," and "*It*" is punctuated by our consciousness. The spirit of Christ is that consciousness, and It has given you your life. Consider carefully, for truly, if this eternal Love we seek does not come from within ourselves, where, then, could you possibly begin to look for it? Let Him guide you to your inner essence and be fulfilled by the Love we share with Him.

In the fear and ignorance inherent in separation, we Droplets nailed the Christ to the cross and created His suffering. The stigma of isolation that creates the need to protect the fragile ego structure, and the fear and ignorance that is inherent in it which can make us do so many stupid things, can all be removed in the light of His love. Remove His suffering and your own, and take Him down from the cross, and let Christ live here and now through you. This world is desperate for the love and compassion that are your birthright and His gifts within you. We have gone very far from the path, and His light needs to shine brightly now, in this Moment. Open yourself to this Moment and to His presence. Become a beacon of His love. Practice your loving and compassion with "random acts of kindness" at every opportunity. You have so much to offer this world. Let go of your fear and restricted identity in which the ego holds you, and be with Him. You won't be sorry. It will begin with the faith in your convictions and the courage to see them through, but in the end there will be nothing left in you to be courageous, and only your Love will endure, as has the peaceful, eternal Love of Jesus the Christ.

> The peace of Christ is the peace of trust in the cause we serve, when service seems to fail of its end. It is the peace of confidence in God when all the forces of the universe seem working for ends that are undivine. It is the peace which can accept unexplained mysteries, which can bear heartbreaking sorrows, which can see natural instincts thwarted, holy aspirations unrealized, Christ-like purpose broken off, yet be unperturbed. It is the peace of a Paul rejected by his countrymen. It is the peace of all those who have given their lives for causes too high and sacred for immediate success and who yet have been able to believe that even their failures were being overruled by God for good.
>
> —Droplet william adams brown

Yours is a vision of unlimited potential and unbounded Love. Imagine a Love within you so great that your worst nightmare, your greatest fear, your unbearable heartbreak would all melt in the warmth of Its eternal embrace. You are that Love shrouded by a veil of illusion that is the defended, frightened, unawakened ego. In seeking Him, you must lose all of your doubt and all of your fear, for they will blind you to Him. You must open your heart and come "near to the fire," and as the illusion of ego and separateness melts away in your loving, what has always been your essence will join with what has always been His, and you will experience a peace beyond imagining. Begin the practice of letting go of your false identity and come to Christ in faith and in Love. Once you have started the "fire," feed it every day and keep the flame of His love alive in you. You alone can bring His love, peace, and compassion to this world as His messenger. You need only become completely present, free from thought and the illusion of time, and you will join with Him as your essence. "Be still, and know that I am God" (Psalm 46:10). So said the Christ, and that "God" lives right here and right Now as the essence of Life within you. His eternal peace is a part of and surrounds all of Life! Let go and be It! Resist nothing.

Chapter X
RELIGION

There is in all the sons of men
A love that in the spirit dwells,
That panteth after things unseen,
And tidings of the future tells.

And God hath built his altar here
To keep this fire of faith alive,
And sent his priests in holy fear
To speak the truth—for truth to strive.

—Droplet ralph waldo emerson

Religion can serve us lost and floundering Droplets very well. Religion offers guideposts and the good advice that can lead us down this rocky road of Life in relative safety. Many Droplets would trip and fall or be lost, their membranes badly thickened and distorted by the temptations and traumas of Life of which religion can steer us clear. Much can be taken from the Scriptures to enrich our lives, guide us, and comfort us in dark times. We can avoid the temptations of the security traps and the addictions that would cloud the membrane—"lead us not into temptation but deliver us from evil"—keeping the potential for our connection with the Holy Spirit alive and in this Moment. Religion can bind us to one another in a recognition of our shared fate, divinity, and humanity.

But religion is not, nor should it be, like any other institute for learning. We must not go to religion to become something or someone, but rather, we go to find the means and the faith to leave all egocentric identity behind. If we, in search of our destination, ask for direction and a finger is pointed in the direction we must proceed, what good will it do us to sit and worship the finger? The adorned temples of our faiths and the limited beliefs that isolate us are the "false gods" that can once again cloud the membrane by satisfying the ego's need for identity and the need to belong and to define the ineffable. In so doing, it keeps us from this sacred and mysterious Moment, for the mind imagines that God can be found only here or there, in some book, or in some previous time, or in some time yet to come, or, worst of all, not until you are dead!

Religion should be offering methodologies to help us unite with this sacred Moment as the *only* reality God has to offer, and not cloud the membrane and isolate us further with peculiar beliefs, differences, dogma, graven images, obscure ritual, fear, and all the other nonsense that can drive us nuts! "Be here now!" is the holy plea from Droplet baba ram dass, and is at the core of all religions. Bringing your total awareness to this Moment is the only *religion* you need to practice. It requires no special place—your body is the temple—and no special thoughts—you must let go of all thought—and no special images, for the sky and the glory of nature are all that you will need.

Why do you think we look skyward whenever we consider heaven? Let's take a moment and ponder the sky. I like to use dark red or amber sunglasses, as they somehow bring further mystery and depth to the visual experience of sky. Know that what you are looking at is eternal. It has no beginning or end. There is nothing beyond it; there is nothing that the mind/intellect can grasp or define. Thought about seriously, it actually hurts and bewilders. Sure, the ego/mind can name the galaxies and begin to measure incredible distances in light years, and science can, as it does with all of nature, begin to break the universe apart: calculate, name, develop theories, and pretend to *know*. But it cannot and will never have the ability to define the final answer here, because there is none, not in terms of ego and mind. *It* simply *is* and *It* surrounds us as the *only* reality there is, a vast, mysterious, endless void, the great abyss that contains within it everything. The essence of God is truly here right before our eyes in a powerful statement of Now that can only be hidden in the chatter of mind.

The limitations of the mind and the illusions inherent in it become clearer as we ponder this great mystery. Looking for an end to the universe reveals the illusion of time and space in which we are all lost. We need simply to bring our full awareness to this Moment in a state of "no mind," and then open ourselves to the Eternal Presence that surrounds us, that *is* us. It is here that we will find the wonder and the mystery that is at the core of all true religion. It is here, from our isolated perspective that we can begin to take a measure of the eternal Love of which we have been deprived, and begin to open ourselves to the eternal, endless Love that awaits us.

Truly, nothing happened yesterday and nothing is going to happen tomorrow; that is only mind-stuff. You live and you die only in this very *Moment*, this vastness that is nothing and everything in one breath. Find your peace in this Moment, find your self in this Moment, find God in this Moment by letting go of all that blinds you to His presence, and bring your full awareness to this Moment, to His level of eternal purity, and you will join Him in this Moment as this Moment. Drop the illusions the mind creates, be open to awareness, and remove the "blocks" that define you and simply Be. ...... Now slow down. ...... Relax. ...... Watch your mind think. ...... Listen to the thoughts. ...... Tell me now, who is watching? ...... Who is listening? ...... Don't you know? ...... Why, it's the SKY! You are the infinite, you are the unbounded, you are the eternal love you are seeking, you are the Now, and you are "*That*"!

Droplet krishna murti likened religions to pools that develop at the edges of a great flowing river. Because they are no longer in the river's flow, they begin to stagnate and smell. Religion must be alive and in this Moment with the flow of Life offering techniques that would allow us to let go and break clear of the illusions that separate us from our most sacred heritage. What possible good can come of wearing special hats, or special clothing, praying in special ways in special buildings, or believing that only we are "the chosen ones"? What tradition or belief that would tie us to the past in a mind-based identity could open us to the glorious experience of Now, free from thought? How many more Catholics need be killed by protestants or protestants by Catholics or Muslims by Jews or Jews by Muslims or Hindus by Buddhists or Buddhists by Hindus, and on and on and on, because of some misleading, deceitful, fraudulent *belief* that hides the reality that we are *all* an expression of this ever-present Holy Spirit, the one and only *God*, and that this *Moment* is the *only* reality that exists, regardless of what you "believe" or in whatever illusion you are lost. ...... Look and see! I know it isn't easy to perceive this Moment as anything other than what seems to be. I know how difficult going beyond mind and the senses can be, for they are powerful illusions; you see trees and rock, earth and sky, and find yourself walking amongst others in what would seem a competition for Life. Your love is conditional and limited to the perception of ego. We *appear* separate and alone and crave security in our isolation. This is the illusion of mind and the betrayal of ego. It is beyond the limitations of the mind, outside the identity we take from thoughts and the isolated illusion of ego, that your heaven awaits. It is here that your unconditional love for all of Life will blossom as you become present, free from illusion in a resounding "yes" to this Moment and all it is offering ...... Now! There is no other reality other than this very Moment whose essence can be experienced in a state of "no mind," yet we spend most, if not all, of our time in an identity that has been created in the mind through the illusion of past and future. This Moment holds a place of perfect peace in the unity and Love that is our shared *Source and Creator*. It is here and Now for all to see. ...... Let go, still your mind. You are holding on to shadows.

Isolated by the mind and beliefs, we are capable of an infinite variety of acts that can defile God and limit our awareness of this Moment. In that isolation and clinging to our beliefs, we were unaware that the Messiah had arrived. He had come to fulfill the true meaning of those beliefs by His presence, but we only saw Him as a threat to our identity, one that had been taken in mind and those beliefs. As He stood before us, how could we remain identified and secured in the faith, the religious doctrine, and the strong belief that *one day* God would send a Messiah when the "Messiah" was standing before us in this very Moment? How could we let go of our identity in mind/ego and become totally present to this Moment and give ourselves to Him? As He stood before us, we quoted from "the book," secured our frightened ego in the words, and obscured the Moment in mind stuff. In our fear of losing our long-standing beliefs and our consequential identity derived from those beliefs, we destroyed the challenge to our illusions that was at once Jesus and the love of this eternal Moment. We chose to worship the "finger" that was indeed pointing to Christ and to remain in the stagnant pool of our beliefs, letting the flow of Life, of Love, pass us by.

All religions are the result of an enlightened master, an avatar, who was in direct contact with the Holy Spirit. In that contact, one basic truth was realized and that is/was that there is only one God, and He is this Moment of which we are *all* an expression. After that, the unenlightened took that vision and verbalized it. Then the ego/mind took over, found identity in the words, and we have the mess that we have today. Was Christ a Christian, Buddha a Buddhist? They had no such need, as they were in direct contact with our Lord, in this Moment, as this Moment, as our Lord. We all share that same potential awakening once the *beliefs* are gone and we can come to this Moment as a pure expression of *"That."*

It would seem the less educated and the more insecure and fearful we Droplets are, the more fanatical we are about our religion and the more "opium for the masses" fits as a definition for religion. It is frightening to witness the violence, terror, and need to control inherent in these "unholy" beliefs. It is equally frightening to watch the ego take on an identity that would try to reflect but could not possibly hold those qualities of the eternal spirit that lies beyond the illusion of ego. Falsely secured by the delusion of invincibility and the prospects of eternal life, the ego becomes a monster, isolated from this Moment, unaware of the true beauty of Life and lost in its narcissistic, self-serving, limited universe. In that isolation, lost and beguiled by deceptive knowledge and an overblown egocentric identity, the worst that we can become is possible.

When they lose their sense of awe,
people turn to religion.
When they no longer trust themselves,
they begin to depend on authority.

—From the Tao te Ching

You must let go of your illusions and limited perceptions with a faith in our Lord and His wisdom. Come to this Moment of miracles free of egocentricity and join with Him. Take personal responsibility for raising your awareness of who you are and how you behave in this Moment as an expression of the Holy Spirit and as a lover of Life. In that letting go, you will live that which will bring all religions and all of us Droplets together, not in the stagnant pools that are the mire of our "beliefs," filled with fear and distrust, but in the flow of Life and to this Moment, grateful and in love. Imagine a planet of enlightened Beings who can only celebrate and be joyful for the glory and richness that is this *Moment* with reverence and thanks for Its creator! Their experience of unity would put them in His loving embrace in full consciousness of their sacred role as witness. Look now at this planet whose beings are lost in the muck of their various *beliefs* and in the insecurity of their isolated, ignorant experience of life, who are still drawn to violence and genocide as a cure for their fear should their brethren present a threat to those beliefs and to that ignorance. You who live in darkness will suffer and die in the pain and sorrow that is that darkness. You who have turned from the living God in the muddle of the mind and the limits of your unholy beliefs perpetuate the "evil" of this world. You alone will be responsible for the "sins" of your ignorance, and you will continue the suffering that is your isolation regardless of the numbers with which you have gathered. You who cannot embrace this Moment in awe, and acknowledge the Mystery and glory of His eternal presence in all there is, will wallow in the misery of your ignorance and suffer the pain of His absence. Your death will be the sting of a thousand scorpions as the transient ego identity you have adopted vanishes forever in His eternal presence and you suffer from the "sins" of your isolation. You will have missed the unity of Love and your soul will suffer that terrible loss. It is only in this Moment that you will find our Lord in the vast stillness and eternal peace of Now. Obscure Him in the constant chatter of mind and in the insanity of your beliefs that defile this Moment of Miracles in ignorance and self-serving quests, and you will surely perish forever in an annihilation of your narcissistic world of illusion and limited perception of self.

Curiously, sports seem to offer a sort of perverse outlet for what religion has failed to fulfill. I do enjoy and participate in sports, but in what can easily be described as a metaphor for life and as a replacement for our spiritual quest, we find good guys and bad guys, hope and faith, the "joy of victory and the agony of defeat," strong ego identity as a "fan," an enormous emotional outlet, the potential for monetary rewards, and even clothing to wear. And you can live it every day! Here is truly "morphine for the masses." Is it any wonder that sports are so popular, why our "heroes" can warrant so much money, and why so many can be so fanatical? The insecurity of the ego will allow it to grab on to any identity that indeed *needs* to grab on to some identity. With sports it is effortless; just choose your favorite team.

So now, just for fun, imagine Life as a huge stadium. We, however, are not passive fans but rather active players. The goal is reunion and enlightenment; the opponent, illusion and ignorance; our game plan, love and compassion; our coach is the Christ Consciousness in whatever form you chose. Now, gooooooooooooo, Droplets! But remember, in this game it *really* doesn't matter if you win or lose, but rather how you play the game. So play it well, with focus and integrity. Bring your Love and Compassion into each "play"; it is your connection to this eternal Moment. Have fun and enjoy! The greatest of God's gifts are here for us all at no cost, and they are here *now* for everyone to enjoy. Pay attention to the play because it's all that there is, and you can truly forget about any goal; there isn't one; you are already here; you have already won; you need only realize it!

Be cautious, for the "religions" of consumerism, money, sex, vanity, substance abuse, work, politics, and anything else that can keep us from ourselves needs to be put into perspective and recognized as potential blocks toward our spiritual growth if we give them too much of our energy and in them find our identity. Ease away from those activities that are purely egocentric in their pursuit, and practice coming to this eternal Moment in full awareness, that is, in a state of "no mind." Begin the practice of stilling the mind in a daily opening to His presence. ...... Simply and completely Be! Initially, you may only be able to hold your awareness open for just a moment or two before mind enters and clouds your perception. But as you continue this practice—and it can be applied anytime, anywhere—you will begin to feel yourself open to full awareness in recognition of and in contrast to the disturbance of mind as it clouds and shrouds the "Mystery." Watch as your mind creeps in and the chatter begins. Watch as you are shrouded in a repetition of past knowledge that can only hold you in illusion. Your witnessing of the obsession of mind is the first and a giant step toward your freedom.

Many years ago, the Droplet bertrand russell's book *Why I Am Not a Christian* came to me. He tore Christianity apart both intellectually and emotionally, and his book left me empty with its brutal honesty. Apparently, it left Russell empty as well, as he spent the last years of his life in frustration and anxiety, and he, too, it seems, had, like most intellectuals, "thrown the baby out with the bath water." Although conscious and courageous enough to take on the Church and its intellectually dishonest beliefs and dogma—certainly not to be limited to Christianity—he had become too intellectual and was unable to come to this Moment and to an experience of his own Christ Consciousness through an open heart and in a profound state of wonder.

As harsh as what I am about to say may be to the "true believers," Christianity has almost nothing to do with Christ, and for all intents and purposes stands as the "anti-Christ." Its focus on the Christ of the past and on His "second coming," its morbid display of His crucifixion and the associated guilt, its extensive muddle of imagery and pageantry, its shallow sentimentalism and the unholy pervasion of fear for a dark and evil force in conflict with our Lord leaves little room for the Christ that lives in this Moment as the ever-present eternal Spirit of Love and Compassion that is the Christ Consciousness. His Spirit cannot be put into a box as an "-ism;" It must be experienced and lived in a *radical aliveness* of this *Moment*. Let no man, no building, no symbol or idol, no fear, no dogma or belief, come between you, Him, and this Moment. They are all the "stuff" of the mind, and although they may hold some comfort for the ego and may even point you in the right direction, they must all be left behind if you are to come to Him. Let go of the beliefs that protect your ego identity, go deeply into your fear with a trust in our Lord, and you will come to His eternal presence, right here, right Now, free of mind, free of beliefs.

Religion needs to be fun and exciting, filled with celebration and ceremony for Life in this Moment. Why religion has such a somber, morose atmosphere with everyone so serious and concerned, filled with the guilt, fear, and shame that seems to come with being human, has always baffled me. We are all a part of this incredible miracle, all unbelievably blessed with this experience that is the gift of Life; why wouldn't we be excited, why shouldn't we be joyful? Why not celebrate? Look what surrounds and permeates us all! This incredible creation does not have to be, and yet it Is, and we are a most spectacular part of it. ...... We are It realizing Itself! We carry within us all of the creative potential of our Lord, a mirror of His possibilities with the most uncanny and most sacred of all possibilities that is uniquely ours to cherish and adore, the magnificent gift that is our Loving awareness! Use it often and be happy. Celebrate this gift of life in full awareness of Its beauty and majesty, free of the thoughts that would limit who you are and the ironic barrier it presents to higher consciousness and to an unblemished understanding of our purpose here. As you blossom into pure awareness of this Creation, you will have realized and fulfilled yourself, and at the same time and in the same space, our Lord. You are here for that sacred reason and that reason alone.

There are many differences that separate us on the surface, and if we are locked into egocentric identity, it is only the differences we see. It is in this most superficial exploration of our lives that we have isolated ourselves. Religion needs to bring us together with emphasis on how we as Droplets of this Great Spirit of Life are all the same in consciousness—in *Source*—and how our quest for happiness is universal. A Chinese mind works the same as an Australian's, a Frenchman's, or a Mexican's, regardless of what is being thought. Our Source and Creator is the essence of this Moment of which we are *all* a part. Religion's purpose and goal should be to bring us to this *Moment* and to remind us of the "Mystery" and of the insecurity we share in ignorance of ourselves. Religion needs to make us all aware of the importance of our inner work, offering retreats for introspection, meditation, and prayer in an atmosphere of "Nowness." It is essential to get away regularly so we can take a look, explore, challenge, and dissolve the ego structures, which have been created in our ignorance, fear, and isolation, especially the "religious" ego structures. We must come to understand and forgive the source of those childhood traumas that may have created a powerful, negative sense of ourselves or for that matter an overblown, egomaniacal sense of ourselves. All of these energetic blocks must be identified, their source revealed, and we must become a witness to them for us to know who we are. It is essential to Being Here Now!

It is written that "For where two or three come together in my name, there I am with them" (Matthew 18:20). Love and our Lord are inseparable. I would urge you to gather together in an awareness of our common bond, and drop the pretense and inhibitions inherent in ego and the fear that restricts you. In friendship and trust, go deeply together into the underlying cause of your pain; find the will and the power to forgive in an atmosphere of spaciousness and eternal Love! Everything that exists in this creation exists as an expression of His love for you. Become a beacon of that love and join Him. Remember that every action of this creation is an act of compassion that will reveal itself to you should you choose to go deeply enough. Come to believe in this "higher knowledge" and have faith in our Lord, and then celebrate *"That."* In His name (and use whatever *name* invokes this Spirit in you) do it with others!

During the past thirty years, people from all civilized countries on the earth have consulted me. Among all my patients in the second half of life—that is to say, over thirty-five—there has not been one whose problem in the last resort was not that of finding a religious outlook on life. It is safe to say that every one of them fell ill because he had lost that which the living religions of every age have given to their followers and none of them has been really healed who did not regain his religious outlook. (emphasis added)

—Droplet c. g. jung

Chapter XI
GREAT SPIRIT

My people's memory
reaches into the
beginning of all things.
　　—*From* My Heart Soars *by Droplet chief dan george*

My searching took me in many directions, but no Droplets have
touched me as deeply as American Indians and the legacy of pain
they have endured. For me, they represent the last great culture of
human beings who managed, through reverence, presence, direct
daily contact, deep religious conviction, and faith, to keep the
"Great Spirit" the focal point of their lives, to give thanks, and to see
His hand in all things without the trappings of books, preachers, or
temples—although reverence for holy men/shamans were an integral part of their experience. Their love of nature and respect for the
land, their deeply held belief that no one could own what the Great
Spirit had created but were gifts from Him, and their utter bewilderment at the behavior of the white man with his incessant need,
greed, and self-centered approach to all that nature had freely
offered, are indications of those Droplets' deep connection with this
Moment and to our Lord. No force on earth has been more destructive to this planet and to the life that abounds on it than the egocentric consciousness of man, which leaves him oblivious to the
majesty of this Moment, lost in the illusion of past, and in an obsessive search of security in a future that can never be. The destruction
of the American Indian culture and the genocide of these proud and
gentle Droplets (ironically much in the name of Christ) remains an

unwholesome blot on the soul of this country and will remain so until we as a people acknowledge our sins and confess our ignorance exhibited in the shallow yet maniacal pursuit of securing the ego at any cost. Unless we learn the lesson here, our national karma will doom us to commit the same sins against our children, our environment, and ourselves, and we will suffer that loss. We must not let this lesson pass us by. In our fear and insecurity, we committed those crimes. In our ignorance and disconnection from our own essential nature and from nature itself, we committed those crimes. In our incessant need and greed, we committed those crimes. In our pompous spiritual arrogance, we committed those crimes. Tell me, what has changed!? ...... For Christ's sake, read *Bury My Heart at Wounded Knee* by Droplet dee brown, or read *Touch the Earth* by Droplet t. c. mcluhan, or read *God is Red* by Droplet vine deloria. The American Indian experience has been passionately captured in these and many other worthwhile books that have come from this beautiful tradition.

The oratory of some of those great American Indian Droplets has yet to be equaled. Listen to the Droplet chief seattle who wrote to the American government in the late 1800s:

> The president in Washington sends word that he wishes to buy our land. But how can you buy or sell the sky? The land? The idea is strange to us. If we do not own the freshness of the air and the sparkle of the water, how can you buy them?
>
> Every part of the earth is sacred to my people. Every shining pine needle, every sandy shore, every mist in the dark woods, every meadow, every humming insect. All are holy in the memory and experience of my people.
>
> We know the sap which courses through the trees as we know the blood that courses through our veins. We are part of the earth and it is part of us. The perfumed flowers are our sisters. The bear, the deer, the great eagle, these are our brothers. The rocky crests, the dew in the meadow, the body heat of the pony and man all belong to the same family.
>
> The shining water that moves in the streams and rivers is not just water, but the blood of our ancestors. If we sell you our land, you must remember that it is sacred. Each glossy reflection in the clear

waters of the lakes tells of events and memories in the life of my people. The water's murmur is the voice of my father's father.

The rivers are our brothers. They quench our thirst. They carry our canoes and feed our children. So you must give the rivers the kindness that you would give any brother.

If we sell you our land, remember that the air is precious to us, that the air shares its spirit with all life that it supports. The wind that gave our grandfather his first breath also received his last sigh. The wind also gives our children the spirit of life. So if we sell our land, you must keep it apart and sacred, as a place where man can go to taste the wind that is sweetened by the meadow flowers.

Will you teach your children what we have taught our children? That the earth is our mother? What befalls the earth befalls all the sons of the earth.

This we know: The earth does not belong to man, man belongs to the earth. All things are connected like the blood that unites us all. Man did not weave the web of life; he is merely a strand in it. Whatever he does to the web, he does to himself.

One thing we know: our God is also your God. The earth is precious to Him and to harm the earth is to heap contempt on its creator.

Your destiny is a mystery to us. What will happen when the buffalo are all slaughtered? The wild horses tamed? What will happen when the secret corners of the forest are heavy with the scent of many men and the view of the ripe hills is blotted with talking wires? Where will the thicket be? Gone! Where will the eagle be? Gone! And what is to say goodbye to the swift pony and the hunt? The end of living and the beginning of survival.

When the last red man has vanished with this wilderness, and his memory is only the shadow of a cloud moving across the prairie, will these shores and forest still be here? Will there be any of the spirit of my people left?

We love the earth as a newborn loves its mother's heartbeat. So, if we sell you our land, love it as we have loved it. Care for it, as we have cared for it. Hold in your mind the memory of the land as it is when you receive it. Preserve the land for all children, and love it, as God loves us.

As we are part of the land, you too are part of the land. This earth is precious to us. It is also precious to you.

One thing we know—there is only one God. No man, be he red man or white man, can be a part. We ARE all brothers after all.

There is some controversy as to whether Droplet chief seattle did indeed author this speech; however, it is of little concern, as the essence and spirit of the American Indian experience is intact here, and that is all that matters.

Having read this, what do you think Chief Seattle would feel if he were here today? What advances in technology can possibly justify having taken this from our children? Think on these things, regret and reject the ignorance and destructiveness that is ego, and then come back to this Moment with Love and commitment in your heart. And for those who have come from this great American Indian heritage, do not forget your past but do not hold on to it in egoistic identification, either. What you can truly share with your ancestors is this Moment and the state of consciousness that made the speech above possible. Bring your awareness to this eternal Now, and you will be forever with the Spirit of Life your ancestors knew and revered, ... free again. Let go of the bitterness and sorrow, and accept what is in a total surrender to Life and to His wisdom. What is Is, as the eternal presence of our Lord, ... nothing lost. Be here Now ...... the Great Spirit awaits you!

Chapter XII

MEDITATION AND PRAYER

Splendor all around me in my solitary seat
I see it raped and wasted in ignorance, deceit
I see the laws of God, of Life, thrown meaningless aside
And man alone does suffer so
In darkness does abide
Too long the truths of Life have lain
Beyond the grasp of man
Time has come to give it back
Let Love again command
Whisper words whose meaning
No intellect has known
Let man be taken deep within
And once again come home
Let Life abound in glory
Let the song of Life be sung
Let Heaven find its place on earth
Let God's will be done

The poem above came through me in 1970 while on my teacher's training course with the Droplet maharishi mahesh yogi. Its message reflects my deepest conviction that meditation is the key to our spiritual growth in the practice of letting go and in a surrender to Life. I had by then tried many different methods of meditation and had come to feel that Transcendental Meditation had much to offer. Its unpretentious, non-invasive simplicity was refreshing. It offered a non-secular, very natural, and effective methodology for leaving the mind behind and returning to *"Source."* I had many profound experiences during that six-month course of meditation and training, not the least of which was my encounter with the sacred sound "Aum."

The typical day for those of us on the course consisted of a practice called "rounding," which basically meant meditating all day and all night, periodically interrupted with the practice of hatha yoga, that is, doing physical exercises known as asanas. On one occasion, somewhere around midday, I was coming out of meditation when I heard and felt what seemed like a huge squadron of B-52s flying just overhead. The *vibration* seemed to fill me and the entire room. I was startled until I realized that I was still very deep in meditation, that I had yet to come back to the "surface." As my conscious mind started coming out of meditation, I realize that the sound, the deep rumbling vibration *aaaaaauuuuuuummmmmmmmmmmm*, was coming out of a small hole at the top of my head and that what I was experiencing was not only the passageway from which the soul leaves the body, but also the sound of Creation, the word of God, the eternal "vibration." As you can imagine, it was an incredibly unforgettable peek into the secrets of Life. It is there for you as well. There is no doubt in my mind that in some galaxy millions of light years from here, sentient beings are at this Moment experiencing this "sound of creation." If they are ready, if they have left the "witness" behind, they will *be* the sound, not a witness to it, and enlightenment will be theirs.

If you would like to preview this sound of Creation, there is an excellent album entitled *Ultimate Om*, produced by Droplet jonathan goldman, which, at least in my mind, reproduces this sacred sound almost to perfection. What of course is missing is direction and intensity. Listening to this sound and having it come from the outside-in can never capture the experience of it vibrating from deep within your being, as your being. Yet listening to this album carries with it a deep relaxation and sense of peace, and you will easily fall under its enchanting spell.

"In the beginning was the Word and the Word was with God" (John 1:1). I've heard about a dozen interpretations of that phrase, and I believe that here the word/vibration is "Aum." This, then, is the word of God, and as He "spoke" it, this creation came into being. But let's consider it as it applies to man, created in God's image.

Man is set apart from all the other creatures on Earth by the uniqueness of his mind, which is self-aware, can reason, and enter a quest for a deeper understanding of Life. His mind has isolated him from his experience in abstraction and made him anxious and afraid. Before he does anything there must first be a thought. The creative impulse of our Creator is indeed a part of man and his thoughts. Just look at the results of the awareness and intelligence man has brought to this world, and all that he has accomplished in just these past few hundred years! Yes, there have been many mistakes made in our ignorance and egocentricity; we are not perfect yet and have much more to learn, but "Oh what a piece of work is man...."

Thought, by its very nature, is a fragmentation process, and herein lies much of the problem. The thinking process is not capable of conceiving the whole. It must take it one thing at a time and in so doing loses what is whole, what is Holy. What it doesn't understand, it names, and by so doing takes the mystery and *insecurity* out of it. "Sky," a simple word heard every day, holds no real meaning at all except to direct us in which way to turn our attention. This "moment" would seem to symbolize something, but it can't possibly begin. Should I even mention the words "God" or "Love" that so many use so often in so many ways with absolutely no understanding? The ineffable is just that. It cannot be spoken because it cannot be understood or explained in words, and to try is to demean and confuse. And so it has been written that, "Those who know don't say, those who say don't know."

True knowledge of *"That"* cannot be obtained from the intellect, nor can it be transmuted through the intellect. I love the analogy that Droplet alan watts used to describe what happens when one tries. He proclaimed that using the intellect to try to describe the true nature of Reality is akin to crossing an elephant with a peanut butter sandwich. What you end up with is either "an elephant that sticks to the roof of your mouth or a peanut butter sandwich that never forgets." These are two distinctly different ways of knowing that cannot be mixed, and as one tries, conclusions become absurd. Reading the Kabala, the Koran, the Bible, the Bhagavad-Gita, or any other "mystical" text can give a profound example of this phenomenon. There is just too much trying to explain the ineffable in an endless banter of words that in the end have no real meaning, raise more questions than are answered, and misdirect our energies to the intellect rather than to a direct experience of our Lord, and to the "Mysteries" of this most sacred Moment.

I know it is terribly presumptuous of me to have you disregard these profound books of wisdom as being too "wordy," and it certainly is not my intent for you to do so. There is much that can be taken from the scriptures that would improve the quality of your life. There is much that can help you understand who you are and the purpose of living. The danger comes in believing you now *know*—that you have found the answer! I have friends and relatives who claim to know God and carry an undying love for Jesus, all taken from their religious beliefs. I have another friend who has gathered enough information from life, been traumatized and suffered "the slings and arrows of outrageous fortune," and witnessed the hypocrisy of religion, and thus has concluded, in a sort of "shock-jock" style, "fuck God." None have actually experienced that sacred ground that lies beyond the mind's concepts and never will as long as they cling to their beliefs in egocentric identity. As you crystallize your beliefs into an identity, it is like putting on a new suit, and in some cases that is literally what happens. Once you have studied, memorized and can quote chapter and verse for an answer to any given situation, you have isolated yourself in *belief*. You may know how to get "wet," what happens when you are "wet," what the advantages are for being "wet," that those who had influenced your scriptures were no doubt "wet," yet you yourself have never had the experience of actually being "wet" or perhaps cannot imagine or believe there is such a thing as getting "wet." The chances are you will never get "wet" as long as you hold on to your beliefs and never venture out into the world of "wet." However, now you can adopt a name for yourself that associates you with those particular "wet" beliefs. You may wear specific clothing that tells everyone

154

that you believe in such and such a way about being "wet." You may live a lifestyle and congregate with others who believe the same way, and there is admittedly a wholesomeness, a simplicity, a close-to-Godliness that I have always admired in the spiritual community life such as the Amish, the Quakers, and the Hasidim enjoy. The temptations of life that can lead us astray have been removed, and a lifestyle of simplicity adopted. But then, I can't help but wonder, where is the passion, where is the quest, where is the desire to get "wet"? Beware of the ego; it will find its identity and security in just about anything, and does not want to be disturbed from that identity once it is established. Any identity taken from the mind will stand as a barrier to yourself.

Herein lies the great irony of Life, for if the truth were revealed to you, you would know that you are already "wet." If you could drop all mind-based identity and come to this Moment empty, you would find yourself immersed in this great ocean of Love, the infinite *Source* of Life that knows no time. But you cannot desire It, for desire is of the mind. Nor should you make mind a problem, for you would be creating a greater problem in mind. You cannot adopt a lifestyle that would lead you to It, you cannot learn more about It and study It. This is all mind-stuff, and will lock you into illusion. Look only to your capacity for unconditional love, for all of this Creation, and to the peace you are feeling in this Moment in simplicity regardless of circumstance. That will be a measure of your ability to let go of ego and thought, the depth of your spiritual awareness and your faith in His eternal presence. It is all you need and why Jesus emphasized simplicity in your life. Let go of all you want and think you are, then come to Him nameless. You will be fulfilled.

No true knowledge can be taken from a book, and no life can be fully lived with a dependence on a book. Advice can be taken, a specific path pointed to, or the consequences of a poorly lived life reviewed. This information can be helpful and reassuring. In the end, though, you alone must make the journey, leaving all you know behind. True knowledge must come from within us in a direct experience of our inner *Source*, in this Moment, as this Moment, beyond the mind, without the beliefs. No text, no book, no words, regardless of how poetic they may read, can bring you this *Truth*; they may even get in the way by creating an ego structure that claims to *know*. You are this *Truth*, and only you alone can come to truly *know* who you are in a direct experience of the Eternal that is within you as *Source*. "You diligently study the Scriptures, because you think that by them you possess eternal life. These are the Scriptures that testify about me, yet you refuse to come to me to have life" (John 5:39-40).

And so, the goal of meditation is to come to *Nothing*, to let go of all the beliefs that would stand in the way of the Eternal. You must come to know and have faith in your Lord as *Nothing*, for it is within this *Nothingness* that you will be blessed with His eternal love. Surrender all to Him so you come to Him as *Nothing*. All that you are holding on to has identified you as to whom you *think* you are and what life is and what stands in your way. This identity is preventing you from coming to this boundless Love and Holy awareness. Meditation will help you let go and be present. No need to create a problem that must be overcome. Simply *Be!*

My experience with Zen has always held a profound state of "opening" for me. The practice of Zen attempts to trick and/or stress the mind and its processes into states of higher awareness through the use of, among other things "koans," those simple questions that have no intellectual answer and attempt to baffle the mind into submission. Listen to one of my favorites: A seeker had traveled many miles and had come before an enlightened master. He asked in earnest, "Master, what is the meaning of Life?" The master replied, "Do you see that cat climbing the post?" "Yes," replied the anxious seeker. "Then ask the post," said the master. ...... There is no intellectual answer here, and the intellect must be left behind; it is indeed a force to be left behind to allow an opening to the possibilities of "Nothing." Here is another of my favorites: After many years of practice, a student was brought before the master, and the master asked him what he had learned after all those years of practice. The student stood in silence, looked at his master and raised his index finger in a symbol of oneness. The master, in a flash, took a sword and severed the finger. With that, the student was enlightened! HA! ...... By the way, what *is* the sound of one hand clapping?

The Miraculous, the "Mystery," is all around us every moment in the "Nothingness" of life; "Just don't do something, sit there!" and you will know. Good advice from Droplet bhagwan shree rajneesh. Meditation is the practice of "letting go" of the processes of the mind and simply being in the silence of Being. It is the practice of "letting go" of the false ego identity and coming to our Lord as a pure expression of His eternal spirit. Any attempt at this inner work intellectually would be like trying to point to the end of one's finger with one's finger. Who would be trying to see who we are? The *experience* of who we are cannot have a witness and so any mental process used to come to that experience would be in the way of that experience. It would be impossible to have a witness to who we are because the witness, the *who we are*, would always be left out! We are then the "witnessing," not what is being witnessed, nor whom we would observe as the witness. We are not our bodies, we are not our minds, we are "witnessing"; that is an expression of *pure consciousness*. What we are seeking, then, is that infinite field of Being which is the *Source* of everything there is, everything that could be. ...... We seek "*That*"!

By putting our attention on our thoughts—or more simply the sound of thought—taking no mind to their meanings, we are automatically taken deeply into the process of thinking and will eventually come to the source of those thoughts, to that field of Being that is *pure consciousness*. The ego/mind is set aside, easily let go of, and only "*That*" allowed to BE! Who you truly are can infuse Its eternal nature into the membrane (mind) and allow your conscious connection with the "ocean," that is this Holy Spirit, the *Source* of NOW. Intellect is, for the most part, a tool of the ego and has no place here as it can only refer to the past and project to the future. It can contemplate, think, and direct (thank goodness), but must be left behind in this process of "union," a process that can only happen in the *Now,* having left all that would isolate us from *"That"* behind.

The illusion of life is formed in thought and in the process of remembering, which gives *our* meaning or at least *a* meaning to the ineffable, and in so doing ironically clouds the membrane with the thoughts which would keep us from *"That."* To *know* Life can only come from a direct and immediate experience of the *Ineffable,* with a joining and surrender into *"That."* The mind, the words, and the memories must be left behind and our essential nature allowed to unite again with this Great Spirit of Life. We have to lift the veil of illusion that the mind/membrane has created and come to an awareness that will illuminate, in this Moment, our *Source* and our Creator as ourselves. This is a transcendental experience that some enlightened Droplets have described as being turned inside out. That works for me, given the analogy of the Droplet. Picture a Droplet that has turned what is inside into what is outside and has merged again with its *Source* unobstructed by the membrane (the mind).

Meditation is an essential tool that allows us to turn our attention from the transient identity of the membrane and come to our true, absolute eternal nature within. Daily practice releases our awareness from the chaos and stress created by the shallow, separate experience of mind/ego, and propels us towards a deeper experience of ourselves as *Source* and indeed towards a deeper awareness and appreciation of all that we experience. Relative life, full of egocentric pursuits, is extremely limiting and a mere shadow of the full richness of Life. Meditation is the gateway to that fuller, richer experience. It has been thought of as learning to die. You might think this rather morbid, but I assure you, "It's a good day to die!" Letting go of the limited, transient identity of ego, which imprisons our eternal Spirit, is the "dying" that can be practiced daily in meditation. In so doing, the membrane is cleared of our superficial identity and our essential nature of pure consciousness is allowed to permeate that identity, shining through a no longer clouded membrane and saturating our daily experience of Life. Inherent in that essential nature is infinite creativity, life eternal, and the bliss of Love fulfilled. The irony here is that in having given up everything, you would have gained everything. The "lower self" would have become the "higher self."

In the Droplet james moody's inspirational book *Life After Life*, an incredibly beautiful, brilliant light is described by all who have had the experience of "dying" and who have been "brought back." That light is also discussed in *The Tibetan Book of Living and Dying* by Droplet sogyal rinpoche as the "Ground Luminosity" or "Clear Light." I like to think of it as Love's pure light. It comes to us in the experience of that radiant field of Being, that pure consciousness, that which we are all an expression of and which is our *Source.* In the simple process of "letting go," and in complete surrender, we will come to *"That"* and to the light of His love. In death we don't have much choice, as we obviously let go of quite a lot. However, even in death we can carry with us the "baggage" of relative life. If we have not learned to let go, if the membrane is terribly clouded and distorted by our experiences in the illusion of separation, if we have not incorporated this "higher knowledge" into our lives, if we have not practiced "dying," that is, the letting go of the illusion of ego, then we can, in death, still get lost in the tangle and confusion of an isolated spirit and miss that final "realization," and our place in "heaven" must wait to be taken. Here, then, is why meditation is so essential and why living a spiritual life has so much significance. Not just in and for the process of passing on, but more importantly in the deeper and richer understanding of our lives in the here and Now.

We will come to learn that we are not our bodies and that we are not our minds, that they are the vehicles to this heightened awareness and that in this awareness we can let go of the petty needs of the ego and the fear inherent in it. Be very clear that this is not a denial of relative life, nor is it a demeaning of our experience of it. On the contrary, it is a complete embracing, an overflowing love for, a total acceptance in, a full awareness of this glorious experience of Life outside the limits and needs of the isolated ego. Truly, in full awareness, heaven will find its place on earth and we our place in *It*!

⁂

With a thickened, rigid membrane, it is impossible to go deeply into experiences, and they are merely etched into the surface of the membrane, like the blade of a knife cutting into granite, never to be forgotten if traumatic, and habitually sought-after if pleasant or of comfort. And so the ego's identity grows, our "story" crystallizes, and the membrane is clouded further. In contrast, an accomplished meditative mind is akin to reaching your hand into a clear pool of water. It allows for an easier, deeper penetration into the experience, thus allowing for a more fulfilling, richer experience with a much clearer understanding of the experience, and yet, once attention is removed, there is no sign of trauma, no need to repeat and no identity formed from the experience.

Recent scientific discoveries have actually confirmed a similar corresponding cellular effect that mimics this "softening" of the membrane. It has been found that the sickened cellular membranes of those Droplets who are experiencing emotional or physical disease become rigid and thickened. The natural intake of nutrients and oxygen becomes difficult, and these diseased cells tend to cluster together in unnatural, unhealthy groups that eliminate "breathing room." When the practice of meditation begins, and a lifestyle that acknowledges "higher knowledge" and the spiritual significance of life is lived, not only does this somewhat metaphorical membrane of ego begin to dissolve, but a very tangible corresponding cellular effect is noted. Cell walls in those dis-eased areas become more pliable and can more easily absorb oxygen and nutrients. They spread apart and begin to radiate health in a spiritual "healing." The overwhelming conclusion would seem to be that the overall effects of meditation and a life that acknowledges, seeks and experiences the "World of Spirit" is well-being.

This cellular unhealthy clustering together is, it seems to me, reflected in our egocentric propensity to gather in overcrowded,

160

unnatural city environments that leave little "breathing room" as ego finds its comfort in ego. Taking this metaphor a bit further, it would seem dis-ease takes comfort in dis-ease, both in the body on a cellular level as well as in the mind that can manifest on a cultural level. In both cases, if a true spiritual awareness of Life is not realized, this dis-ease can destroy the whole organism in an unwholesome quest for security. Misery would indeed seem to love company. In contrast, a reverence for life in the natural world has been the experience of those whose awareness has brought them close to our Lord.

Contemplation and concentration use "thinking" and our intellect to try and understand our lives through the thought process, a magnificent process I would not want in any way to demean. For it is this thinking process that is an essential element in this glorious process of becoming aware as we gain our knowledge and wisdom from it. However, meditation takes no interest in the meanings that may arise from thoughts, but rather focuses on the process of thinking itself so we can come to the *Source* of thought. We would come to that ineffable field of Being that transcends and is the creative *Source* of all that is. In meditation, we let thoughts come and thoughts go like images on a screen and take no mind to them. In meditation we effortlessly attempt to bring our awareness to this "*Source*" of thought, this creative field of "Beingness," which is the *Source* and essence behind all of this Creation. Becoming a pure expression of "*That,*" to be a vessel for the Christ Consciousness in this body, is the ultimate purpose of meditation and our destiny as spiritual beings. Only a radiant *you* will survive the loss of ego.

Raising our awareness to "*That*" is not so much a process of doing *something*, as there is truly nothing to do. *It* is already with us! *It* is our *Source* and our essence; we could not be here without *It*. Rather, it is a process of undoing, that is, removing that veil of illusion that clouds your vision of your eternal spirit and your unity with all of Life. In the illusion of separateness formed by ego, we can only continue to suffer in ignorance of our true nature. Meditation is, ironically, the contradiction of making an effort to do ...... absolutely nothing.

To wait without hope
To wait without Love
There is still hope and Love
But faith is in the waiting
To wait without thought
You are not ready for thought
The darkness shall be the light
And the stillness the dancing

—Droplet t. s. elliot

MEDITATING

The ideal time for meditation is in the early morning before you begin your day, and again just before dinner; however, you can and should meditate any time it feels right or you have the opportunity. Allow a minimum of twenty minutes to a half-hour for your morning and evening practice. If there is more time available, take it. In my mind, there is no such thing as too much meditation unless you are using it to escape your responsibilities. Meditation without activity will not allow you to incarnate and live this inner presence, so taking action in this world of form is as important as communion with the world of spirit, with enlightenment becoming the product of both.

As you begin your meditation, find a comfortable, quiet place where you will not be disturbed. I see no point whatsoever in sitting in a position that will make your back ache or your legs fall asleep. This will only keep you on the "surface" with thoughts that are focused on the body's pain or the discomfort you may have created by sitting that way. The only physical requirements are to not let your head rest on anything, as it needs to be able to move easily during the process, that you do not eat heavily, and that you make use of the bathroom before you begin. Of course, the use of *any* drug is detrimental to this process of going within and should be avoided. Clearing the system of the effects of some drugs can take considerable time and so are all best avoided. There is no drug that will benefit you in this process. Their effects can only be detrimental to the overall balance and functioning of the nervous system and can only further cloud the membrane. If the drug is an addictive one, your egocentric identity will then be linked to it, and you will have a difficult and unnecessary barrier to undo.

In some meditations a mantra is used to help turn the attention from the meaning of thoughts towards the thinking process itself and ultimately to the *Source* of those thoughts. A mantra is simply a sound, a *vibration* with no intellectual meaning but with tried and true qualities that contribute to this "turning within" process. A mantra gives the random chaos of the mind's processes a center to return to, a place of no meaning to put your awareness on, a simple vibration to follow back to *Source*. At the end of this book, you will find a list of mantras and some instructions to follow that will give you your own mantra, along with further instructions on how to establish its use, should you choose.

Some meditations use the breath, or, more accurately, put the attention on the breath as a methodology of letting go of the meanings of thoughts by offering a "thoughtless" place to return to. It allows your attention to move from the head into the body where an awareness of your being can be felt and where intellect is of little use. Thoughts and their meanings keep the mind active, and your awareness on the "surface" with their endless flow. These thoughts, regardless of their high and mighty content, are merely a reflection of the superficial mind's illusions and manipulations. They must be left behind in the dynamic activity of opening your awareness. Whether you use a mantra or pay attention to the breath, or both (it can easily happen), it is and should be an effortless process. Just a shadow of the mantra need be in your awareness and returned to when you realize your attention has strayed into the meanings of thought. With practice, you will be able to meditate in almost any situation as you become proficient at "letting go" of thoughts.

Now, let's have a look at what a typical meditation would be. Begin by making yourself comfortable as described above. Close your eyes and simply be. Take a few deep breaths and relax in their release. Bring your awareness to your presence in the room or space in which you are sitting. Know that you could not be where you are if not for the presence of God as your *Source* and essence. Feel His eternal presence in the consciousness that has given you and all you know life. Listen to the "ringing" in your ears that is your nervous system given life by *Source*. Extend your awareness out to the infinity that surrounds you in all directions: in front of you, behind you, above you, below you, all around you. As you are "bathing" in this eternal presence, easily introduce your mantra and begin to effortlessly repeat it. It may come as a gentle whisper or in a clear forceful pronunciation. As long as no effort is used, it is coming as it should.

As you begin your meditation, the thoughts of the day's activities will naturally come to mind. The stresses, the problems, the joys and the sorrows will all be there in thought as well as in feeling. These "thoughts," no matter what they may contain, will, in time, become simply a part of the "thinking process" as we silently observe them and let them go. It is an integral part of the meditative process that thoughts not be repressed, as their expression becomes the mechanism that allows the stresses and knots formed in the nervous system from these various life experiences to release, and a sort of emotional "clearing" (not to be confused with scientology!) is obtained. The release that is this "clearing" is accomplished through the thought process and should not be consciously interfered with. As we experience the thoughts and at times the corresponding physical sensations and emotions that may accompany them, tension is released and our awareness released from the limitations of those stresses. Simply put, the "energy" can flow.

As the process of meditation continues, our thoughts will naturally slow down and we can begin to turn our attention from the meanings of thought toward the *Source* of those thoughts, using the mantra as our vehicle. We come to the final "who" who is witnessing, to that field of pure consciousness of which we are all an expression, as is all that we are a witness to. Once we have removed what is being witnessed and the separate "who" who is witnessing from our experience, then only *"That"* remains, and we will come to know through direct experience that we are and have always been One with the eternal Source of Life.

I must emphasize that no concentration or mental effort is used to shut out thoughts in order to stay with the mantra/breath, regardless of how uncomfortable or annoying they may be. Any mental effort would be a thought process, a function of mind/ego, and has no place here. Slowly, as your meditation proceeds, the thinking process will slow down, as will your breathing, as you begin to take "no mind" to what is being thought or to their meanings. As an example, the thought that says to you "I can't do this, I gotta get up" may come but must have no meaning nor can it be acted upon; however, it must be allowed expression and your awareness should be free to focus on any physical sensation that comes with that thought (tension in the neck or back, anxiety or simple nervousness). Given time and attention, the tension will ease, the accompanying thoughts will be gone, and your awareness will move on. You may then have the thought, "Why, I am relaxing and my breath is becoming shallow," but the "meaning" is not focused on and our attention is brought gently back to the mantra. The thought "I must find no meaning in thoughts" may be remembered, but let it go, too, and return gently to the mantra. They are *all* only thoughts here, and as they come up, they are let go of unless their intensity and the physical/emotional sensation which will accompany them is too great, in which case you must allow your attention to simply stay with these feelings until they are relieved. You will know when it is done, as you will find your mind wandering somewhere else. When you realize this, simply return your awareness to the mantra, easily, without effort. This is a time of trust and a faith in the eternal presence of *Source*. In our meditation we relinquish our control and give ourselves over to this higher intelligence. Our "higher selves" will know where to go and what needs to be done. We simply set ego aside and allow It to happen.

If you consciously react to your thoughts as they come up, you will lose your open awareness of this Moment in the "reference library" that is your mind. What you "know" can never bring you to an understanding of this Moment. Your thoughts and their meanings can only keep you from that awareness. Consciously letting go of thoughts and returning your attention to a meaningless sound will open you to this Moment and to the glorious *"Nothingness"* that has allowed your life to Be. You will go deeply into your consciousness, naturally and easily by simply "letting go" of thoughts and returning your attention gently to the mantra.

At some point in the process of meditation we may "transcend," and our awareness bathes in its infinite *Source*. There is no longer a "witness," only pure "witnessing." This is initially a "none experience," a blank that may be experienced as a loss of time. However, as you come back to normal waking state consciousness, you will feel deeply rested and refreshed. Some residue of that "bath" remains and is incorporated into your activities as heightened awareness.

As you prepare to come out of your meditation, remain silent with your eyes closed. Again, sense yourself in the space in which you are sitting. Sense that you are conscious, and become aware of being aware. Isolate awareness, be conscious of consciousness as the incredible *Source* of who you are, and marvel at what it is to be alive! Within you and all of our kind lies the light of awareness that can embrace this entire universe and give it meaning. Know that *you*, as an ego structure, have no part in the creation of this miracle, that you have been graced with this gift of Life, and that our Lord is here and now as your essence and the light that is your consciousness. Begin and end your day with an awareness of the miracle of which you are a part and to which you are a witness, and be joyful! You are the light of the universe! Be grateful. Now, just before you open your eyes, rub your hands together briskly, then put them to your eyes. It will create a soothing transition from your inner to your outer experience of Life.

Because there is no effort made in meditation, what may be needed is allowed to come. That may at times be sleep, so don't be surprised or disappointed. As you will see, transcendence and sleep are two very different experiences.

Curiously, in this effortless process, problems that you take into your meditation will often be solved without effort in a "knowingness" that defies explanation and cannot be willed or manipulated. This is the creative aspect of our Lord that dwells within us, known to all who have ever created. Those who have accomplished great works of art, who have come up with new inventions, made medical breakthroughs, or have gone beyond the ordinary in any way, know that the thinking mind had little to do with their "genius" and was, in fact, more often in the way than a help. Let this then also be and be thankful. However, be certain not to *use* your meditation for any purpose and expect nothing from it.

As meditation becomes an integral part of your everyday life, the clarity, depth, and creativity of your thinking process will improve as you release the traumas of the past and are open to your potential. You will begin to "incarnate" your essential nature into your experience of this Moment. You will become more aware, more "present," and more joyful as you come in touch with and express your own true nature.

Meditation allows your awareness to go beyond the superficial meaning of thoughts to the *Source* of those thoughts, indeed the *Source* of all that there is. Daily practice allows for the release of the stresses of life that cloud the mind/membrane and take you from yourself. The qualities of this transcendental field of Being, our "*Source*," are allowed to permeate our relative activities making for a deeper, wiser, happier, more loving, creative, in-tune Droplet.

It should also be emphasized that not all meditations will be deep, relaxing experiences. At times major stress blocks from our past experiences may be released and the mental activity and/or the physical/emotional sensations of that release may be uncomfortable and intense. This is a most profound step in the right direction and should not be regretted or avoided; it's okay! Don't stop your practice because you think it's "not working" or something is wrong. These blocks *must* be unraveled for the "flow" to happen, and you gain the ability to go deeply into the meditative experience, to come to who you are. Stay with those more difficult or intense sensations/emotions and come to a direct, non-intellectual experience of their underlying cause. You will gain insight into what is in your way and into the process of letting go. You will come to a deeper understanding of your awareness as *Soul* and to the source of your suffering as you continue to "let go" and explore the cause of your pain. You will end the sorrow of your exile as you allow your eternal nature to free itself from the bonds of illusion and join with the eternal Presence of this Moment.

Be patient; do your meditation without expectation, without purpose and without hope. Simply let it be and accept whatever may come as it comes in a surrender into *"That."* ...... But be sure to do your meditation!

Meditation is an experience that cannot be found outside of meditation. As Droplets of this Great Spirit, we owe it to ourselves and to our Creator to practice it daily. ...... Jesus has already told us to "Be still and know that I am God." Now it can be said to "Be still and know that you are God"!

≈⊙≈

PRAYER

A single grateful thought toward heaven is the most complete prayer.
—*Droplet gotthold lessing*

Prayer can and should be a humbling experience. To give thanks need be the only reason one prays daily. By giving thanks for *all* that this day has given us is an acknowledgement that His hand is in *all* that we have been privileged to experience, that He is the *Source* of that experience and it has *all* been given for our benefit. The Lord can work in mysterious ways and even the most horrifying or heartbreaking experience can be a gateway that will bring us closer to Him—that indeed will need to bring us closer to Him. To be simply and truly grateful for your life, no matter what, can be a powerful healing and an important first step towards the peace of enlightenment.

The effects of prayer can be extraordinary if we are able to leave the egocentric needs behind and come from that place deep within where we can *sincerely* surrender. We come to that field of Being where anything and everything is possible. Being in touch with our true nature puts us in touch with *"That,"* and in *"That"* in touch with God's love and God's wisdom. It is here that all things are possible. By bringing the spiritual, that is the "unseen," into conscious focus through our prayer, we are creating an atmosphere in which miracles can happen. We are going beyond the limits of the mind/ego with a faith and belief in that which the mind cannot comprehend as we open ourselves to the "Mystery."

Pray till prayer makes you forget your own wish, and leave it or merge it in God's will.

—Droplet frederick w. robertson

As difficult as what I am about to say may be to understand, know that it is possible. You need only truly pray once in your life and "salvation" will be yours. To come to the Holy Spirit, to Jesus, to God, completely naked, that is, having given up everything, completely clearing the membrane, having dropped the ego through love, devotion, and humility, to have, in effect, become "saintly," it would be then that your union with the Holy Spirit would be complete. The Droplet falling back into the ocean, having lost its illusion of a separate identity—that is egoless—it can now and only now be Everything! Ah, but here's the rub. If the ego has formed its identity in martyrdom or in a burning desire to return to our Lord, what then? The ego is very tricky and will take on *any* identity in order to survive. I have met far too many "seekers" who have formed their identity in the search, in the words and in the form of a spiritual life that has now become the greatest barrier to their liberation. It must all be left behind and all desire abandoned, even the desire for enlightenment. Enlightenment can never come from desire. It is only available in this Moment through our surrender and through the practice of unconditional love. Let your gratitude and love be the only impetus for prayer as you open yourself to the possibility of Grace.

He prayeth well, who loveth well
Both man and bird and beast,
He prayeth best who loveth best

All things both great and small;
For the dear God who loveth us,
He made and loveth all.

—*Droplet samuel taylor coleridge*

Use the gifts of meditation and prayer daily. Bring awareness to your thoughts, to your actions, and to your presence in this world as a conscious being. See the "Great Spirit" in the eyes of every Droplet you meet, and reach out to It, remembering that we are all fallen angels who have forgotten how to fly, that we are desperate and suffer in our loneliness and fear and are longing to come home. Their suffering is truly your suffering as it is our Lord and Creator who is suffering, the One and Only in ignorance of Itself. Feel His presence in the Mystery that surrounds you as you bring His love and compassion into this world. Know that you and all you survey are our Lord, as an expression of our Lord, with all the unimaginable potential of our Lord, and be grateful for every breath of Life. Be clear in your understanding that we could have only come to know our Lord out of a state of ignorance, just as it is the darkness that reveals the light. What you see, what you hear, and what you feel, all of the senses are His gifts we share with all of His creation in search of Him. Forgive the ignorance of this world and know it could have not been otherwise. Now, in the silent stillness of your being ...... listen and know ...... you are the lover, ... you are the Love. Turn on your "light" and identify whatever is isolating you in egocentricity, then gently let go and let *It* Be, and as you do, forgive. Be grateful for life, be grateful for love. Now listen and know, you are the lover, you are the Love. Let go and let It be!

Chapter XIII
NATURE

Hail to thee, good living tree, created by God, just like me.
—An American Indian greeting

There is little, if anything, in nature that is "self-conscious"; we the exception. As a result, what is happening in nature is happening as the pure expression of this Great Spirit. No trees are manipulating the growth of fish, nor are there fish wishing they were birds, nor are there birds afraid of heights. What is simply Is. "God's country" is truly *"That"* in all the magic and majesty of an unbelievably creative parade of animals, plants, and insects, and their basic instincts, all linked and dependent on one another for survival in an ever-changing, dazzling display of creativity, balance and codependence.

I need not shout my faith. Thrice eloquent
Are quiet trees and the green listening sod;
Hushed are the stars, whose power is never spent;
The hills are mute: yet how they speak of God.
—Droplet charles hanson towne

An extraordinary creative intelligence permeates every aspect of nature. It has taken us "intellectually superior" Droplets a very long time to just begin to understand, in our terms, what is going on all around us. We are only just beginning to recognize, thanks in large part to the works of those like Droplet richard attenboro and those of the National Geographic Society, the Sierra Club, the Wilderness Society, Green Peace, etc., the damage we have done as unconscious, detached beings whose egocentric drive towards trivial pursuits has left the very foundation of our survival in jeopardy. Alas, a very necessary step in our evolutionary process, for it would seem we Droplets are unable to appreciate the immediate blessings of Life until they are gone. In the sadly prophetic words of Droplet joni mitchell, "But you don't know what you've got till it's gone. You paved paradise and put up a parking lot." We have lost enough to our overindustrialized world of need, and to our ignorance and greed. The time has come to understand, respect, and protect this home of ours and center in on the true and lasting values of our lives. These are simple values that require little more than our attention to be enjoyed. Yet, they are the foundation of our quest for happiness, which induces a reverence for Life and a love for the Creator.

For us Droplets to begin to understand something, we must spend time with it, focus our attention on it, make our attachment to it and become *aware*. With nature, not only are we dealing with something we are struggling to understand outside of ourselves, we are also dealing with something that we are a physical expression of and are uncertain of our place in. Like it or not, we are the "human animal," and an expression of the natural world. Not to spend time reuniting with this energy is denying who we are on this physical plane. That does not mean running upstate in RVs with TVs and stereos aboard, nor does it mean reading the *New York Times* outside! Taking on a challenge that will "conquer" some aspect of nature doesn't cut it, either. What it does mean is slowing down to nature's pace; developing your intuition and instincts by shutting down the incessant chatter of the mind; finding and respecting the purpose of every insect and every plant; knowing the special qualities that each creature on earth contributes to the whole; realizing that God does not make mistakes and all that is, is for a reason; watching the slow revolution of the earth as sunset happens; and becoming awed at the majesty of the night sky.

Here again, the intellect can take us on a fascinating journey of discovery into the many intricate and mysterious aspects of nature, and can be cherished as a part of your experience. The Droplet joseph wood krutch's wonderful book *The Great Chain of Life* is one such journey and is a must-read for those who would open to this energy. I would also strongly suggest the insightful work of Droplet thomas berry, *The Dream of the Earth*, which will open you to the wonders of this extraordinary planet with an emphasis on our sacred role as witness and as guardian to this sacrament Earth. But ultimately, the intellect here, too, must again be left behind, and we must simply learn to Be an expression of what we are hoping to one day understand and to bring that sparkle of a knowing, loving, open, and aware witness to the glory of this Creation and complete our return to Eden.

[As I] sit quietly, doing nothing Spring comes and grass grows of itself.

—*Zenrin Kushu*

The eternal, creative mystery that is our Lord is present in every aspect of nature, as it does what it does, waiting for our awareness. Consider for a moment a simple apple seed. Truly, here, is God at work! For if this seed is planted and nourished, the miracle that is an apple tree will grow. Within that simple seed was the incredibly complicated genetic imprint for this new tree, and all the thousands of apples that would be produced by that tree over time. Within each apple, dozens of seeds would be produced that had within them the genetic imprint that could produce yet dozens of more trees with the ability to produce thousands of apples and hundreds of thousands of seeds that would produce still more trees and more apples and more seeds and on and on and on. ...... All from one simple seed!

What, then, is our fate? Are we all truly children of God created in His image with unlimited potential, or are we just a momentary blip in the grand cosmic scheme of things, created as parasites on this planet whose purpose is to take all we can while we can? My experience is that our Lord does not produce mistakes, and so I believe we are *all* an essential element to the fulfillment of this creation. We have within us the uncommon ability to become AWARE and to *know*. It is our sacred role in the fulfillment of this glorious creation to do so! Don't let It down, He is counting on you!

Nature/the environment is not someone's plank in a political platform. Nature is the pure expression of God's work and should be considered sacrosanct, period! Every effort must be made to respect and preserve His creation. The egocentric aspects of greed, need and corruption create the poisons that pollute our environment as surely as they do in our consciousness. Much of what seems wrong or has become unbalanced in nature is no doubt what is wrong and unbalanced in ourselves.

The illusion of separateness and the superficial egocentric drives to secure and maintain an isolated identity keeps us unconscious of our connection to the earth and to the creatures we share it with. That connection cannot be made solely through the five senses; it must also come from a heart-felt reverence for the world of spirit and a holy awareness of the loving, creative force behind this creation. Clearly, if we continue on this unconscious course, we will soon and necessarily suffer the terrible consequences of our ignorance, and what has become unbalanced must necessarily make adjustments. These "adjustments" will no doubt devastate our way of Life and force us into a new consciousness. The world will be a very different place as man comes to Now. As we are forced to let go of ego and the physical structures of ego are abandoned, living will be far more in harmony with and respectful of the natural surroundings God has created as we elevate our status from a blight upon the earth to that of wholesome witness who can truly understand and enjoy this sacrament of life.

The same awareness, with all the love and compassion that we would bring to our dealings with our children, must be brought to bear on our dealings with Nature. No profit margin or "consumer need" would be allowed to jeopardize the safety of our children, nor should it take precedence over the purity of God's creation. We have no such right. Free will does not give us the right to destroy; it is His gift that gives us the ability to enjoy this world in many different ways. We are the keepers; as a species we have very little more than our awareness to offer this planet. If we can destroy this most splendid home which God has given us to evolve in, then we can and must make effort to save and protect it for and from ourselves.

A human being is a part of a whole, called by us "universe," a
part limited in time and space. He experiences himself, his
thoughts, and feelings as something separated from the rest ...
a kind of optical delusion of his consciousness. This delusion is
a kind of prison for us, restricting us to our personal desires
and to affection for a few persons nearest to us. Our task must
be to free ourselves from the prison by widening our circle of
compassion *to embrace all living creatures and the whole of*
nature in its beauty. (emphasis added)

—*Droplet albert einstein*

Chapter XIV

RELATIVE LIFE

Woe! Woe!
Thou hast destroyed it!
The beautiful world!
Woe! Woe!
Thou hast destroyed! Destroyed!

Create! Create!
Build it again
In thy heart,
The beautiful world!
Create! Create! Create!

—*Goeth*, Faust I

Let me remind you now of the Droplet plato and his cave analogy. Even those many years ago, we Droplets were able to transcend the relative world of illusion and come to the eternal presence that is this Moment as our brother Plato demonstrates. In his analogy, Plato saw everyone in chains, and their awareness was bound to focus only on the rear wall of a cave that had projected on it the shadows of all that went on, being cast by the light from the mouth of the cave behind them. Those in the cave could never turn around and see what was truly causing the shadows, so their life was limited to the experience of only the shadow images. Occasionally, someone managed to break the bonds and turn to see reality as it truly is, with all the glorious light, color, and spectacle that is Life. They would then come back and try to explain what was actually going on to those who had never had that experience. It naturally didn't go over very well. Knowing only shadows and having become accustomed to life in that way, those in the cave were not easily convinced that their experience of life was merely an illusion and that everything they knew as real was actually only a "shadow" of the true nature of reality. Herein lays relative life and the dilemma.

It doesn't take a lot to see that the "shadow" concept can be easily replaced by the "membrane" concept, as both represent a partial, incomplete, limited awareness of our situation, and when focused on can replace the true nature of reality and limit our identity. This world of shadows is the world of the "lower self"—the ego. Keep in mind, though, that in both cases some aspect of the true nature of reality, the "higher self" is being projected out and is infused into the illusion, which does give life to the illusion. The shadows were cast by what was *real,* or there would be no shadow. As Droplets, our desire to join a church, political party, or motorcycle gang, or to initiate a corporate merger or to find someone to love are clearly inherent, "higher self" qualities of our essential nature—that is to seek that which will gives us happiness, security, and will bind us to something more than we are. It is this impetus that will eventually lead us back to our Lord, to "*That*" which is the ultimate pleasure, the source of our happiness, the final security, and the fulfillment of the Love we seek. So what we are living does incorporate some aspect of the true nature of reality, which does give it meaning, substance, and format, and even though much more needs to be *realized,* we can all begin with what we have and where we are ...... *Now*! Enlightenment is a possibility that exists for everyone, all of the time, anywhere, as an essential part, and in fulfillment of this Moment.

In stillness recognize and in faith let go of the world of illusion and come to the glorious presence that is this Moment. Come to the silence that surrounds the world of form and bathe in the peace that is the gift of being totally Present. We know now that being completely present requires a state of "no mind." In that state, all the concepts and ideas of our relative identity vanish in quietude, and our awareness is allowed to open to its eternal nature, free from words, concepts, and the machinations of mind. Go outside and get an inkling of that which I am speaking. Recognize the eternal nature of the sky that surrounds you, become aware of the miracle of existence, and watch your mind fall into the stillness of awe, if only for a few seconds. Your practice will leave you open to the eternal in longer and longer intervals until you have achieved Nothing. Let go in Life, let go in meditation. The peace of His presence will call to you. As it begins to remove the illusion of mind and egocentric identity, you will be a reflection of the eternal Love and peaceful presence of being here Now.

Most of my adult life I have worked as a carpenter/contractor in and around New York City. There was some relief from that while I was in charge of the New York City Transcendental Meditation center and during my brief encounter as a student, enrolled in NYU's film school. I am awed by and love films. They can be powerful tools for learning and can broaden and mirror our experience of Life. The avatar and saint Meher Baba recognized this extraordinary aspect of film and encouraged their use for introducing spiritual truths to the public. While watching a film, we are absorbed in someone else's experience of Life. The raw film itself serves as consciousness, the director the mind/ego, the camera the eyes and the screen a temporary membrane that mimics the "illusion" of our experience, only this time outside ourselves. The images projected are still only the "shadows" of reality being manipulated by the creative impulse of the director. But his vision of Life and the corresponding "words" can take us to places we have never been and open us to our potential. We—our awareness—becomes the "silent witness" to the life unfolding before our eyes, a life in which we cannot participate but only observe. Watching a film can be a powerful exercise in understanding consciousness and to the process of becoming aware.

I salute those Droplets who direct and act and who have reached inside themselves and produced films that reflect a deeper understanding of who we are, and have put important values into their work. Whether through the good and evil fantasies of *Star Wars*, *Willow*, and *Lord of the Rings*, or the love stories *You've Got*

Mail, As Good as it Gets and *Love Affair,* or the insightful tales of *Family Man, Powder, My Life, It's a Wonderful Life, Little Buddha* and *A Beautiful Mind,* or the heroics of *Saving Private Ryan, The Matrix,* and *Dances with Wolves,* or just the simple meeting of two friends over dinner in *My Dinner with Andre,* Life and all the glorious aspects of good and evil, joy and sorrow, lust and love, adventure and challenge, sacrifice and tragedy; and the drama, the mystery, the quest, and the comedy that is Life are there for us to open ourselves to and to grow.

I have equal contempt for those who would exploit, glorify, and perpetuate the "evil" that is inherent in separation and ignorance with films that promote violence for its own sake, demonize innocent aspects of nature, which too often leads to their abuse, defile the act of love in egocentric pursuits, exploit and demean the sacred role of women, glorify egoistic insensitivity, and mock anything deeper than their own shallow, egocentric sense of self-importance. The most lasting impression I took from film school was that what one puts on the screen is a direct and intimate reflection of whom one has become. The narcissistic need to reflect the trauma and perversion of one's life in a film should be dealt with in therapy and the inner work of self-actualization, not projected onto a screen that subjects us all to the unresolved distortions and perversion of one's experience of Life. This doesn't mean that only Disney films are acceptable here, but gratuitous violence and deviant sex have no place in "entertainment," and do little to raise our awareness when glorified. We live in a troubled time, and the consequences of our actions should be reflected in film so we can raise our awareness and come to understand why. Films like *Once We Were Warriors* are riveting and brutal to witness, but have powerful messages that can raise our awareness and broaden our perspective.

Another excellent example of the power of film to entertain and inform can be taken from Droplet woody allen's provocative insights as he quests for a deeper meaning to his life, a struggle presented honestly and with delightful humor in his film *Hannah and Her Sisters.* Watch as ego suffers in isolation and as the intellect grasps at straws, frantic for identity in the shallow arena of city life, longing for acceptance and the unity of Love it feels will fulfill it. It is a love we are all seeking with hopes of putting an end to our exile; however, we rarely look beyond egocentric desire for fulfillment or to the underlying cause of our pain. The focus is always on someone or something outside ourselves to make us happy with far too much emphasis on the intellect and the "story" of our lives and not nearly enough time taken to look at our *lives* and at the miracle of Being.

The beauty, mystery, and depth found in the simple act of "witnessing" in so many of the wonderful documentaries that are truly the fulfillment of this media is awe-inspiring. Films like *Blue Planet*, produced by the National Geographic Society, bring a conscious and compassionate "witnessing" of the phenomenal aspects of nature. It can awaken us to the "Mysteries" of Life and the desperate need there is for compassion and Love in our dealings with nature, all of which seems to have been lost in this screwy world of ego, greed, and beliefs.

Film-making belongs in the hands of those who are responsible and aware, just as anything with great power and influence does. This is an industry that is still in its infancy and whose potential I can only joyfully imagine.

⚜

In "relative life," I have met many Droplets that I will technically describe here as "assholes." (Pardon the construction worker in me.) Not an easily recognizable spiritual term, but one that pretty much says it all when describing certain Droplets whose membranes have become severely clouded and distorted. Membranes thickened with ignorance and weird, disturbed information. Self-serving egos without conscience or compassion, locked into the darkness of their narcissism, incapable of any kind of relationship requiring self-exploration and/or sacrifice. Droplets of greed, lust, and corruption who defile life around them through exploitation and abuse. Although not impossible, reaching them is very difficult, especially if they are surrounded with power and money or some fanatic religious belief. These unfortunate Droplets can be found, to one degree or another, everywhere. How troubled or dangerous they are depends on just how clouded the membrane has become, the depth of their ignorance and greed, how distorted the information they carry is, the degree of trauma they may have endured, and how loveless their family life has been; additionally, the influences of karma play an important roll here as well.

Parents, or the lack thereof, can have a particularly influential role in creating these disturbed individuals. If disturbed themselves, what they can pass on to their children is magnified in intensity. The gift of parenthood is not one to be taken lightly. Wanting children is simply not enough. We must be prepared for this sacred role. So much pain has come from those who were simply not spiritually prepared to handle this most important responsibility and who were not capable of giving or did not have the time to give the unconditional love and sacrifice that is such an important part of raising children, indeed of living. Many simply cannot find the love and dedication in themselves to do this job properly, but those who can MUST! It is our future as a race of spiritual beings and a priceless beginning for our children!

Droplet robert bly in his book *The Sibling Society* eloquently points to our very serious social dilemmas wherein parenting has taken a back seat to technology and to social programs. We have condemned stay-at-home moms and elevated "professionals" with nannies; fathers have been made unimportant and unnecessary; women have lost touch with the feminine energy that would bring balance and harmony to all of this; single parenthood has become politically correct; children have become little more than "pets"; and out-of-wedlock births are just an alternative lifestyle. These are *very* serious issues that will have a devastating effect on our future. We have given in to the shallow, selfish, superficial, and ultimately destructive needs of the isolated ego that demands its own way, and to hell with Life. This world is blinded to the "Mystery" and glory of this Moment in the muddle of words, shallow and limited beliefs, and short-term desire. ...... We are, I'm afraid, asleep in Paradise and unconscious of our role in It! We need to wake up, take a look around, explore, and bring witness to the ignorance and the pain that is so much a part of our time, then open our hearts. We must begin to care and to live who we are!

This male ego-oriented world has put tremendous pressure on feminine energy, on its importance and on its survival. Many women have given in for security and for the power of "acceptance" in this aggressively male-dominated society. There is an epidemic of women's health problems that have historically been associated only with men. Heart disease is now the number one killer of women. Putting career before family has not only attributed to infertility, it has mutated the feminine energy into a highly structured, control-based psyche that is no longer in touch with itself. The feminine "receptive" energy is far more dynamic and infinitely more open to this "Mystery" that surrounds us and to the spiritual significance of Life. Pregnancy, birthing, and child-rearing demand a surrender to Life and a willingness to relinquish control. With that humility comes a faith and an openness to the process of becoming, in the Now Moment. As such, a purely woman's perspective should be given priority in all major decisions that govern the family, society, and international politics, for that very same reason. In some American Indian cultures, *only* the women were allowed to choose a chief, which created a natural balance between the "yin and yang," or the male and female energies of their tribe. A woman's natural tendency toward compassion and tenderness, so much a part of the female experience, is the conscience and soul of any culture and is as important to the survival and growth of that culture as it would be to the good health and balance in any individual.

The Dancing Animal Woman by Droplet anne hillman has opened the awareness of many women to their power, their strengths, and to the beauty and grace of their feminine heritage. She has shown us that having the wisdom, strength, and courage to be who we are on this earth as an expression of our Lord's love without the influences of an insecure frightened ego, is true maturity and the path to fulfillment.

We have witnessed the destruction of innocent life and the havoc that the worst of these detached/disturbed Droplets can reap. We have seen their lust, greed, and perversion do unspeakable harm. There is a saying that for evil to grow, all that is needed is for good men to do nothing. It is interesting that in the ancient Indian caste system, the warrior was placed second only to the saint. It is the warrior who is willing to put everything on the line, as is the saint. There is, unfortunately, a time for war, a time for confrontation, a time the "good fight" must be fought, and corrupted membranes, like a cancer, removed. We need only identify the perversion of these Droplets, which can allow them to commit the atrocities we've witnessed against other Droplets, against nature, and against God, in order to justify whatever is necessary to bring an end to their "sins." It is equally important to acknowledge and support the need for our law-enforcement programs and those committed to it.

There will always be "assholes" to one degree or another; it is part of the evolutionary process. It is simply the insecure ego expressing its ignorance in the illusion of a separate identity in search of identity, and it can manifest its destructive energies in individuals as well as in groups or even nations.

There must always be Droplets willing to defend and protect the innocent, the helpless, our freedom, and the environment with a conscious course of action that honors Life and freedom and not one driven by hate and vengeance—that is, one dedicated to "fight the good fight." Their role should be honored and deeply respected as should the role of the saint who would have us turn the other cheek with love, compassion, and in full awareness that we are all a part of the same Spirit and share the same destiny. This may seem a contradiction, but I assure you it is not; it is simply the way it is.

I am certainly not an advocate of war, and I foresee a time when war will be obsolete, our collective consciousness raised high enough to prevent violent conflict entirely, a time when our differences are not so clear and the "illusion" lifted. This, however, looks to be a long way off, and I pray we won't destroy ourselves in the interim. But alas, "to everything there is a season," and as Droplet richard moss points out, there is no time more spiritual than war time. Life and death are very real then, this Moment very precious, and our suffering is great. Questions are asked, concepts challenged, and one's faith is put to the test. It is a time when we come together and put our values in order, a time when the simple God-given gifts of Life become sacred, a time when the darkness of our ignorance is so horrifyingly clear.

⁂

Relative life can be very difficult. Issues of health, money, family difficulties, death and dying, tragedies of all kinds, are real and they surely hurt, but they need to be explored, felt deeply, and understood, not run from. Bringing the understanding that comes from the experience of our own true nature into relative life is a bit like inheriting a bank account with unlimited funds available. Until then, our funds were limited and as each expense—stressful experience—came to us, we were pressed to pay the bill. Any major tragedy or extreme stress easily depleted the necessary "funds" and left you "spent." Ego identity is very restricted, short-lived, and dependent on external events for identity, and so is fearful, insecure, and easily devastated when things go wrong. Opening to and living our eternal nature in the Moment would allow for an enjoyment of life of immense proportions as we gain access to these "unlimited funds." The "bills" would still need to be paid, and that could easily be done; however, you would still have available to you unlimited funds and would never be devastated by external events. You would no longer be confined to the needs and restrictions of a limited ego, and could open your heart to all who suffer without fear or restriction. Unrestricted, our understanding, love, and compassion would grow as we embrace all of life. Our limited ego identity would become insignificant in the face of this boundless presence, yet would still be maintained as an aspect of our being and personal identity.

In relinquishing the illusion of ego and the powerful limitations to which it confines you, and guided by this "higher knowledge" toward that place of expansiveness, you would heighten your awareness, raise your consciousness, and open yourself to the wonder of being and to who you truly are, and what Life is, as your "bank account" becomes limitless. You would no longer be confined to the relative identity that is the body and the mind, but would become more conscious of the common "*Source*" to which all of your expanded awareness is now a witness. In that awareness, your pain would become compassion for those lost in the struggle of a limited ego identity that isolates and limits them in ignorance and suffering. Your fear of death would be lost in a new identity, outside of body and mind, in the boundless Love that surrounds and permeates all that is as your eternal heritage reveals itself to you. The sorrow of loss would be healed in His presence, which can only lovingly embrace all of His creation. Only an isolated, detached and transient ego can suffer loss. In that state of expanded awareness, you could begin to witness the majesty and wisdom of the eternal stately ebb and flow of God's work and go beyond the egocentric need for instant gratification and "happy endings." We are becoming a part of something much, much bigger and infinitely more fulfilling. Have Faith!

> The Tao is like a well:
> used but never used up
> It is like the eternal void:
> Filled with infinite possibilities.
> It is hidden but always present.
> I don't know who gave birth to it.
> It is older than God.

> —From the Tao te Ching

We Droplets need to be free to explore Life and challenge limitations. Those of us fortunate enough to have been born into freedom should cherish this most precious gift that was understood and was the driving force behind our founding fathers' rebellion. When the expressions of passionate Droplets are repressed, all of us suffer in the darkness of ignorance. Tyranny and fascism by the ego-maniacal few has never contributed to our growth and spiritual awareness, at least not in a positive way. With freedom comes the challenges and insecurities of Life for each individual. From the insecurities come the quest for meaning. From the quest comes our passion, our faith, and the fulfillment of our destiny.

There is great wisdom to be taken from the insecurities of life as illustrated in Droplet alan watts's insightful book *The Wisdom of Insecurity*. To attempt to structure a life that would secure the illusion of ego is a denial of our Lord and would shut us off from our own unlimited potential in a limited and needy identity. Much can be learned during difficult times. Our discomfort, anxiety, and fear are reminders of our need to come home and find our fulfillment in the spirit of Life that lies at the core of our being, that which is the essence and *Source* of this eternal Moment.

Nothing can truly secure the ego, for the ego is based in illusion and we will forever suffer the anxiety and fear of being lost in that illusion. By saying "yes" to all that life is offering in this Moment, you deny the restrictive energy of ego, and it will open you to Life's infinite possibilities and to your own glorious potential. Our attempt at securing the fragile illusion of ego has brought us to the very brink of destruction, for that identity holds no reverence for the unity of life and our sacred role as Lover.

The story of the Buddha illustrates how important our need to know and the freedom to explore Life are and what can be realized once the limited desire to secure the ego is abandoned. As a young prince, the Buddha was not allowed to leave the confines of the castle. His father had been warned by the in-house seer that he would lose his son, and he feared that he would suffer great harm if he were to go out into the real world. So he kept his son confined to the castle, where he lived a fantasy life in which death, poverty, and anything else that was "negative" were all kept from him. The time came when the Buddha could no longer stay imprisoned, and he left the false security of his father's castle to explore the true meaning of Life. Enlightenment was neither his goal nor the impetus for leaving; freedom and simply to "know" were. The result speaks for itself. From the "insecuring" of ego in a quest for higher knowledge, enlightenment was attained. The biblical story of Droplets adam and eve is similar in theme in that they, too, *had* to leave their *father's* home and were given the freedom to explore life in a quest for truth. ...... So, how are you doin'?!

Yes, you are Adam, you are Eve, you are the Buddha in exile from paradise where you once existed in an unconscious union with our Lord. You have been gifted/cursed with the freedom to find out who you are and you will suffer the sins of your ignorance until your return to this eternal Moment in full awareness is complete.

With that return, you will become enlightened with the experience that will not only satisfy the longings of the Soul in its quest for the love of our Lord, but you will have made our Lord joyful in the ecstasy experienced as you realize your true nature. Your life is not a choice, only what you do with It is. Do you want to remain ignorant and suffer in that ignorance? Or are you willing to be courageous enough to let go of your false identity and make your way back to the "Kingdom"?

With freedom comes responsibility, not just to ourselves, but to others as well. We cannot have government dictate our emotions. To live passionately and to freely give to those in need are the hallmarks of freedom and an enlightened society. When government sets the rules and demands our generosity and compassion, *we* are left out of the process and our country is weakened. The dictates of communism and socialism may espouse caring for all of the people, but a false sense of security and the need to control are inherent in these ideologies. Only a democracy allows all of its people the opportunity to become all that they would like to become, and in so doing strengthens the country. "In God We Trust," if applied to all that has been said, would mean that the Holy Spirit, the essence of this Moment and whose essential nature is inherent in all Droplets, will prevail if given the chance. Freedom is that chance.

There is, like everything else, an egocentric dark side to this as well, for freedom without discipline is chaos, as surely as discipline without freedom is tyranny. Finding a balance is the role of an enlightened government and has been done well by our founding fathers. We must have the freedom to drive wherever we want and whenever we want, but we must also have and obey the rules of the road in order to ensure our safety and the safety of those around us.

Our enlightened founding fathers have left a legacy that still endures and will always endure as long as freedom is cherished and the role of government is limited. "Life, liberty, and the pursuit of happiness" in the hands of an *enlightened* government would catapult our race towards our spiritual destiny. But beware, for an *unenlightened* government that has been influenced and has adopted the egocentric aspects of fear and separation and the need for comfort, security, and distraction, can and have fostered the insane levels of consumerism highlighted by the exploitation and abuse of the natural world. The greed and corruption of those involved can be far more tyrannical and a much greater threat to our freedom than any fascist dictator. "In God We Trust" must be our moral, ethical, and spiritual commitment to Life, and not another hypocritical, self-serving, egocentric slogan.

⚘

Living the simple life doesn't necessarily mean throwing away everything technology has given us and finding a cabin in the woods to live in, although you could. Our fulfillment is in the spirit of Now and not dependent on the superficial trappings of Life. Like it or not, the "good old days" are gone and were, for the most part, unappreciated given the state of our progress at the time. In those bygone days, our inability to manipulate the physical world left us in awe of it, and we projected much in the way of mystery into our experience because of our ignorance. As we learned how to manipulate, as we learned the folly of our fears and projections, the mystery became lost to us in ego pursuits and the complexities of the mind. The sanctity and spirit of nature was consumed by egocentricity. The best we can do now is to become aware of what made the "good old days" good and incorporate that knowledge into our experience of today. Certainly the importance of simplicity would be part of that knowledge, but perhaps more important would be finding and living the "Mystery" of Now again. It will come when we recognize that we still have no *real* knowledge of *anything* or *anyone* around us and that to truly know this great mystery that lies beyond the pretense of mind and ego is to open oneself to the unimaginable beauty and grace. This, then, is the purpose of your Life: To become AWARE and be humbled by this great Mystery of Life as a grateful witness.

We can "manipulate" life and abort a fetus or build horrifying weapons of mass destruction to "improve" and "secure" our lives, but in the process we end up obscuring the fundamental Mystery and beauty that is this sacrament of Life in the illusions of egocen-

188

tricity. In the superficial gratification of the limited ego, we have obscured this miracle that is our lives. Truly, the "time has come to bring It back and let Love again command." Remove or at least acknowledge the stigma of ignorance in which we suffer. As we let go of egocentric pursuits with the gaining of "higher knowledge" in the Now, we automatically develop a reverence for life as the true mystery that is this life unfolds before our eyes. All that is Holy will grovel at your feet in the joy of recognition as you become aware of the majesty of this Creation and bring fulfillment to It in your sacred role as witness. This can only happen Now, free from illusion.

※※※

Technology has given us many comforts that have freed our lives of the constant need to survive and the stress that can result. We have available to us more information than ever before—information that can deepen the value of our lives, information that can make our lives healthier and have us live longer, information that can clearly show us where we've gone wrong and may even point a finger back to the "path." As Droplet sigmund freud noted, it is, after all, "the truth that will set you free." This is an evolutionary process we are going through. We are ever so slowly growing, becoming more aware, and coming out of the ignorance and inability to realize the glory that is this Moment, and we are becoming content to *simply* be fulfilled by It, through It, and in It. I have developed a deep faith in and for this process of "becoming" and in the hand that guides it. All that was in the way of Its recognition was taken from me, and I have come to wonder at Its mystery and marvel at Its grandeur. You, too, can discover the wonder and find your faith in this Moment, free from the limits of the ego, should you choose.

Ask and it shall be given to you. Seek, and ye shall find. Knock, and it shall be opened to you. For whoever asks,

*receives; and he who seeks, finds; and to him who knocks, the
door is opened.*

—Jesus, Matthew 7:7-8

But you must learn how to ask and how to receive. It is not in
and through the intellect that this knowledge will be received. It is
not through casual inquiry that these important questions are made.
It will come to you as you, that is, your "higher self," as you bring
your awareness to this Moment in full recognition of the Mystery
that surrounds you, and you humble the intellect with this "higher
knowledge" in prayer. Intellect cannot give you this answer; however, it can take you to that sacred ground where it can be received.
That sacred ground is revealed once we can acknowledge the Mystery and all we don't know and finally become humbled and silent
in that glorious state of "no mind." It is here you will experience the
Mystery of this Moment and come to the sacred knowledge of
Being. It will come from a place that is beyond the mind, the ego,
and the senses. It will come from that intuitive, super-sensory part
of who we are that knows how to ask and can be open to the
answer, to that place where mind, ego, and intellect have no role as
you become a pure witness to this miracle that is consciousness and
can bathe in the mystery of Being. Ask from here, seek from here,
listen from here—from Soul, the All and the Nothing. Become
silence! Here you will not be denied; you cannot be denied.

~

I love going into supermarkets and seeing all the variety that
nature has provided for us. I love going online and tapping the
amazing resources of information available. I also love sitting and
watching honey bees work so hard with such devotion and passion.
Simplicity is not so much a way of life as it is a state of mind. We
can take all that is available to us and create an ego structure out of
it that can be very complicated, mesmerizing, and difficult to see
beyond. There are those who have perfected the manipulation of
this world of "shadows" and have secured a relative "successful" ego
identity from it, but will have much trouble leaving it behind in the
pursuit of Truth, for "it is easier for a camel to pass through the eye
of a needle than for a rich man to enter the Kingdom of Heaven." Or

we can marvel at all that "God is doing now" and has placed before us, enjoy and learn as a child would, and then let it go without creating an identity in those "things," but rather recognizing and appreciating, through expanded awareness, what has come through us as gifts. This is truly simplifying our lives. By creating a fluid membrane that can go deeply into experience and return without identity in that experience with only love and gratitude for having been blessed with the ability to have the experience is the goal of the meditative mind, the key to simplicity and the joy of keeping the "Mystery" alive!

"To walk through the snow and leave not footprints." Within this Zen koan we can begin to intuit a state of consciousness that would allow us to take action in this world but not become identified with the results. Becoming egoless is to become fully aware of who we are, unrestricted by mind and the identity it seeks, completely open and united with the Spirit that has given us Life. Yet we still remain a part of and active in this world with "nothing lost and nothing gained in living every day."

⁂

Relative life can become a prison without the relief of meditation, prayer, and an inner exploration of who we are beyond the limits of mind/ego. Normally, as we experience Life, we take these experiences inside ourselves and they become a part of who we are, our identity. Some experiences may seem good and some not so good; either way, they create a reference library that defines the rest of our lives. Let me give you an example. Suppose you enjoy taking walks. One day as you are walking, you are set upon by a frightened dog and bitten. Your pleasant and peaceful walk is ruined. There is now a stressful event that has become a part of who you are, and each time you approach the place where you were attacked, the event comes to mind. Your awareness becomes limited to the past and to the trauma of the event and fearful of a possible future reenactment, so you lose your openness to the "Moment" and the joy of freedom.

Imagine hundreds of thousands of events doing the same thing to your open awareness, and you have relative life and why this world seems to be such a maze of conflict and confusion. Should we ignore the lesson of the frightened dog and be bitten again? Of course not. But to never take a walk again or to walk in constant fear would be worse. If we go deeply into each experience and to the emotions they may provoke, there is something to learn in everything. In prayer we can acknowledge and be grateful for the opportunity. In meditation and in the practice of being here Now, we can create a fluid mind that can experience life deeply and come out unshaken and unidentified in our eternal role as witness.

In truth and from a broader understanding of our lives, nothing good or bad happened on your walk that day; rather, the "energy" of life expressed Itself to you. It was perhaps, too much "energy" to absorb in that moment, and you were left in a state of tension and distress, perhaps "spent." Unexplored, it will remain a "knot" of tension/energy that could better serve you elsewhere. This is *all* energy, all *"That"* simply being *"That,"* and all we experience are a part of *"That."* ...... Don't take it personally! Karmically, perhaps the dog was a deer or rabbit you killed for food in a past life or some other aspect of nature whose needs where ignored or taken advantage of. Perhaps the dog's owners were abused directly or indirectly by some unconscious act. The karmic possibilities are endless and to truly understand *why* is an enormous and unnecessary challenge. But to have that basic understanding of the workings of karma is so very essential to a productive life in the realization that whatever is happening *has* to be. To quote again from *The Seat of the Soul* by Droplet gary zukav, "There is not one act in the Universe that is not compassionate." To simply know of and to have faith in this process of *becoming* is enough to keep you open to this Moment of possibilities and to allow you to accept events as gifts for your awakening.

Bring your faith and this "higher knowledge" to each day, and accept that all that will come to you this day is coming for your growth and spiritual awareness. It will open you to this day of miracles and to its possibilities in ways you could never have anticipated. Your anxiety will be eased in Faith and your fear will be replaced with a Love that will grow in understanding. What will come *must* come. ...... Accept, be grateful, then let go, and if necessary, forgive. It will allow you to come to this Moment completely present, here and now, with no expectations, no wishes of what could be, no worries of what might be, no fear of what was, and no projection of what should be, ... completely *aware, present and in Love*. Being aware does not mean being "smart," but rather being completely present and mindful of who you are as a conscious sentient being, in this Moment, with no baggage, and with an open, receptive heart— simply and essentially *you*. Your intellect will find its true expression from your heart and find its peace in this Love.

I have always admired the deep faith in life and in our Lord that the Christian Science religion displays. Their total acceptance of the misfortunes of life and their desire not to interfere with "what God is doing now" brings a conscious awareness of the *Source* of all that is happening and relinquishes all egocentric desire to that "higher power." And yet, it seems they may be missing something equally as grand, something equally as "holy" by ignoring what our Lord has gifted us with. Free will and our desire to return to him requires some effort. Bringing a compassionate and loving heart to an unfortunate situation is to bring our Lord's will to it as well, as we, too, are an expression of "*That.*" Faith is an aspect of life we could not properly live without, but we must not lose faith in ourselves. We are an expression of His love and compassion, and are obligated to use them in times of need. If your child has broken a bone, would you not seek out someone who knew how to set it properly? If knowledge can put an end to suffering, then we must seek it out and apply it, for if we can put an end to the suffering of a soul in need, then we have put an end to the suffering of our Lord.

There is a story I have always enjoyed that illustrates our need to Be Here Now. A terrible flood was reported approaching a small community. Everyone was warned to leave but one very righteous man who had lived a good life refused to leave, believing God would care for and protect him. As the flood waters grew, a motor boat arrived at his house and offered to take him to safety, but he refused, saying, "God will save me." As the flood waters grew higher, he was forced to climb to the roof of his home, at which point a helicopter arrived to rescue him. Once again he refused help, believing God would keep him from harm. As the flood waters grew even higher, the man was swept away in the torrent and drowned. As the man came to God in the afterlife, he was confused and disappointed that his undying faith in his Lord had not "saved" him, and so he asked why. God replied that had the man listened, He had sent an early warning so he would be spared, and if he had paid attention and had he been present, he would have noticed that God had sent him two opportunities that would have saved him from the flood. This story illustrates the need to free yourself from your beliefs and to Be Here Now! You might be very surprised at what God is offering you for your salvation at this very Moment.

If you listen carefully to the voice of the Lord your God and do what is right in his eyes, if you pay attention to his commands and keep all his decrees, I will not bring on you any of the diseases I brought on the Egyptians, for I am the Lord, who heals you.

—*Exodus 15:26*

Life is rich with the wisdom of our Lord, and every aspect of the natural world reflects His presence. There is no doubt there is a "higher knowledge," an intelligence that rules and permeates all of life. It needs to be explored, understood, and gained faith in. Herein lies the majesty and importance of the human mind, for it can, if not influenced by fear, bring us to the very threshold of that Divine Intelligence and strengthen our faith. I was honored to have known Droplet dr. robert mendelson, first through his book *How to Raise a Healthy Child in Spite of Your Doctor*, then through his public lecture series, and finally through direct phone conversation wherein he made himself available to anyone in need. He was a high-ranking physician who, among other things, stood on the physician's licensing board in Chicago. His charismatic presence and good humor were a joy to witness. At the end of his long and distinguished career, he had come to the unorthodox conclusion that there is within the body an innate intelligence that would be better left alone to do its work. Our role should at best be to understand, have faith in and, if possible, help it along, not so much by doing something but rather by having the faith and courage to know when to do nothing. Of course, the medical community has contributed much to the betterment of mankind and it is not my intent to make its contributions insignificant. But Dr. Mendelson had become aware enough to know when enough was enough, and he condemned the intrusive role that his medical profession likes to play and made clear the long-term negative effects it can have on healthy living. His controversial yet adamant opinion that vaccinations are a serious threat to our children's' well-being is being supported daily with discoveries that link immunizations with many serious and debilitating long-term diseases.

Dr. Mendelson's passionate and heartfelt advice was that love, faith in our Lord's work, simple cleanliness, and good nutrition can do amazing things for the health of our children and for ourselves, and echoes the wisdom of 1 Corinthians 2:5: "That your faith might not rest on men's wisdom, but on God's power." This "power of God" is the essence of this Moment, which is revealed to us as we become unencumbered by mind and ego. It is who we are and carries with it a deep, ineffable understanding of Life with a profound faith in the innate wisdom of the body as a part of His creation.

We have a responsibility to life to ease pain when we can, but we must also gain the wisdom to know when we cannot. Life is a grand meditation, and there are times we must suffer through and release the karmic consequences of it. There are times that only our faith can bring us through, a faith that can accept the circumstances of Life as the will of our Lord, giving us the strength and wisdom to let go when we must.

We are not our bodies; we are not our minds. We are much, much more than either of those gifts would hold us to. Sometimes the gifts must be taken from us so we can see *"That."* Sometimes the gifts must be taken from us so we can be *"That."* Have faith in our Lord and in His creation. There are no mistakes; there is nothing wrong. There is only the will of our Lord and His impeccable wisdom.

Let meditation refresh you and keep you open to the possibilities of Life. Allow yourself to go deeply into your essential nature and simply "Be." There is a goal to the martial arts: "to be prepared for everything, but to expect nothing." That is, to balance your life with the wisdom of your experience and the freedom of your open awareness. I also like: "Be prepared for nothing and expect everything." That is, know that none of this *had* to be and be open to the wonder of it all! (You're gonna have to spend some time with that one!) Don't limit your identity to ego/mind and the fears and beliefs inherent in them. Be open to the infinite possibilities of this Moment beyond those superficial identities. You are so much more than you are holding on to. ...... You are Nothing!

Watch for ego and the need for it to find identity. If it cannot come through the front door, it may find its way through the back. Here is an amusing illustration. One day a student rabbi walked into the temple to find his rabbi and mentor prostrate on the floor in front of the altar. He was wailing and pounding his chest in a surrender to our Lord, "I am nothing, I am nothing," he cried out. The student, inspired by this display of humility, joined him and began pounding his chest, also wailing, "I am nothing, I am nothing." Soon after that, the janitor entered the temple and observed the rabbis. He, too, became caught up in this show of surrender and joined the rabbis in their wailing, "I am nothing, I am nothing." With that, the rabbi stopped his wailing, turned to his student, and said, "So, look who thinks he's nothing." ...... Watch out for ego!

There is another story I have always loved passing on, which illustrates the power of mind over us. Once there was a highly revered monk who had journeyed with his student/disciple to a neighboring village, and they were on the way back to their monastery. It was raining heavily as they approached a small town about a day's journey from home. At one side of the street was an extraordinarily beautiful and voluptuous young woman. Knowing the strict vows of celibacy all monks had taken, the disciple was astonished to see his master go out of his way to approach this woman and ask her if he could carry her across the muddy road. The woman accepted his offer and after a brief exchange of gratitude, the monk resumed his journey. For the entire way home, the disciple could not speak to his master. That evening he could not sleep with his disappointment. Finally, the next morning he went to his master and confronted him. "Master, yesterday on our way home you went out of your way to carry that woman across the street, knowing the vows we have taken. I am very troubled by this." The master eyed him closely and replied, "It was perhaps my sin to have carried this woman across the street, but yours is the far greater sin to have carried her all the way home and through the night."

"Know thyself": go beyond the superficial, the transient, the "mind-stuff," and be free. Open yourself to the majesty of Life and to the role you are playing in it. Be free of yesterday and don't worry about tomorrow; you are only whole Now, you can only be present Now. ...... Be free!

Finish every day and be done with it. You have done what you could. Some blunders and absurdities no doubt crept in; forget them as soon as you can. Tomorrow is a new day; begin it well and serenely and with too much high spirit to be encumbered with your old nonsense. This day is all that is good and fair. It is too dear, with its hopes and invitations, to waste a moment on yesterdays.

—*Droplet ralph waldo emerson*

"Honor thy mother and thy father." This is the commandment that evokes much resentment in so many. So many of us did not have the perfect parents who gave unconditional love, perhaps just the opposite. So many of us carry the wounds of abusive or missing parents. So many of us cannot function well in this world as a result. How, then, can we "honor" them; how can we stop the pain?

What must be honored here is not so much their actions but their intent. As distorted and misinformed as their actions may have been, their quest was no different than yours and their pain no less; only the path they had chosen differs. That path can and should serve as a stunning example of what can happen in separation, and it can be a beacon for your quest, should it be honored. Putting their life in order with the use of "higher knowledge," whether actually or in theory, will bring order to your life. The chaos and traumas of a difficult childhood do stand as blocks to your spiritual growth, as they most likely were for your parents, and have been placed there for a reason, a reason that must be explored. Understanding how they came to who they were/are is essential, as they have in effect paved the way for us. We are not separate from them, and their efforts were our efforts. Indeed, as a part of who we are, understanding who they could have been and where they were/are on this journey should be honored and explored, and their mistakes forgiven! It will ease your pain and deepen your experience of Life.

No other Droplets will have as much influence on who you become than your parents. No other Droplets have more of an influence on who you are than your parents. Believe it or not, you were the one who chose them to be your parents! Your karmic tie to them over the course of many lifetimes is the most profound of all. Your choice to incarnate with them as your parents came from a recognition of what needed to be dealt with as we reviewed our former life before reincarnating into this one, not just for your spiritual growth, but for theirs as well. To not honor and love them is to deny and misunderstand who and why we are here and leave the karmic debt unpaid. You will have missed the opportunity for serious spiritual growth as a victim of the ignorance that is both yours and theirs.

To keep the anger, hate, and resentment that may be a part of your experience, will only strengthen the ego's illusion and keep you in your isolation and stagnation. Our parents, especially our mothers, took us from that state of consciousness wherein we initially could not differentiate between our experiences and ourselves. We came to know who we were through their eyes, for our egocentric identity would be born and crystallized out of that experience with our mothers. Whether that experience was a positive one or a negative one, ego was formed and would one day need to be understood so as to release ourselves from the illusion of that mind-based identity. This relative (pardon the pun) identity can obstruct the flow of the ever-present "life force energy." As a negative experience, these blocks create an imbalance in your body and your mind that can eventually manifest as disease. A very real relationship has been established between cancer and those whose relationship with their parents had many unresolved, painful issues, leaving the "energy" with no other outlet except disease to express itself. The strong-willed, highly intellectual egocentric identities are curiously far more susceptible to cancer. These powerful relative identities create a barrier to the Soul's expression, and the repressed energies often manifest in disease, should these identities only serve to protect the ego. On the other hand, the weak, suppressed, or defeated ego often manifests in a schizophrenic personality as a means of escaping the confines of an unpleasant identity. Curiously, their expansive, undif-ferentiated experience of life leaves them statistically far less prone to cancer. These few statements are foundations of yet another book, and I will not go into them here. But be reminded that your body, your mind, and the emotions that are the result of the interac-tions of both are barometers of your state of awareness and must be paid close attention to. Listen to your body and become aware of blocked psychic energies of fear, anxiety, and depression that can cause discomfort, pain, and disease, both on a physical and mental level. By the simple act of bringing your attention to these negative emotions, the energy they carry will be transmuted into the light of awareness. Focus on them and become aware of the underlying emotion. Open yourself to that "unlimited bank account" that is your inner essence and free yourself of negativity and the false iden-tity of ego.

To "honor" does not mean to worship or become subservient, for we are all Droplets of equal status here, truly all children of God. But we must take the time to know them as that and to love and to honor the path that has brought us to where we are now. They, too, have suffered in egocentric pursuits, and in their ignorance they may have caused you suffering. We are all in exile and have adopted the illusion of ego as a means of dealing with the pain of that loss. You must go to your "higher self" and acknowledge that they have done the best they knew how with what they had, and love them for that and forgive—"Forgive them Lord for they know not." ...... Then, take on the challenges ahead, perhaps guided and strengthened with the knowledge of their mistakes. There is never nothing to learn from someone, and there is much to learn from those you are closest to. Learn the lesson of souls lost in ego identity and then let go in love and forgiveness. Come to this Moment whole, and release the tension of a mind-based identity. This is your work for this lifetime and a pathway of liberation for you and for them.

For you as parents who may be suffering the terrible loss or tragic illness of a child, or for that matter, any of you who may have suffered the untimely, premature loss of a loved one, you must come to understand and appreciate the sacrifice they have made for you and for your spiritual growth. There are no mistakes in the world of Spirit, only different ways to learn, and the most profound lessons of all can be taken through tragedy. Their sacrifice was their gift to you, one meant to open you to the world of the Spirit and to the Love that resides there. It is a sacred gift that was willingly and lovingly decided on in a time and place you had both forgotten as you entered again the dream of life. It is a gift that must be cherished and explored in the Now Moment, for it was here that this gift was intended to bring you. Every tragedy in life can be a gateway to the eternal if you can allow yourself to go beyond the sorrow of loss and the egocentric identity being challenged and be open to your eternal nature and to love. The material world can take many unexpected turns and is loaded with hazards and dangerous curves that can wreak havoc in your life with little or no notice. It is in this drama of Life and the beautiful sadness inherent in the loss of form where Life plays itself out and where our suffering is the greatest. By becoming present, free from ego and fear, you can feel your sorrow deeply and through it begin to feel His eternal presence in all there is, as what is. His love will rise within you and heal the pain of your isolation. Your sorrow will disappear in the warmth of this Love as you come to understand the true nature of your Life. Go deeply within ...... Now. Trust and surrender to His wisdom and become grateful for *all* He has set before us as it is *all* a means of knowing who we are as we continue on this glorious journey of Love, as we continue on this glorious journey that is our Lives!

I had completed this book and felt it was once *again* ready for submission to my editor for review. One day during that review period, I had tuned into a "New Age" talk radio show, and a woman's voice caught my attention. There was something about her voice and her manner that drew me to her intently. The radio show was having "technical difficulties" and the telephone connection they had with her kept being interrupted and was finally lost. I did, however, get her name and the gist of what she was there to talk about, so I went to the Internet and found that Droplet brandon bays had written a book entitled *The Journey*, an account of her spiritual awakening and extraordinary self-healing.

For Droplet brandon bays, this journey began when she was diagnosed with a large, cancerous tumor. By her becoming simply and completely present—that is, not turning away from her pain and her fear, accepting all that was set before her as a gift from our Lord dedicated to her growth, and then completely exploring its source—she was able to transcend her pain and dissolve her tumor in an awareness of her eternal essence within. This was a radical departure from her "New Age, self-help" movement that had consumed much of her time, similar to ones I have come to deplore as they do little more than boost and encourage the ego to "do more and be better." My wife and I decided to take the "journey" and participate in a three-day intensive that was fortunately being offered at a nearby retreat within just a few weeks.

Brandon's clarity and deep understanding of the human spirit and her genuine desire to bring the love she has found to all who suffer in ignorance is truly remarkable and an inspiration. Her approach is unlike any standard "therapy," as it does not allow the participant to dwell on the verbiage that can arise as those deeper layers of emotional trauma are revealed during the course of the journey. It does little or no intellectualization of them as they are "peeled away" and their underlying causes discovered. Rather, her approach looks to and bears witness only to the emotional underlying source of each layer. For instance, a tumor or any debilitating emotional issue once explored might evoke feelings of anger or repressed rage (although truly anything is possible). That rage explored might evoke feelings of abandonment. The abandonment explored might bring up feelings of worthlessness or of not having been loved as a child, and once those feelings are explored there may well be even subtler feelings that reflect our deepest insecurity and fear. We could then come to the very essence of what it is to be human and sincerely ask, "Who am I?" We are finally faced with the unknown, the abyss, the great Mystery of Life, ... the who I am. As the finite ego comes face to face with this vast, eternal presence, it can no longer comfortably remain as an independent identity. That encounter is marked with an initial pulling back in fear. However, once this fear is also embraced and the *letting go* of that fear is allowed to happen via the "journey" process, the participant is able to come to that *something* that is so much more than our limited ego identity. Most of those who participated experienced a place within themselves that dwarfed the ego and the pain it carried and brought them to an overwhelming experience of peace, love, clarity, expansion, and wholeness as they became aware of those eternal qualities that lie deep within ourselves as ourselves.

The "journey" concludes with a natural and easy "forgiveness" of all who may have wounded us in their ignorance, partially in a recognition of the wounds they, too, had endured, but more from this place of boundlessness and freedom. The associated dis-ease that had manifested in physical and emotional illness can now be released, eased, on a deep, cellular level. The participants can begin to live up to their full potential, unencumbered by the physical and emotional blocks that had limited their awareness and obscured their true Selves. We witnessed a rather large, diverse group of "ordinary" people burdened with physical and emotional issues—stemming in large part from their parents' abuse—use those issues and their suffering to come to *Source* and experience the overwhelming presence of the Eternal that is at the core of our Being. Incredible stories of tumor remissions and emotional self-healing are reported once the participant is led to this inner awareness of *Self*.

We can repress, hide, deny, and run from a great deal that is ugly and uncomfortable in ourselves. We can and have introduced many ways to escape those unwanted feelings and cover them over with "feel-good," addictive, or compulsive behavior. But unless we deal with them and listen to the Soul as it suffers and speaks to us through our bodies, these unresolved issues will continue to create the *dis-ease* that puts limits on our potential, on our ability to enjoy this Life, and to truly know who we are. Truly, blessed are those who suffer, for it is the Soul that is crying out to be free; you need only to listen.

Enlightened souls were not the product of that weekend, but an awareness of our eternal essence had begun to manifest in many who participated. I would sincerely hope that you explore Droplet brandon bays's work, and that it becomes a significant part of your growth process, and that you embrace this very aware and loving Droplet as I have.

> *Others told me to open my heart and let God in. I suffered still. The Journey guided me to open my heart and let God out. I am free.*
>
> —*from* The Journey

Through the deep relaxation that meditation can bring, the mind can become more "fluid" and the stresses of those different experiences of life can be relieved in daily practice, thus allowing a gradual clearing of the membrane, reducing the need for egocentric protection, and a fuller/deeper appreciation of the Moment acquired. In prayer we can give thanks and acknowledge His hand in all we have been graced with and been witness to, and for those experiences that we have had as learning tools and as events that can, if explored through methodologies like *The Journey*, break the patterns that have limited our awareness and open us up to Life. By acknowledging His hand in all that we have been privileged to experience, we are left grateful, open to Life, fearless, and in love. We can become empowered by His presence and open to the possibilities of being instruments of His healing. Come to Now empty and be filled!

There is nothing that could exist without His presence. Look deeply into every aspect of Life and you will find Him here, in the Mystery, the majesty and the splendor of it all. He is the One. Drop the mind and become present, if only for an instant. Practice coming to this state of "no mind" as often as you can remember to forget. In faith, humility, and gratitude, you will grow closer to our Lord in this open state of Presence. As the ego dissolves in the power of love and in the grace of Presence, you will let go of the illusion of separateness as the tension between your mind-based identity and "*That*" eases and you come to recognize that all of this Life is an act of Love given to us so that we can *know* who we are.

On the day before my wife was to go to a Zen Buddhist monastery for a week of meditation, a friend came to visit. She told my wife that she would never go to any place that did not hold Jesus Christ as their Lord and Savior. The obvious fear from her Christian indoctrination, which she was so painfully living, was all too clear. I could only wonder what a relief to the fear and pain of her life it would be if she had the knowledge and faith that He is not limited to *anything*. That He has always been with us, and is in all things, everywhere, regardless of what we *think* and regardless of what we *believe*! If we could have the faith to let go of the false idols of our beliefs and so raise our awareness in this Moment, to this Moment, and so become *mindful* and aware of this Moment and our role in It, we could then join Him in His eternal presence, no matter where we were, no matter what we do, fearless and joyful for the simple grace of Being.

"I tell you the truth, anyone who has faith in me will do what I have been doing. He will do even greater things than these, because I am going to the Father" (John 14:12). So promised the Christ to those who would believe and have faith in the spirit of His presence as He joined again in total union with and as our Lord. "Before Abraham was born, I am" (John 8:58). And that presence, "I am," is here and is Now in the timeless essence of Life. Silently repeat these magical words to yourself, "I am," and feel His presence as the core of your existence. Have faith in this process of "Becoming" as He did and let your awareness and this "higher knowledge" bring you to Him ...... Now! Indeed, greater things than these will be yours as you discover the glorious emptiness of your inner essence and join

Him in eternity. Life will continue to evolve and we will continue our "journey" back to Him. It is the purpose and the joy of this Creation. So be happy, do what you do consciously, and enjoy, as truly, "life is not a problem to be solved, but an experience to be lived." Live it fully in awareness and in Love, and for Christ's sake and your own, ... *enjoy*, not in the superficial, hedonistic needs of the ego, but in the playful innocence of a child, in awe and in gratitude, in faith, in surrender and in love. Don't you see what you have?! ...... Try not to get so caught up in what you *fear* or what you *want* in the critical, doubting, demanding energy of ego, for truly it is the meek who will inherit the earth. Let go, come to *Now*, and open yourself to the presence of our Lord in all that there is, as who you are.

In India, now amongst us, there appears to be a Droplet whose close connection to our Lord is making for many a "miracle." Droplet sai baba is astounding his followers with miraculous acts of healing and the manifestations of whatever seems to be needed. Indeed, when "That" connection is in place, all things are possible, as all things are at hand. But there is no need for you to run off to India for your "miracle," any more than a fish would wish to be wet. We are all swimming in this same ocean of miracles. You can make your connection to the Eternal through Sai Baba here, there, or anywhere, given enough faith.

That we are all connected is illustrated by the events of human consciousness that seem to spontaneously leap to the next level all at once, all over the world. Even bacteria seem to display this same "connectedness," confounding scientists with their ability to develop resistance to new antibiotics all at once, all over the world. The complete presence of a Sai Baba and other Droplets as deeply connected to the Christ Consciousness, yet not so well known, can raise the consciousness of humankind by the simple grace of their presence on Earth. The concept of holy men living in caves, or deep in the jungle, or in an apartment in the East Village, affecting the mass consciousness of humanity is not far-fetched. These "saints" can and have lifted our collective awareness, even without our knowledge of their existence. We are all a part of and an expression of one unified field of Being that is this mystery we are calling *Source*—the nothing and the everything of this infinite ocean of Consciousness, doing what It does as this Moment. If the word "God" did not have so many bizarre meanings and connotations to so many people, I would use it here to refer to that ineffable presence, the eternal *Source* of Life at its core that simply cannot be known through mind nor defined by intellect.

Of course, being in the presence of enlightened souls such as Sai Baba can be a remarkable experience, as we are truly coming close to *Source*. But be reminded, the experience is only remarkable because *you are there*, that you, in your quest, have brought your awareness and your witnessing to the Moment. Take some time now, look within, and think about this. Come to see how important you are to this Creation and why raising your awareness is so essential, your witnessing so miraculous, your complete *presence* so incredible and so desirable. Open to this world of miracles by letting go of your limited ego identity, and experience your destiny as a fully aware witness. Don't limit your awareness to the self-indulgent ego and its superficial needs, fears, and insecurities. Yours can be the world of miracles Sai Baba knows.

We as Droplets, that is, as an expression of and as a part of "*That*" all carry within us the unlimited potential that is "*That*." "He (meaning you in faith and surrender) will do even greater things than these." So said Jesus and so He meant. Our choice is whether to choose the "light" of heightened awareness in a realization of who we truly are, or to choose the "dark side" and remain on the egocentric level, unconscious of "*That*" and a victim of ignorance. By choosing the light, we are attempting to remove the limits of ego and its protective layer of illusion, and are opening ourselves to all that this Moment holds as an expression of the Holy Spirit. We are then accepting it as such without the distortion of the limited experience of ego that can only demand, criticize, condemn, be fearful of, and on and on in its state of isolation. That does not necessarily mean we are choosing only to be "good" or "spiritual," whatever that means.

Droplet carl jung wisely stated that he'd rather be whole than holy. What it does mean is that we have chosen not to limit ourselves to some ego identity that stifles our growth, limits our awareness, and attempts to define our Lord. This would ultimately only comfort and secure the needs of a limited and fearful ego and further cloud our awareness of this Moment, thus keeping us imprisoned in mind, ... fearful, insecure, and isolated.

Open up and become present in that glorious state of "no mind." Look to this Moment in stillness. Let go of the fears and traumas that burden you, and surrender to Life. You will be fulfilled by your complete presence in a total acceptance of this Moment. You will come to recognize the presence of the eternal spirit within you that has given you your Life, that is, who you are and what you seek once you have let go and surrendered to this Love.

We are all special Droplets, each a unique expression of the Holy Spirit, who have been given something of a choice, the darkness, isolation, and pain that is inherent in our ignorance and detachment, or the light of "higher knowledge," the humility and grace of awareness and a life lived in Love. You *can* choose! It is your choice! Look to your actions and determine whom they serve. The more isolated and unaware of this Moment you are, the more your actions will serve only your illusion of a separate self and the needs and fears of an insecure ego in the constant chatter of mind. The more aware and connected you are to this Moment and to the Love that surrounds and permeates your being, the more your actions will serve our Lord in the peaceful, loving silence of Being.

As you become more connected to this creative and loving energy, your desire and the will of our Lord will become inseparable. All that you need and don't need will come and go from you in the perfection that is this Creation. You will come to find out that every Moment is perfect, that there is neither a grain of sand out of place nor a single instant to regret as you come to the realization that all of this is perfectly "*That.*" Here the heart is master, compassion the sign, and your peace the reward. Let go in Love and come to the incredible Mystery that is this Moment, that is your life, and surrender to It. It is right here, right Now. ...... Believe me.

Life is something that happens to you when you're making plans to do something else.

—Droplet john lennon

Lennon is credited with this insightful and delightful definition. Life experienced from an isolated egocentric identity would appear to be "something" other than that experience and is indeed how most of us view our lives. In its isolation, the ego can make plans and play in its illusions, but God is not some static concept found in books and theories. He is the dynamics of this *Moment,* the very essence and *Source* of all there is. Life and the grander picture it paints for us will prevail and will, at times, spoil our egocentric "plans," but always for the greater good, even if at the time we may suffer in it and cannot understand. We can choose to limit our awareness to the pursuits of the ego and the limited convictions of our *beliefs* and remain unconscious to the mystery of Life that surrounds us. But sooner or later the bubble will break and Life will have its way; for our sake it must. "Not my will but yours be done." So said the Christ as He surrendered to the Almighty in full recognition of His eternal essence.

Be grateful, have faith and trust in the process of Being. It is perfect. It is magnificent. Nothing can go wrong. ...... "You can't always get what you want, but you always get what you need." Make your choices well. ...... Make them from the heart.

Imagine Jesus has come to you. He stands before you as an enlightened being to whose presence you are witness. He is the love and compassion that permeates all of Life personified. He reaches out and touches you, and you are overwhelmed with a deep sense of peace, serenity, joy, and love. Try to feel this intensely. ...... Feel the power of this beautiful Being's presence. ...... Now tell me, where is the love you are feeling coming from, how is it you can sense this presence? Yes, Jesus has inspired it. He is *"That,"* and

208

holds incredible power. But the love that you are feeling is resonating from within you as your "higher self," your connection to Him. You are also "*That*"! This "higher self" is that state of being you must acknowledge you have all the potential of becoming. He could not invoke this Love, this presence, this awareness, from a door knob. Jesus has come to us as a symbol, as the personification and the perfection of our Love and our spiritual heritage—as a mirror of our potential. Through belief and faith in Him, we are acknowledging the power of the Love and the Christ Consciousness that resides within each of us. Through the act of unconditional loving, we are, in effect, taking Christ down from the cross and giving Him life in this Moment through us. The Christ you seek and the love He has for you is the essence of who you are NOW and have always been. To know this is not so much a process of somehow doing something that would bring you to that understanding, but rather it is a letting go of that which clouds your awareness of that eternal presence and separates you from your true essence and essential nature. "Don't just do something, sit there!" Seek this truth in "no mind." Come to the silence, the eternal stillness that is His presence within you. Surrender to His Love.

You may not wake up tomorrow "enlightened"; you may not wake up religious; you may not wake up in love with Jesus; but you will wake up capable of loving. I know. I've seen it in your eyes. You can choose to love or not to love. You can choose to remain ignorant to your "higher self" and remain locked into the pursuits and limits of the ego. You can choose to remain unaware of the miracle that surrounds you and remain a slave to your egocentric identity. Or you can take the risk to let go, open up, and be present. Get in touch with your love, practice your loving, be the lover, be the Love. You can choose to do the difficult inner work of recognizing and removing the "blocks" that cloud that vision of hope and renewal and become aware of your potential. Don't be misled; it can take a great deal of inner struggle that can cause discomfort and at times pain; the ego is very frightened and has gathered many defenses in that fear, and letting go can be a difficult process. However, everything you think you are or want to be will come, and it will eventually go in the transient superficiality that is the ego, but not the Love. It is the Eternal, it is this Moment, it is who and what you are, ... what God is. ...... Join Him ...... Now.

It has been said that those who are enlightened do not see what I would describe as dust particles, "floaters," that float through the eyes and your field of vision when you look toward the sky. Imagine them gone and there is a direct connection between what's in and what's out. Imagine that you have become this Moment, that the membrane has dissolved, that what you are inside is what is outside, ... that your identity has become your inner essence of an infinite, unbounded, eternal Presence, ... the Source, ... Consciousness manifest. If you can begin to imagine this, then you can begin to imagine enlightenment ...... but only *just* begin. For imagining is an aspect of the mind, and *you* are not.

Spend time outside, consider the sky and its infinite nature as often as you can; it will still the mind in awe. "Lighten up"; let the presence of the Eternal bring joy and comfort to your experience of this Moment, and enjoy your life Now. The clouds that may distract you from or block your view of the Eternal are no different from the thoughts that do the same to your open awareness and the recognition of who you truly are. Take heart, though, for even on those *rainy days* that can bring pain and sorrow or great ideas and deep inspiration, they will all be nourished and will bring joy to our hearts once the "seeds" of Love and "higher knowledge" have been planted and we come to see that all of this is *"That."* Without that "seed," though, things could get a little "soggy," and once the sky is clear, there will be nothing to grow toward the Light.

Do revel in those bright blue skies when you have them, feel and be awed by the presence of the eternal One, and come to the "Mystery" that surrounds you. You, too, are that Mystery. Remind yourself often of the miracle that is your life with the simple statement "I AM." Use that simple statement as you are taking a walk or enjoying some part of your day, or for that matter any time you remember to, and watch yourself become present and aware of the miracle of Being. As your focus shifts from all that is outside you to your body as it breathes and moves and IS, you become more and more present, and a tickle of joy will accompany the awareness of that *Something* that lies beyond the mind into that eternal timeless presence of "I AM." As your consciousness shifts from the accustomed mind-based identity to the eternal presence of the Moment that has given you your life, you will lose the anxiety and fear inherent in the illusion of mind as you feel yourself merging with the one thing that can fulfill you: ...... yourself!

I remember as a boy watching the movie *The Incredible Shrinking Man.* I was spellbound as he got smaller and smaller and then finally could no longer be seen. I spent hours imagining what had happened to him and what he must have experienced. Now *you* imagine; imagine taking your awareness to that microscopic world, then to the subatomic world, and finally to that space described in *The Dancing Wu Li Masters* by Droplet gary zukav, where matter becomes energy and seems to vibrate into existence out of nothing. Now go further, and leave even that behind to where mind has no purpose. Come to the "Mystery," the infinite, absolute void that makes all of this creation possible. ...... Then feel the timeless, vast presence and the complete perfection of Nothing! ...... Now return and project your awareness out into deep space. Leave Earth and our solar system far behind and travel beyond the farthest galaxy hundreds of billions of light years from here. Leave even that behind and come to that same "Mystery," the infinite, absolute, endless void that makes all of this creation possible. ...... Now, again feel the timeless vast, ever-present and complete perfection that is Nothing! ......

No matter if you take your awareness deep within or reach out beyond the known universe; you will ultimately end up here, where you began, where you are, in the mysterious, eternal, timeless presence that is this Moment. It is the *here and now* and is the only reality there is, the only reality there could ever be. It is who you are, and in It you will find His peace. Look to the silence that comes between the words, in the pause between your breathing in and your breathing out. Look for Him in the peace that surrounds all that is, in the mystery and magic of Being, here in the middle of Nowhere, where each of us and all that is *exists*. Come to Him, to His eternal, timeless presence that is at once His eternal compassionate Love and the great abyss that surrounds you. There could not be one without the other, and you would not *Be* without them both, this ineffable beauty, this miraculous, incomprehensible mystery that is your Life. Allow *nothing* to get in the way of that vision and you will come to know.

There was a time in our not so brilliant past when we believed thunder was the grumble of disgruntled gods and that stars were pinholes in the fabric of the sky, which allowed the light from heaven to shine through. We believed the earth was flat and that the moon was made of green cheese and that God was some supernatural being endowed with incredible creative powers, often taken to fits of anger and wrath.

Confronted by the unknown and the fear that accompanies it, our first instinct is to try to put whatever is unknown into terms with which we are familiar to ease our anxiety, and so "green cheese" became the substance of the moon and our Lord a saintly character with a long white beard. We would still believe these things and still be wallowing in the mire of our ignorance and superstition if it were not for the inquisitive mind of man and the relentless integrity of science in its quest for truth.

There is, therefore, much to thank science for, as its desire to truly *know* has brought us out of our ignorance and has opened us to a world of seemingly endless possibilities. And yet there is much to regret, for as the world became more familiar and we began the manipulation of the environment around us, we lost that fundamental Mystery of Life and became arrogant, feeling superior to nature, flaunting our "genius" and new knowledge.

The theory of evolution stood in the face of Genesis and Adam and Eve. In this inevitable process of evolution, we cast much of what was superstition and myth aside and embraced the new "religion" of science and declared, "There is no God." The ego had found its security in the intellect and in "knowing," and we lost our inno-cence in the frenzy of the modern world and matter-of-factly debunked the intellectually dishonest dictates of our faiths. And so we found ourselves having to choose between what made sense and our place in heaven. Where, one would ask, would the Soul be bet-ter served—in the power of the mind and its control over the mate-rial world, or in the intellectually dishonest dictates of our faith? The answer would be in neither, as long as the "answer" remains a concept of *mind* where only ego would be served.

The knowledge of science is a fascinating yet superficial knowl-edge based in the physical world and in a manipulation of that world. The essence of the transcendental *Source* of that world is unobtainable through intellect, and the true nature of the unseen world of spirit is left untouched by the logic, theories, beliefs, and manipulations of an inadequate mind, and, in fact, is demeaned and trivialized whenever any attempt to understand "It" intellectually is made. In spite of all we *know*, the essence of the unseen world of spirit remains an unfathomable mystery to the intellect. This most splendid reality does exist peacefully outside the confines of mind, waiting for our awareness in a knowing that transcends and is totally unlike the machinations of mind and intellect. Only an "awakened one," that is, one who has left the limited intellect behind and brought that inner core of pure awareness, an unblemished pure "knower" to this transcendental field of *Source*, can truly come to realize the glorious nature of Life and embrace Its Mystery com-pletely. You hold within you all that is necessary to realize and experience that potential. It will happen by your simple and com-plete presence, free of mind. You need and must do ...... nothing.

<hr />

"As above so below." So it has been said of the unseen world, the world of astral travel, the world of spirits, spells, and alchemy. This world of the "occult" is, no doubt, fascinating. But far too many mys-teries beckoned me to this Moment of miracles, and I see no good reason to go to the mere manipulation of yet another world whose *Source* could only be "*That*" and whose fulfillment could only be in "*That.*" Here, too, isolated egos with self-serving goals can be found and must be avoided. Here, too, suffering in ignorance of our Lord's will can be found, and lost souls know the pain of His absence. Here, too, many interesting and charismatic spirit entities abound. And for you misguided souls who would worship the "dark lord" from this plane, you are more than likely worshiping nothing more than the equivalent of a cyberspace junky getting off on screwing up your computer with a virus, only in this case the computer is you and the virus the temptations of power and/or immortality that are longed for by an isolated, needy ego!

So it is that our Lord's creative spirit knows no bounds, and I would be less than truthful if I said my own spirit didn't rise in awe and wonder at the possibilities. Can "magic" be done? What of alchemy? Can we alter destiny? What of the "Devas" and the "Elementals," those subtle spirit entities that represent, guide, and protect individual aspects of nature? Can we change form and encounter spells? It surely is interesting food for thought, but food we must be ready to digest! It is a food that can dangerously lure and nourish the ego on a plane more difficult to navigate than this one, with the prospects of power and immortality taking us even further from ourselves and our purpose here. Not to mention the incredible amount of charlatans that abound and must be avoided in this "industry" of the occult.

Truly, you will find no greater mystery in this universe than in the simple act of your breathing in and your breathing out. No entities are more graced with His spirit than those you have seen all day. No alchemy is more miraculous than an open heart filled with Love. It is here and now that you will find yourself and where your focus need be. The world of the unseen will open to you as you come closer to our Lord, and your ability to "see" becomes a natural extension of your growth—"and all else will be added unto thee." Many have foolishly entered here before they were prepared, and suffered in the premature experience of these unfamiliar, overwhelming "energies" of the world of spirit. Trust and have faith in our Lord and His wisdom, for so it is above as it is below, and what will come to you will come when needed.

Listen closely now to the wisdom and experience of Droplet st. paul.

Though I speak with the tongues of men and of angels, and have not charity, I am become as sounding brass or a tinkling cymbal. And though I have the gift of prophesy, and understand all mysteries, and all knowledge; and though I have all faith, so that I could remove mountains, and have not charity, I am nothing.

And of course by charity, St. Paul is referring to a Loving heart. This, then, is all that will matter in your life and all that you will need.

UFOs?! ...... Oh no! So where is this coming from, you ask? Well, my father was fascinated with the UFO phenomenon and his enthusiasm rubbed off on me. I believe I have read most of the books published on this subject and see a link that can be developed here. I began this book with a "vision" which gave a base from which to build and a measure with which to weigh information for its veracity. If UFOs are "real," then they must be reflective of the basic premise set forth. Let's explore!

I have always envisioned life as spirals within spirals within spirals: each individual life, spiraling from infancy to adolescence, adulthood to middle age, and finally to old age, and that process spiraling within the context of many lives spiraling within the grander evolutionary spiral that could very well be spiraling within a more complex spiritual spiral. As a race of sentient beings, it has taken us humans here on Earth about a million years to reach the point we are at now. As mentioned earlier, we as a race appear to be somewhere in our adolescence on that broader evolutionary spiral, with some knowledge, far too much power and with very little experience. Yet it is possible, as the spiral goes, for any one of us at any time to experience the full extent of this evolutionary potential through enlightenment.

This glorious "Song of Life" has been singing for billions upon billions of years, and our Lord has manifested Himself throughout the incredible expanse of this diverse universe, as this universe, for all that time. A race of beings who have evolved for, say, three millions years (a drop in the bucket, all things considered) and have perhaps reached "adulthood" on this grand evolutionary spiral would, it seems to me, have evolved beyond the illusion of a separate ego identity *toward* something much closer to the experience of Unity and in a much more intimate relationship with our shared *Source* and *Creator*. The "membrane" would be very transparent here, and their close connection to our shared *Source* of creative intelligence would be a dynamic influence on their activities. Heightened awareness and will would have been taken to the very threshold of the unseen world of spirit through this process of evolution in the relentless desire to know and return to our Lord. It is here at this juncture of spirit, matter, and will that *alchemy* is possible. It is here it would seem that anything is possible.

If, indeed, as the theory goes and as Droplet edgar cayce demonstrated, thought is faster than light, and if that intricate energetic web of life that binds all of life is maneuverable by thought and not influenced by time, then being close to *"That"* would allow for considerable mobility. It would also explain the incredible maneuverability and speed of those physically subtle vehicles of light sighted, in that they were being controlled by *thought* and free of the physics of the natural world.

And further, if indeed the eyes are the "mirror of the soul," then these evolved beings would have reflected in their eyes the close connection they would enjoy with the Eternal. The experience of those of us who have had "close encounters" report a powerfully deep and unnerving peek into the "great abyss" and a complete "undressing" of their psyche—a loss of ego—as they peer into these beings' eyes! Others have reported a profound peace in their eyes and in their presence, with a desire and ability to communicate telepathically on deeper spiritual matters. And yet, still others have had traumatic experiences marked by forced abductions and intrusive, painful "examinations" by those beings who may perhaps be somewhere on the down side of that evolutionary spiral mentioned earlier, who may not be so conscious and compassionate and who may still be limited by a narcissistic self-identity (assholes even here?!). "As above so below" would certainly seem to apply. I don't know about you, but I am fascinated and delighted with the possibilities here, and encouraged about our future as sentient beings and this gloriously creative process of evolution in which we are all engaged.

Droplet rudolf steiner writes in his book *The Spiritual Hierarchies*, "If one fails to recognize the ascending development in human evolution, one also fails to recognize the most spiritual deed that has occurred in earth evolution, the deed of Christ." And perhaps that "deed" has not been missed by our "alien" visitors, or perhaps in some cases longed for. The compassion and love of a Christ may have been passed over in their evolutionary process, one where intellect and mind dominated, creating a wound that needs to be healed, a void that needs to be filled. If so, our evolutionary process would be of great interest to our cosmic brothers and sisters, especially at this juncture.

However close these "aliens" are or how far they are from "angelhood" is enchanting food for thought. Droplet keith thompson's book *Angels and Aliens* is a fascinating look into the unlimited possibilities and potential of this evolutionary process and the "Beings" that may have evolved in it. But be assured, for whatever their experience may be and no matter where they may be in this glorious process of "Becoming," we share with them as we share with all of Life the same *Source*, the same quest and the same potential for Christ Consciousness. Enlightenment is truly a universal experience that has only One meaning, one that binds all of life to the Love of our Lord.

So does it fit? I like to think so, but unlike the rest of this book, which has come from the heart and from direct experience, this is pure speculation and conjecture. Take it or leave it as you will. In the end, extraterrestrials may be purely the magic of myth. But there is much to wonder about and much to learn. As I claim no direct contact with the "supernatural," I can only say that it has been fun to explore and to *wonder!* It was Droplet joseph campbell who insisted, "The first function of myth is to open the heart to the utter wonder of being." Certainly, the intellect and the ego have been challenged by this phenomenon, and a new and fascinating chapter in the process of self-discovery is unfolding.

The limits of language and the inadequacy of words have deeply struck me as I have tried to write this book. So much of the same *verbiage* used to explore the unseen world of the spirit and bring our awareness to the mystery that is this *Moment* must also be used to describe the UFO phenomenon making them, at least in terms of language, strange bedfellows. ...... Or are they? If we have (and we have!) let language and the use of words narrow our perception of Life by attempting to define and give meaning to the Ineffable in a convenient twenty-four-hour format, and in so doing have shut down our open awareness and limited our ability to explore life, then haven't we in a way done the same here? Perhaps this UFO phenomenon is not any more "other-worldly" than our initial encounters with chemistry, physics, and astronomy, which required a whole new language to be explored and understood, a language we have yet, in this case, to develop. Perhaps it is a world that is right here and right now in this Moment of miracles, but for now beyond our vision and understanding.

"As above so below" keeps ringing in my ears, beckoning me to open more to not so much to the world of UFOs, but to the infinite possibilities, to the mystery and to majesty of this most extraordinary *Moment*. So I would have you wonder and open to this Moment of worlds seen and unseen, and as you open to *wonder*, put no limits on the creative potential of our Lord, and keep your faith in His wisdom and believe in His love.

> *There is more in heaven and earth than dreamt of in your philosophies.*
>
> *—Droplet william shakespeare*

Did you know there are more stars in the universe than there are grains of sand on all the beaches of the world?! While I was in college, I took the opportunity to join the astronomy club. The professor who directed the club was a young, enthusiastic idealist whose love for astronomy was inspirational. At one of our meetings an extraordinary, very well done film was shown that took us on a journey from Earth out into the farthest reaches of the universe. At the end of the film, I saw genuine awe and confusion on the face of the professor. In this moment of sincere humility at what appeared to be our insignificance in all of this, having only just begun to experience the incredible expanse of this unbelievable universe, he turned to us and asked with true sincerity, "Why are we here?" At that moment, I became acutely aware that we are here to give witness, that our expanded awareness is an essential part of the joy of this creation and will fulfill It. I realized that without the witnessing, without awareness, without the recognition, Life would have no purpose and that we are His witness and His fulfillment.

We are all the jewels of this creation, the final ecstasy, the *reason*. Each of us carries within ourselves the potential of knowing and experiencing the hallowed essence and source of this entire universe. We have within us the ability to realize and give witness to the majesty and beauty that is this Creation, the glory of this Moment, and the magnificence that is our Lord and Creator. It is our destiny; it is our heritage and truly the sacred purpose that is our humanity to become His enlightened witness.

> *God revealed a sublime truth to the world when He sang, "I am made whole by your life. Each soul, each soul completes me."*
>
> *—Droplet hafiz*

We have come to know the speed of light to be 186,000 miles per second, plus or minus a little bit. If we could send a ray of light from New York to Los Angeles and back again, it would make the round trip about thirty times in one second. Because the universe is so big, the only way to begin to measure it is in terms of "light years," that is, the distance light can travel in one year. We can have a peek and marvel at how far light can travel in a second or two, but the distance is incomprehensible when considered in terms of thousands, millions, and even billions of years. Recent Humble images have discovered 100,000 galaxies, each two to three billion light years in diameter and tens of billions of light years apart, hundreds of billions of light years from Earth, all hidden behind a single galaxy a mere seven million light years from here in a universe that presents itself as endless.

If we were to take the time to contemplate this never-ending aspect of our universe and go deeply into the ever-present concept of nothing, we would discover that this "nothingness" could not be anything less than never-ending and that in the timeless presence of this "nothingness," we would be in the presence of the Eternal. We would find that nothing could exist without "nothing" and that all things must necessarily come into existence out of Nothing. Within this eternal presence of "nothing," how could there be time or space; it is, after all, NOTHING! What exists, then, can only exist Now in the eternal embrace of "nothing," Now and only Now, free of the illusions of time and space. "Nothing," then, is as much a part of our true nature as the color of our eyes and the longings of our Soul. As we come to a pure experience of Now, unfettered by mind and empty, or should I say "unattached to" any relative identity, we would come to know "That."

The subtle blending of molecular energy to create new substances, the incredible intricacy of an aphid's leg, and the immense grandeur of galaxies in collision are and can only be in the here and Now as the ever-present spirit of our Lord in His endless display of miracles. All that is can only happen here and Now as Him. As you come to this eternal presence in the endless void of this mysterious universe, you will come to know His eternal Love and the *Source* of human goodness. It is from within your unconditional embrace of this eternal void that His love will be revealed; all that is, is within you, and you contain within your Soul the eternal, limitless presence of our Lord, a Nothingness that will draw from you the only power in the universe that can fill and fulfill It, ... your unconditional Love. Come to Now! Come to His eternal presence in nothing, through nothing, and free your eternal Spirit through the power of Love.

Our Lord has always been here as the essence, the presence, and the creative spirit that is this Life. The Christ Consciousness is the eternal, ever-present "Great Spirit." As He sang the song of Life and the Earth took form, He was that form, but it could not *know* of It. When Life began, and the one-celled creatures multiplied, and Life became abundant, He, too, was those creatures, only they could not *know* It. And when the journey to "reunion"—that is to "Loving"—

that began with the volvox, the first one-celled creature on Earth to need or perhaps to want a mate to reproduce, He was those creatures and that desire, only they, too, could not *know* it. And as Life relentlessly evolved and we came to the form that is human, He was that form but we knew It not. And as we became "self-aware" and found ourselves surrounded in mystery, out of our fear and isolation, the ego was born. He, too, was the cause, but we could not know of it. And when we became the first to want and to need Love as an essential part of our lives, as the core to our existence, He was that core. He was that Love, but still we knew It not. When we were lost in the tangle of thought, self-awareness, the philosophies, religions, the beliefs, and the fear, He came to us as Jesus, the "Way," and He let us know who we were and what our destiny is. We are truly all Droplets of this great ocean of Love. The time has come for you to truly *know* that "I am That, you are That, that all of this is That," the eternal, ever-present Spirit of Life fulfilling Itself. Know that and be grateful, know *"That"* and be fulfilled as *you* create the joy of recognition. You are not alone and the world can never be abandoned. He is the spirit and the essence of all that you survey, all that you are and all that you love. Love It all, love all of His creation, love every blade of grass, every cloud, every thing, and love yourself as the wholesome witness whose sacred role will be revealed as lover of this glorious dream of Life.

He is always with us as our *Source* and our essence; we would not *Be* otherwise. We know It not, but we are getting closer—we *are* getting closer! He is the laughter of children, the song of the birds, the wag in a puppy's tail, and the flight of the eagle. He is the beauty of the lily, the fragrance of the lilac, the humming of the bees. He is the warmth of the sun, the changing of the seasons, the sparkle in your lover's eye. He is the silence of the forest, the scent of the skunk, the patience of the saint. He is the swarming of the maggots, the thunder and the storm, the colors of the rainbow. He is the dawn, He is the sunset, He is the almighty expanse of this incredible universe, all that you desire and all that you fear. He is the beating of your heart, the consciousness and sacred Love that we share. He is *all* things always. In the isolation that is the ego we can only suffer and be destroyed outside of that vision. Our loving is the impetus and the way to return to Him. Becoming *aware* of and enjoying the Love that surrounds and permeates us, *realizing* and reuniting with our Lord as the mystery and miracle that is Life, is truly why we are here. We serve no other purpose than to bring our heightened awareness and our joy to this Moment. It is truly our destiny to know what He knew, to see what He saw and most of all, to feel what He felt in this Moment, as this Moment. ...... It all begins with you. "Seek and ye shall find; knock and the door will be opened to you." Still your mind. Take your awareness beyond the limited needs of the ego and open yourself to the mystery and wonder that is this Life, that is *your* Life, Now.

In the final analysis, it is you for whom you are looking, and only you who stand in the way. Within you lies the essence of all of Life as yourself, shrouded by a veil of egocentric identity in the illusion of time. Your relative identity—that is, who you perceive yourself to be—taken from all the experiences you have lived in this body, is merely an expression of who you truly are and will limit you in time, and you will suffer the inevitable loss of that transient identity should you go no further. Like those in Plato's cave, you are holding on to shadows. Your relative identity is of little significance in your quest for truth and can become a difficult barrier to undo if you have crystallized your sense of self in it. Whether you perceive yourself as a doctor, an entertainer, or handicapped, whether you have become identified as a housewife, a construction worker, or a patriot, whatever identity your mind would hold you to, know that your eternal nature stands outside the limited perception you would have of yourself and the illusion of time inherent in mind. You are swimming in an eternal ocean of Love isolated by a membrane that has become the "who" you believe yourself to be. As you quiet your mind and come to what mind can only perceive as "Nothing," your focus will shift from the transient nature of mind and you will allow the Love of this eternal presence to rise within you, as you, and is where your conscious connection to "That" is found. The Droplet has returned to the "Ocean" and now realizes itself as "That." You have lost nothing but your ignorance.

Your love is your connection to "That" and to all of Life expressed in "That." You can and will begin to bring this unconditional Love and forgiveness into this world with forgiveness and love for yourself. All of your sins were done out of fear and in ignorance of your "higher self"; know this and forgive. Bring kindness, compassion, and a forgiving heart to this Moment for yourself and all you behold as you too are the perfect expression of this "Great Spirit" as it is in this Moment. Not in the egoistic arrogance of "I'm perfect," for indeed it is "the meek that shall inherit the earth." Rather, take that journey within and find the grace of humility and the sanctity of gratitude for this miracle you hold and for the divine eternal intelligence that has created it. Practice dropping the transient needs of the lower self and the superficial ego identity. Look to avoid anything that would keep you in isolation. Simplify and let go! For in simplicity, in those quiet moments away from the chatter and the relative never-ending needs of the mind/ego, you can begin to know who you are and that you embody all there is to know. Become prayerful and grateful for this miracle that you hold. Know that you need look for no greater miracle than your breathing in and your breathing out. This Moment holds all that you need for complete happiness in the simplicity of total awareness, in the peace of complete silence, and in your total surrender into *"That,"* to the *Mystery*, to *Life*.

Practice meditation and prayer and so bring awareness and mindfulness to your actions. Take the "journey" and explore your pain; it will lead you to the Eternal. You can only suffer in ignorance of your true nature; it is the impetus to let it go. In His presence you can suffer no longer. Find your forgiveness and come to the peace of this Eternal Presence. You will begin to find your actions and desires supported by this Moment, in this Moment, as you come in "tune." Practice coming to this Moment completely present, with what has been referred to here as "no mind." Watch as your mind can't help but open the library of accumulated knowledge and define what it "thinks" is going on. Be prepared for the natural tendency of the mind to look to the future and bring anxiety, fear, and even hope to your experience. Both past and future are not real, they do not exist, nor can they exist in this; the only reality that exists ...... the Now Moment.

Pay attention as to how you react to situations, to what is going on inside you as things come up. It is far more important to see how you react to situations than the situation itself. Only this very Moment truly exists, and anything that would keep you from it must be acknowledged. As a witness to the machinations of mind, you will fall easily into a space that sees them for what they are, and you will become aware of the silent, ineffable, eternal presence that peacefully surrounds and permeates all of Being.

Know that you are loved and are Love. Be playful, be happy, and bring a joyful mind to this miracle that is your Life. Be open to the Mystery and Wonder that surrounds and permeates every aspect of It and be with that Eternal Presence. It is here and now, waiting, in the joy, in the play, in the eternal nothingness that surrounds you and in His everlasting Love. You are not alone when you are loving; you cannot know loneliness when you are present; you cannot suffer in the light of this eternal Love.

And people would ride from far and wide just to seek the words he spread. I'll tell you everything I've learned, and Love was all he said.

—*From* Boy with the Moon and Stars on His Head,
by Droplet cat stevens

Chapter XV
A NEW CONSCIOUSNESS, A NEW WORLD

You are here to allow the divine purpose of the universe to unfold. That is how important you are.

—Droplet ekhart tolle

The mystic, philosopher, and yogi Sri Aurobindo became aware of a powerful spiritual, cosmic energy that was infusing itself into the earth in the early part of 1967, and proclaimed it the beginning of a new age. I remember the date well, as it corresponded with my Kundalini awakening and I attributed it to this infusion. Certainly, I was not the only one affected by this energy. The '60s and '70s were marked with an enormous amount of spiritual activity. Ramdas had declared "Be Here Now," and his words were echoed in the works of Krishna Murti, Alan Watts, Gopi Krishna, Satchitananda, and many other self-proclaimed gurus. There was no doubt that something was going on and that many would be influenced by its presence. The relentless evolutionary process had begun to take us out of the illusion of egocentric identity, into a realization of our true nature. We began looking within, with a recognition that there was a deeper meaning to life that went well beyond the limits of the five senses—and none too soon, for the needless and senseless destruction of human life and the wanton destruction of our environment that chronicles our history could soon be outdone with the irresponsible use of technology in the hands of lunatics and madmen.

Change and growth are threatening to the ego and to the beliefs and structures it has created to preserve itself. With this movement toward higher consciousness, there was a simultaneous surge in the ranting of "right wing" religious zealots who declared the devil was at work here and condemned eastern mystics, yoga, and meditation as evil. It seems the nature of growth in awareness has to necessarily be challenged by a corresponding demand to remain ignorant in the confines and security of "beliefs."

It is fear and ignorance that have created the violence and ego-maniacal monsters that have laced the history of humanity, too often supported by hoards of equally frightened and insecure Droplets. Yet, what is happening now is truly outside the confines of mind and belief. Our Lord and His presence cannot be denied, and so it seems that indeed a new age has dawned. We are evolving into a new consciousness or perhaps it can be better said as "moving into the next phase of perceiving consciousness." We are beginning to experience life from the perspective of Soul, outside the limitations of ego and mind, into the freedom and fulfillment of "Being."

This "new consciousness" is manifesting a sacred yet ancient wisdom that emanates from deep within the silence of Being. It has brought with it a realization that ego/mind are not where the answers to life can be found; rather *they* are now the source of "evil" that has enslaved our spirit in the illusion of separation, in the endless banter of yesterday's memories and in the pitiful hope of tomorrow. A true awareness of the Now moment has been lost to the mind's fixation on the illusion of our egocentric identity and in the thought patterns that would falsely define who we are. This process of securing the ego would soon destroy this planet if allowed to continue in the madness, ignorance, and greed that is inherent in that identity, unconscious of *Source* and oblivious to the sanctity of this Moment. That almighty presence is here and is Now in all we perceive and have been blessed with. We are beginning to know *"That"* in the here and Now as more and more are becoming Present to the beauty, peace, and fulfillment of this Moment, as we are awakening from the dream of life and the illusion of mind.

We are, I believe, mercifully, although it would appear painfully, evolving beyond the influence of ego and the enslavement of mind, and finding our identity in the Now, this sacred eternal Moment that holds all and is the *Source* of all. We appear to be going through the pain of a "birth" that is heralding a new consciousness and perception of Life. We are learning to let go of the fears and insecurities of mind as we come to the great abyss. The "Nothing" that has always been a threat to our sense of self in a death that only ego can experience is now offering fulfillment in "*That*" and an awareness of our eternal nature. There have been many Droplets who have called to us before with this sacred wisdom, many earlier "blossoms" of consciousness that have awakened to our true nature; however, we are now in great peril and that "call" has become louder, more frequent, more intense, and clearer as our suffering and the danger of our demise has increased.

A most powerful example of this awakened call has come through the gentle yet complete presence of a most extraordinary Droplet, eckhart tolle. He has quickly become an inspirational spiritual guide whose depth of wisdom and clarity of thought on the nature of man and the spiritual significance of life has not been equaled perhaps since Christ, and yet he remains humbled and awed by this eternal presence with which he is now at peace. His awakening came to him suddenly after many years of suffering and mental torment. His awakening and his teachings are proving to contain a timely yet timeless and powerful spiritual message that has captured the hearts of many followers. If you have not yet read *The Power of Now*, I would certainly recommend it as your next book. Eckhart's awakening has brought with it a depth and fluidity of thought that is inspirational, and he offers to all who might become present more insightful techniques for being here Now, and many more good reasons why we must.

We could continue on this unholy course, locked into the past and anxious about our future, sacrificing the sanctity and fulfillment of this Moment of Miracles as we become further lost and entangled in the madness of mind. Or we can begin to realize how little mind truly knows and how limited the intellect is at finding out and, one drop at a time, abandon this seemingly unstoppable freight train of ignorance and greed that is hell-bent on our destruction in the endless desires of ego to have more and be more. We can and will begin to become more present in the silent stillness of Now and in touch with a wisdom far more powerful and fulfilling than mind and intellect can offer as we leave the madness behind and enter again the sacred grounds of Eden.

Tell me, now, can you truly give any direct insight, outside the banter of religion, as to how or why you are here? Have you experienced the great Mystery that is this universe and the miracle of creation? Do you know your face before you were conceived, and do you know what will happen to you once you have died? How is it that your eyes can see, you ears can hear, your heart is beating? Where does the eternal aspect of the sky come from? Can you answer any of the questions that concern the true nature of reality and the mystery of Life, or have you become content to remain in the fog of your illusions, pretending in a Life that has been "made up" in mind and played out in the false relative identity of ego? Now the time has come for you to choose. Do you want to know who you are, or are you content to remain ignorant, playing the suffering game? You will lose nothing but the illusion of Life as you come to Nothing and allow your awareness to be free of the endless banter of mind, and open to the Miracle of Life. To achieve this, you need to do absolutely nothing. There is nothing you need to add to your experience. Adopt no religion, wear no special clothing, and practice no belief. Let go of all that binds you to mind and ego and simply Be.

This is the dawning of a "new consciousness," free from the enslavement and illusions of mind. What once imprisoned us has become the vehicle that has brought us to the threshold of a deeper understanding of ourselves and must now be gratefully taken down from its role as lord and placed in its proper role as servant. All that would keep us from this Moment and from the power and grace of this new consciousness must and will be understood—all that would bring us to Now recognized and practiced in a reverence for Life. Yours is an incredible opportunity to have our shared consciousness and the potential for a deep sense of presence become the guiding force in your life. It would be through the practice of coming to Now, described in numerous ways throughout this book, that you will come to the glorious experience that is found in the presence of our Lord. Take your place in this new age of awareness, one that would end the suffering of humanity, one where human beings will no longer be blinded by the illusions of mind and the painful "story" of their lives with the violence and destruction inherent in ignorance and fear, one that is completely present to the miracle of Life in a profound union and total acceptance of Now, free from fear and unshaken by events. Not even the prospect of the total destruction of this glorious planet could disturb the peace of this presence.

Let go of your isolated identity that can only see you struggling to survive and in competition with life. That which has given you life is what is all around you as Life. Relieve yourself of the need and desire to have and to be more than you are right now. Stop and accept what is yours Now and end further desire. Truly, nothing more need be added and you can finally relax. It is all so simple. In that freedom, come to this Moment of miracles and become It, and in that presence you will know you have and have always had all there is to live and all you need to love.

As you release yourself from the restrictions of mind and open to the eternal presence that surrounds you in an awareness of our Lord as the *Source* and essence of this very Moment, you will know that you and your expanded awareness were the reason for this creation and that the blossoming of your love was the sacred purpose for your existence. You will truly be here Now in touch with the only reality that is ...... free! No need to leave family and friends behind. No reason to quit your job or leave the comforts of home. No need to find a silly droplet-shaped hat to wear or brandish a droplet pendant around your neck in support of your "belief." You are now living the eternal truth of your being and you will shine with that eternal presence. Cherish all the gifts of Life, but let yourself be free from identification with those gifts. Nothing will be lost but the chaos of mind and the illusion of a separate ego as you come to realize nothing can belong to you, for you are already It. You will blossom into your eternal nature, at peace with Life and in Love.

Face your death Now and let go of all that would perish in it. What will be left is the wholesome purity of a Soul in union with our Lord, a soul that is free, a soul In Love, our Lord fulfilled!

CONCLUSION

Knowledge is happiness, because to have knowledge—broad deep knowledge—is to know true ends from false, and lofty things from low. To know the thoughts and deeds that have marked man's progress is to feel the great heart-throbs of humanity through the centuries; and if one does not feel in these pulsations a heavenward striving, one must indeed be deaf to the harmonies of Life.

—Droplet helen keller

I am not a scholar, nor do I hold any degrees. What came to me was from an altogether different school. I am not a guru, nor do I want to be. I have come to know the perfection that is this Moment and know there is nothing here that I need to "fix." I do not consider myself a "holy man." I am kept busy in my roles as husband, father, and contractor, and although I would like to think I am becoming a whole man, I don't know what "holy" is except in what I sense as Jesus and my "higher self." I sometimes quarrel with my wife, yell at my kids, argue with my subcontractors, and still appear to struggle with egocentric issues. I can witness as mind creeps in and becomes the critical and doubtful nerd that would remove me from this Moment. I can watch as I become judgmental and the isolation of ego takes over. But it quickly disappears like a ghost that haunts but has no substance, for my constant companion is the silent stillness of Being and the peace of our Lord in all that is as this Moment.

I have seen the perfection of this Creation and have known the peace of His eternal presence. I have come to *feel* how incredibly important and integral the role that Love and Compassion play in the fulfillment of our Lord as they manifest in our hearts, in this Moment. It is clear that we all hold the key and are the instruments of that fulfillment, and that our destiny and our purpose is to come to that awareness. We are all Droplets of this great ocean of Love, endowed by our Creator with all that we need for complete happiness. I am compelled to let you know that. Do with it what you will.

Yes, every moment is perfect, and yes, there is not a grain of sand out of place, and yes, we Droplets have all we need in this Moment to realize *"That"* as compassionate and loving mirrors of our *Source* and *Creator,* however, for this to happen, we must make some effort. It is with these magnificent and mysterious gifts of free will, self-awareness, and intellect which are at once the source of our suffering and the vehicles to the ecstasy and to the rapture of knowing who we are—to knowing *"That"*—that we will come to *Source* and will know and live His Love. Use them mindfully from the heart and you will use them perfectly. Be very clear in your understanding that nothing *more* need be added to your experience in order for fulfillment to happen. You are not "missing" anything. Simply clean the "mirror" and be Still. ...... You will come to know who you are and why you are here as you and Life simultaneously explode in the overwhelming joy of recognition.

There was a time when it was very difficult for me to be in this world and to function, a time when the "Kundalini" energy had brought me "close to the fire," and although it was a time of enormous insight, you gotta eat! So I learned to play the game again, and believe me, it is a game. In the "game," one renders unto Caesar that which is Caesar's and renders unto God that which is God's. Of course, it turns out that this is a completely relative assignment, for in the final analysis, *everything* is of God and only the ego structure can make any other distinction. Beneath this distinction, though, there is despair, for the ego unconsciously knows of its deception and of the terrible game it is playing, a game it can never win. But the illusion is strong, this world of ego very demanding and unforgiving, and in it one does have to eat and protect oneself and those for whom we are responsible. Although the Eternal is all that there is, as is our experience of It, the play of life goes on with all the drama, tragedy, love, sorrow, and laughter that is Life. It is a glorious and wondrous experience, no matter how the cards may have been dealt. If you have trouble with that, then imagine It simply never happened and all that is your life and all that you have learned from it never was! Who said you *had* to happen or any of this had to be?!

Your life is purposeful, and your desires meaningful, for in your searching and in your suffering, your quest will eventually find true meaning in your relationship with our Lord. With this in mind, you cannot serve two masters, and your relationship with our Lord will be the only relationship that truly matters. Our Lord is in all that you experience as that experience; when you suffer, He suffers; when you laugh, He laughs; when you cause suffering, He again suffers; and when you bring His Love to life, He is fulfilled. Recognition of that is happiness, ignorance of that is suffering, and the road to find "*That*" out is your Life. ...... Enjoy the journey, be in this Moment, and come to love your life!

In my line of work, one comes up against some very strong egos, Droplets that have become rigid and shut down, whose fears are great, whose faith is weak, and who are driven by the illusion that money and power will secure them. Here again, their quest is no different than mine, only the path that they have chosen is. So clear, too, are the traumas of childhood that have wounded and isolated these souls and have hidden them far from themselves, hardened their hearts, and left them strangers to the softness of love. I have seen the "wounded child within" on the faces of so many and have felt the pain and fear of their isolation so clearly seen in their eyes. They have lost in themselves the wonder and mystery that is this Life and limited themselves to manipulation, control, and acquisition too often marked with violence and perversion as distraction and means. I pity them for the price they have paid and for the soul that suffers their ignorance.

I have been around long enough to witness many of us who have retired and the accompanying utter bewilderment as to "what to do now." For many, there is not much to look forward to, as the next "big event" in their lives is dying. They may live vicariously through their children or in the nostalgia of past accomplishments and find themselves "hanging out" uselessly, waiting. They have lived lives in the isolation of egocentric pursuits and now find themselves strangers to this Moment, without direction, outside the arena of ego and desire, waiting and afraid to die. In many there is a vague belief in some kind of afterlife, and they may even come to religion; however, this is more out of fear and as a comfort for the ego than in a quest for understanding the journey they have made or in gratitude for the privilege of having been allowed to make it. For most, the ego identity is being lost, the body is failing, and many become bitter and resentful in the glory and potential that is *still* this Moment. There is one very significant piece of information I did take from Droplet yogi berra, and that is, "it ain't over till it's over." *This* Moment is loaded with the same prospect of enlightenment and the healing power of His Love, regardless of your age or physical condition. Never give up your faith or your quest; it is never too late! He is with you now as He has always been with you; you would not *be* here otherwise. Open your heart to His presence in this Moment of Being. Loving is always possible, always there. Let go, become present, and be happy. ...... Why not?!

My ego structure is not as demanding as most, and I have had my difficulties being as aggressive as I sometimes need to be, although I must say "going with the flow" has served me well. I have learned how essential a sense of humor is and how important it can be at times to have a good laugh at ourselves and to never take ourselves too seriously. This foolish world has taken the illusion of itself far too seriously and has created untold suffering in the terror that is the ego. Let it go; there is so much more awaiting you.

Laughter does not come from the logical and knowing mind; it comes out of the breaking of patterns and the introduction of the illogical and unexpected. Every "punch line" I've ever heard was funny because it wasn't what was logical or expected. It is good and essential for the mind to find joy in the jubilant breaking of patterns and the laughter that arises from it. For that brief instant, the mind is set aside and the cheerful gaiety of Life revealed. It is so good for the soul to know laughter. It has been said that the experience of "enlightenment" begins in resounding, uproarious laughter. Why not start practicing?!

> But I [Jesus] laughed joyfully when I examined his empty glory.

>   —From The Second Treatise of the Great Seth

I have learned that some are ready to hear what's been said and some are simply not, and that the illusion and delusions of the ego are just too powerful, and, as a result, I have learned to watch out for "assholes," that is, ignorance personified. Theirs is a world locked into an ego identity that has them as the center of the universe, a very limited, needy, and selfish universe. I do what I can as an example and I don't run from the challenges they present. God's work comes in many faces, and there is always something to learn and the need for love; so be it. I do, however, "tie my camel" when necessary, as should you.

Watch for and be cautious of ego structures that seem full of themselves and present an image that cries out for attention. They have lost sight of the God Head within them in a relative identity that is capable of enormous evil and the infliction of untold pain and suffering as it seeks to secure itself.

I know how much "faith" plays a role in our quest for peace and reassurance. Here again, the mind must be left behind, as faith is believing *without* knowing. Once we have taken the mind to its limit and come to the Mystery that surrounds us, we can only be left humbled. Until we experience the loving presence of our Lord, we can only look within at our *desire* for that Love and live a life that reflects the faith and trust in the power of that Love to fulfill us. You know and I know there is nothing else that will. Have Faith,

He will come. ...... Have Faith, He is here! ...... Have Faith and let go of your fear and all that you are holding on to for protection. Go within and drop through the emotional layers that bind you to ego identity and come to that Holy, eternal Presence that is your Life. Believe and have faith in the power of Love and forgiveness.

I have learned to learn from every experience I encounter, no matter how trivial, for how I react to each experience is an indication of the strength of my false ego identity or of how close or how far I am from the Eternal. I have learned to look into myself, trying not to take my own relative self-image too seriously, to be thankful and to BE who I am on this Earth as an expression of the Holy Spirit. That is not always "good," and I make plenty of "mistakes," but it always is, and I do try to "do the right thing." I know that I am "perfectly becoming" and can forgive myself if I'm not quite there, making forgiveness of others easier and genuine. I make a sincere effort to try to love something new every day. It is so easy to do now. Do the same, whether it is a flower, a sunset, or your neighbor. Be grateful and bring your love to this Moment and find your peace in It. Learn to be joyful for the miracles of Life and to forgive. Let go of the false identity of ego that only holds you in suffering and must one day surely pass. What have you got to lose?!

I know how important spending time alone is and the absolute necessity of getting away. In those quiet moments, as I feel myself seeing, hearing, and breathing—every time I blink, or sneeze, or take a shit, when I realize that my hair is growing, my heart is beating, and that I am dying—I know that He is with me and that my life is not an act of my will but rather exists by His grace alone. He is the life within me, He is the consciousness and the source of my Being. He is my love of Life.

"Repent, for the kingdom of heaven is near" (Matthew 3:2). Indeed, it is in your hands and you need only repent—that is, grieve for and regret the ego structure that is in the way of your loving. Remove the influence of your isolation and the Kingdom will rise within you. It will require your complete attention, your deepest faith, and your total openness to this Moment, to being here Now. Just the paying of "lip service" to a spiritual life or performing ritualized, habitual ceremony at predetermined times and places may satisfy the ego but will not take you very deeply into the experience of this Moment, into yourself and into the ever-present "Mystery." Get away and spend time with yourself, with nature, in meditation and prayer. It is essential!

> To me every hour of the light and dark is a miracle,
> Every cubic inch of space is a miracle,
> Every square yard of the surface of the earth is spread
> with the same.
> Every foot of the interior swarms with the same.
> To me the sea is a continual miracle,
> The fishes that swim, the rocks, the motion of the
> waves, the ships with men in them.
> What stranger miracles are there?
>
> —Droplet walt whitman

As the "baby boomer" generation, we have shaped much of the energies that influence this world. Now that energy needs to be put into a graceful surrender to the Eternal One. Through the practice of introspection, guided inner journeys, meditation and prayer, and with our newfound desire to bring all the love and compassion so needed at this time into this world, we would conclude this journey in faith, with the love and compassion that will bring you to our Lord. Putting aside the ego structure that is becoming desperate and insulted by the aging process will be much easier now. Let go of the superficial identity of the ego and let the body age gracefully, and you will gain a strength of presence you never had before—not one of egocentricity but rather one of Being and acceptance.

The need for cosmetic surgery, hair dyes, and young lovers are the last gasp of the ego's shroud of illusion and can only keep you in your isolation. Don't allow yourself to become bitter and resentful; that, too, will only deepen your isolation. This is not the time to boost the ego, and you will be missing an important and powerful opportunity to surrender the illusion. It doesn't mean "giving up." It means "opening up" to something much, much more. Continue to enjoy this gift of Life, which by now can only have been made richer through your experiences. As an "elder" you have much wisdom to offer. Stay fit, continue to explore, but put your emphasis on your surrender to the Eternal in the Now. Be grateful for this gift of life, in awe and wonder to all that is still around you and to the Love. Everything you have lived for has brought you to this Moment; don't miss It!

<hr />

Strangely, as much as the mind/ego is in the way, it is nevertheless the vehicle to our salvation, for without one that has grown either in faith or in the acquisition of "higher knowledge," the Miracle would be missed. Without that core of intelligence, that deeper "knowing," and the purification of the "knower" in the total presence of Now, the final *Realization* could not be attained as the witness would be unavailable. The "knower," obscured within a shroud of illusion, would have no vision of the sacred "Mystery" and our Lord would be left unrealized and unfulfilled. This awesome mystery, this incredible contradiction that is this magnificent gift of intelligence, and the coming to *know* that we all have been blessed with is nothing short of ...... mind boggling! It is at the core of our Faith, the means to our surrender and the tool we will use to demolish the temple of egocentric isolation and open our awareness to the Divine presence that lays outside the walls of ignorance.

Truly though, I've come to witness the nature of the illusion that is the "membrane" (mind/ego) and how powerful that illusion is and how desperately lost this world is in it. The exhibition of the fear, violence, perversion, and destruction that is so prevalent in our time is nothing more than our having lost—perhaps not having found yet is more accurate—our connection with the reality of this Moment and the divinity that surrounds and permeates It. I don't pretend to know God's plan, but I see much suffering and pain ahead as we are beginning to evolve beyond our identity in ego. This ego of ours is the necessary "bud" in that process of becoming, and we are beginning to open and flower into the "golden blossom" that is this new consciousness. Attachment to the "bud"—the vehicle of ego—is very strong, but if you don't begin to let go of that false identity, it will make your experience of Life seem hopeless and lost in the inevitable destruction it must go through for this unfolding to happen. But like the inherent nature of water to "seek its own level," we Droplets of this great ocean of Love have within us our own inherent nature to seek "*That*" which we are and return again, this time fully conscious, to the Love that is our *Source* and Creator and the final "who we are." No matter what may seem to be going on, no matter how difficult it may be to let go and become aware, we are in that process. Have faith, open your heart to His love within you and allow yourself to blossom. ...... Know that every moment is perfect and that we are all perfectly becoming. There is no reason to fear when you have nothing to lose.

It is clear, too, that only through a direct transcendental experi-ence—that is, taking the mind's processes of analysis, reflection, and logic to their limits and then leaving them behind in a deeper, unfet-tered awareness of Now—can we come to know the majesty of this *Moment* and to the experience that we are not separate from *It*. In our letting go of ego, the mind, and the subsequent illusion of time, we allow ourselves to become present as we open ourselves to an awareness from that level of "Soul." Here, outside the influence and illusion of mind, in a state of pure consciousness, we will come to know directly that we are all Droplets of this same Ocean of Love and that all of this Moment is God's work in progress, and in It our differences should only be cherished as His creative spirit. But don't take my *word* for it; this is not the only time it's been said. I have included quotes from just a few who have come to know. For cen-turies the ineffable has come to many other Droplets through this transcendental experience, and although the words may differ some, the experience is universal. That experience reflects the complete and unconditional Love of our Creator. It brings with it the realization that we exist, that our eyes see, our ears hear, and our hearts beat because of the "God Head" that is at the core of our existence and brings us Life. We will come to *That* by becoming *Present*, that is, becoming acutely aware of our presence in this Moment, aware of that miracle within us that gives us our life, aware of awareness without the influence of mind, in a state of mind that has become still and has fallen into the silence of the Eternal. It is here where we will come to know the Soul and our connection to God. It is here where we will come to the "cause" and in whose recognition we will find the ultimate purpose for our lives. This Moment is *"That"* and we and all we experience are also *"That."* The *One* and the *Only*. In faith, be assured that you are loved and being cared for, that you can and need to bring your loving into your experience of this Moment. It is your connection to *"That"* and to His eternal Presence. Your practice will make you perfect. Come home, you are needed! There is nothing to lose and *Everything* to gain.

⁂

I have used the words *"That,"* *Source*, Christ, God, Soul, Great Spirit, the Buddha, It, Toa, Him, this Moment, and so on to refer to the Ineffable. Droplet ralph waldo emerson used "the Oversoul"; you use whatever *word* does it for you. Our Lord won't mind what word you use, revere, and cherish to keep the Mystery alive and bring you to Him. But KEEP THE MYSTERY ALIVE!!! It is all around you, who you are and all that there is in this very Moment! Be very clear that the "words" don't have much to do with what is going on here and can certainly get in the way of your ultimate knowing. I can and have used the words "magnificent, majestic, mysterious, Holy, sacred, ineffable, miraculous" and on and on, but they *mean* absolutely nothing without the experience. Do not make *anything* familiar with words. "Knowing" something or someone is ultimately and truly impossible with words alone and can only remove the mystery and wonder from your experience. That doesn't mean you should remain ignorant and not bring some understanding to your experience, as it is with the mind's exploration and in the knowledge gained in that exploration that you will eventually come to the Mystery, provided you go far enough. But try to remember and behold the magic it was to be a child or when you met your beloved for the first time. Eventually, in the pursuit of truth you will come to that same experience of awe and wonder. In the interim, take caution, for letting the mind/ego come into and define experience can create a stagnant atmosphere that severely limits the depth of the experience, the richness of that experience and eventually creates the *boredom* known only to the ego in this Moment of pure mystery and wonder. Too much "knowing" can make for a very unhappy Droplet by breaking your connection to the mystical cosmic energy that lies beyond mind. Not in and by the process of finding out—that *is* the joy of life—but rather in the illusion of believing you now "know." It is *all* mystery, after all, found only in an ineffable transcendental experience of unity of which the mind and ego are simply not capable and to which they are in fact a barrier.

It is essential that as you live each day you acknowledge the importance of living a spiritual life and in a way *unlearn* what you think you *know* and keep your experience of this Moment open to its Mystery; that you let go of the "shadows" and go beyond the world of ego and form into the unseen world of spirit and grace that is our heritage, our *Source*, and our fulfillment. Through your meditation, in your unrelenting focus on the underlying Spirit of Now and by the power of your prayer, "let life abound in glory, let the song of life be sung, let Heaven find its place on earth, let God's will be done."

However mean your life is, meet it and live it; do not shun it and call it hard names. It is not so bad as you are. It looks poorest when you are richest. The fault-finder will find faults even in paradise. Love your life.

—Droplet henry thoreau

Should your experience of Life overwhelm you with fear and panic, or if what you are experiencing is too painful and your sorrow too deep, then it is the time to go deeply into your pain and into your fear; do not try to escape them, for they have much to teach you. Accept them as gifts from our Lord for your awakening.

Let go of all effort, resist nothing, embrace, and go deeply into them and to their source. In your total surrender you will come through your pain and your fear to an awareness of the Eternal within you ...... to the immense silent stillness, ... to our Lord and His Love. Let go and be reminded that all of your fear originates from your isolated and ignorant ego's fear of dying. Know that you are not your body, you are not your mind, that they are the gifts, the instruments to your enlightenment and to the realization of your eternal essence, and that you are that essence outside the illusion of ego and the banter of mind.

"Blessed are those who suffer for theirs is the Kingdom of Heaven." Your suffering is your guide, and I have come to know that those who suffer the most are those who are the closest to Him. Those who are the most fearful and anxious have already seen It and have contracted their awareness in that fear and anxiety. Ego by its very nature is weak; that is why we try so hard to protect it. But if it is weakened further by trauma or circumstance and it is allowed to come to the "abyss," now aware of something more, something terribly more than what it perceived itself to be, it will contract and desperately cling to mind. And so, to protect, some become fanatical in their beliefs, compulsive in their behavior, or seek escape in substance abuse or in a "savior" outside themselves. You have come to the "Fire," and now would be the time to let go of what is so clearly in your way, go deeply into your fear, and become aware of the eternal within you and allow the peace of that presence to radiate from your soul. Your lower self has felt and been terrified by the Eternal. It is within you, as your essence, your higher self, or you could never have come to know it. You cannot escape what you are. Let go of the fear that binds you to ego and you will be filled with the Love of this eternal presence.

Know that It has always been here waiting. Should you accept and acknowledge your limitations and have faith in your potential, it awaits peacefully in your surrender, yet you will lose nothing but your isolation, nothing but your fear and ignorance, nothing but your desire to be anything more than you are right Now! Take the time to explore your pain and in your solitude find its source. ...... You will come to Him as you let go of what you fear and embrace

It. The power of His Love will heal you and the darkness of fear cannot stand in Its light. The alternative can only leave you isolated and desperate, in the hell of your fear, in pain and in the sorrow of your isolation that is a life without Love, a life without faith, a life without our Lord. We so desperately cling to form and the limited, painful identity of ego for no other reason than our ignorant fear of whom we truly are an expression of.

❧

I was blessed with a glimpse of what Is, and I know of what I speak. I apologize if I have done too much "preaching," but I needed to try to put what I was feeling into words for you and for me, not as an answer, but as inspiration. Take the inspiration and let the words go. There is no final "way" for everyone; our Lord is far too creative for that. You must know that you already know the truth, that you already have the answer. Nothing that's been said would have meaning to you otherwise. I have said nothing you do not already know. I have only been a reminder. This is your journey and only you can make it ...... with a little help from your friends. Listen and know, for "no meaning that comes from outside us is real. The Buddahood of each of us has already been obtained. We need only recognize it. Thus the Zen master warns his disciple, 'If you meet the Buddha on the road, kill him.'" (This good advice is from the book of the same name by Droplet sheldon kropp.) This is your journey, no one else's. Let no one or nothing come between you and our Lord as this Moment. Find this sacred wisdom within yourself. It will come to you as it has come to all who have become present, in the silent, peaceful state of "no mind." Simply practice being here Now in the stillness of Being and surrender to It. Open yourself to our Lord as this eternal presence, the who you are, and be free.

❧

As a boy, my love for Jesus was intense but even that was removed during the Kundalini event. In time, though, Christ slowly rose again in my heart, only this time with far more meaning and so much more to give. He waits for you here in this Moment as well, not in idols or images or in books or ideas but in the Love, in the

Eternal, in the Mystery that is the Life, which you hold and embody as the essence of this miraculous Moment that is "*That*." The Christ in history who walked among us in flesh and blood was "*That*" in full awareness of God as Himself. "*That*" is the eternal, ever-present Spirit of our Lord and Creator who lives here and is now in all that is, beyond the illusion of time and space. "Split a piece of wood, and I am there. Lift a stone, and you will find me there." So said the Christ as He brought His presence to us in all that is as what is, in this the only reality that is ...... the Now Moment. Christ was never born nor shall He ever die, for He is the eternal ever-present spirit of the God Head within us. At Christmas, celebrate His eternal presence now born within your awareness as yourself. It is His gift to the world, and through It you will find your fulfillment. At Easter, celebrate what He has shown can never die within you, and become aware of the ignorance that would shroud you in a veil of illusion and isolate you from His presence.

⁂

I know this book is not complete as surely as I know I am not complete, as every time I felt it was finished, something more came to me and surely something more will come. But it is essentially complete and it has been my joy. Truly I know that trying to put *It* into words is impossible and in a most profound way a betrayal to the experience. Please remember that. Thank you for taking this journey with me. I sincerely hope that with this your pain will be eased, that you have found some peace in a difficult world, that you have been inspired to go within and to become present, that your perception of Life has been enriched and that your faith in our Lord and Creator has been deepened, if only for a ...... *Moment!*

Hail to the divinity within you!

THE WORD

I believe in the importance of ceremony and in the giving of thanks, especially as it concerns spiritual matters. Below I have listed four sets of sounds/mantras that have been handed down from a long line of saints, dating back to before recorded history. I cannot begin to name them; however, I can experience their presence and the eternal consciousness we share in the Mystery and beauty of this eternal Moment. I am asking you to take some time and, in your own way, surrender in gratitude to the Eternal One and give thanks for what you are about to receive.

The "Bija Mantras" are particular "seeds" of sound that can be planted in our consciousness. Once planted—that is, once their pronunciation is taken from an outward verbal expression and brought into the mind—they are never spoken aloud again. Like a seed that is planted, digging it up will only weaken the developing root system.

I am deeply grateful to my dear friend Droplet john beaulieu for his research and his insightful work with the Bija Mantras, and for his help in passing them on to you.

The Bija Mantras are the most potent of all. They definitely belong to no language and are not found in any dictionary. They are a combination of letters that represent the relationship between the Kundalini (life energy) and the supreme consciousness (sacred sound). Any attempt to understand them intellectually will be futile.

—Ushabudh Arya

There are numerous ways of imparting a mantra, but what is most important is he/she who is receiving and the attitude they take with them to the process. For some, the ceremony and structure of a specific location may be the only setting in which they feel they have gotten the "right" mantra. If this is you, then seek out such a place. However, if you feel comfortable and can take the time to open to this "energy," then by all means continue. I am of the strong opinion that the introduction to the practice of meditation and the receiving of a mantra must "feel" right for the would-be meditator. Be assured that what is to follow is a powerful and effective methodology for your initiation into the practice of meditation.

In this application, after your sincere ceremony of gratitude, I would have you find a comfortable place to sit where you will not be disturbed. Take a few deep breaths; they will help you relax and become present. Look at the mantras listed below and "sound" them out loud without expectation and with as little mental processing as possible. Don't concern yourself with the worry that you may not be pronouncing them correctly. However they come to you is correct, be assured. As you sound them, take notice as to how they resonate, how they affect you, how you *feel.* Do not study them; just a few soundings will intuitively give you your mantra. You will *know* which one is right for you. Simply adopt the one that *feels* best. Trust your choice. No one knows better than you.

Once you have chosen your mantra, say it out loud a few times, then begin to whisper it, softer and softer. Little by little take its pronunciation to no more than just a breath, then close your eyes and begin to say it mentally. Do not focus or concentrate on it, simply let it be a part of you. Let it happen without effort. As you are repeating it, your mind will eventually and naturally wander. When you realize your awareness has strayed into thoughts, that your mantra is no longer there, simply "let go" of the thoughts, and easily come back to the mantra, letting your awareness be with it again. It does not have to be a clear pronunciation, although it may be. It can be just a shadow or a sense of its presence. However you perceive your mantra, however it may come, is okay. Continue, *easily,* just this way, with no expectation, without effort. ...... You are meditating.

Once you have chosen your mantra and have begun using it, do not attempt to use another. Your initial choice was correct and your need or desire to change it may simply be the result of an unpleasant release of stress or of having let mind into the process. Let go and trust. Please refer back to Chapter XII and the heading "Meditating" for a review and further clarification of the technique.

THE BIJA MANTRAS

Set 1:

ai-dha (eye-eee-dah-haa)

ja-ma

au-ra

ssh-pa
sha-yam
ai-nam (eye-eee-nam)

Set 2:

i-sha (eye-sha)
ah-ma
o-da (oh-dah)
ah-ying
ah-nam
ssh-kham (ssh-ka-ham)

Set 3:

ah-sa
e-la (ee-la)
m-pa (mmmm-paa)
o-tham (ooo-ta-ham)
sha-ya-ma
ai-sa (eye-eee-sa)
ss-ta

Set 4:

o-ta (oh-tah)
ja-pha (ja-pah-haa)
ssh-tham (ssh-ta-ham)
u-ba
va-da-ra-tam
ah-tha (ahh-ta-haa)
ssh-ma

In a way, I would ask you to use this book as a mantra, not something to be quoted and studied, but something to have a sense of as you live your life, a gentle whisper that is a reminder to let go of thought and become present and aware of the eternal essence of Being and *Source* of Life, no matter where you are or what you are doing. Let it be a reminder to you that you are surrounded by and are a part of Miracles that can only be realized in your pure, non-judgmental, "thoughtless" experience of Now! Please feel free to visit my web site at *www.dropletsjourney.com* with any questions or concerns. I would love to hear from you and see "how your doin'."

POSTSCRIPT

I had, coincidentally, felt that I had finally finished this book (again) on the morning of September 11, 2001. The job site I had been working on had an unobstructed view of the World Trade Center, and I watched in horror while the most heinous act of terror ever to have been perpetrated in this country (Oklahoma City notwithstanding) unfolded before my eyes. I watched with a sorrowful heart at what God was doing now, what God *had* to do now. Remember, we are a part of this process of Life revealing and fulfilling Itself, and that process may at times seem cruel and from a source of "evil" and not from our beloved God of Love. But like any dis-ease that creates pain, it must be understood and the cause explored if we are to enjoy healthy living. If only limited self interests are looked to and an awareness of a grander theme is left unseen, our suffering will be great, our reactions shallow and unproductive, and our isolation will deepen. As I came to understand the circumstances that created this tragedy, I came to see how prophetic this book had become.

The limited "fundamentalist" view cannot come to this *Moment* with a realization of the mystery and sanctity of Life, as it is locked into the past and into the mind with its beliefs and dogma. There is little freedom to explore Life and challenge limitations whenever strong *beliefs* prevail. Those isolated souls can only strike out at a world that has continued to evolve, leaving their view of life behind and their egocentric identity threatened. As said, a threatened ego is capable of incredible acts of horror in order to secure itself, especially if it is uneducated to the world and "fanatical" in its religious beliefs. What wouldn't an ego do if it thought it could live forever in glory?! The attack on the World Trade Center is a very sad, yet profound, example of what the fearful, misinformed, narcissistic ego can do. Threatened by the "infidel" and our way of life, threatened by change and consumed with hate, these terrorists struck out. These are misguided Droplets whose view of life and whose actions present a cancer on this Earth. Their ignorance, fear and fanaticism are their own worst enemy, which leaves them void of the Mystery and blind to the sanctity of Life that ironically lays at the core of their religion. With that enemy in control, they can never hope to come close to our land of the free and the home of so many of those brave heroes who unselfishly perished in that cowardly attack.

We, however, are not without blame, for in our own fear, ignorance, and fanaticism, we, too, have defiled the sanctity of this Moment of Miracles in our pursuit of egocentric security in those superficial material "things" with little regard or reverence for the purity of Life around us. We have much to learn from this tragedy about ego and arrogance, and about our place in this world and in the values we keep. We have now become a nation of fear, for we have lost our faith in the Eternal One and have been corrupted by the limits of ego.

This has also been, ironically, a sacred time that has brought us back together through national pride and with a love for this great nation, its foundation of freedom and its people. For some, especially those close to the tragedy, it has served as an awakening to the simpler, deeper values of life, and has initiated a radical change in lifestyle.

There was one such woman who witnessed the brutal deaths of many who were forced to jump from the inferno above. Her initial trauma kept her from sleeping and had devastated her life and her ability to function. With some extraordinary help from an enlightened therapist, she began to explore why. Why had she been chosen to witness this terrible tragedy? What could possibly be learned from this horror? And then she remembered watching and witnessing the "explosion" of light that occurred as each soul came to earth. She then recalled being comforted by one of those souls who

Thanks for shopping with us! We are located in quaint Powder Springs (a suburb of Atlanta) and hope if you are in the area you will stop in and see us;o)

We are glad we could have you item available for you to purchase and if you have an issues with it, please contact us BEFORE leaving feedback as we are sure we can help with any problem.

Please return to see us via online, by phone or in person;o)

Susan
The Book Worm Bookstore
4451 Marietta Street
Powder Springs, GA 30127
www.thebookwormonline.com
like us on facebook to see our daily specials and ask for free shipping with your first purchase of $10 or more!

http://www.facebook.com/TheBookworm.PowderSprings

assured her they were all right and that she had no reason to fear. A deeper, richer, and far more spiritual life began for her that day.

We must be reminded that this great nation does not exist without *us*, and that we do not exist without *Him*, and that *He* is this great Mystery of Life expressing Itself throughout this *entire* planet in so many different ways. Whatever course of action we must take, awareness of "*That*" must be kept in our consciousness. Otherwise, all those who have died will have died in vain as victims of our continued ignorance and isolation. Let the memory of those who perished that terrible day be a reminder of the sanctity of Life and to the love and beauty of the Spirit within us all. Jesus would ease your anxiety with the words: "Do not let your hearts be troubled" (John 14:1). Come to Him now, in this Moment, and understand why.

ABOUT THE AUTHOR

Steven Pfister is not a scholar. He holds no degrees or titles. What came to him came without notice or desire, from a source that transcends intellect and the illusion of relative life. He has spent most of his adult life in pursuit of deeper awareness and understanding of the *gift* he received those many years ago. He earns his living as a carpenter/contractor and lives in upstate New York with his wife and three sons.

Printed in the United States
1356300004B/259-294